"These nineteenth- and early-twentieth-century
biographies, now republished by Chelsea House,
reveal an unsuspected significance. Not only are a
good many of them substantively valuable (and by
no means entirely superseded), but they also evoke
a sense of the period, an intimacy with the
attitudes and assumptions of their times."
—Professor Daniel Aaron

ORCHARD HOUSE, CONCORD, MASS.
Home of the Alcott Family, 1858.

L. M. Alcott.

LOUISA MAY ALCOTT
EDNAH D. CHENEY

INTRODUCTION BY
ANN DOUGLAS

American Men and Women of Letters Series

GENERAL EDITOR
PROFESSOR DANIEL AARON
HARVARD UNIVERSITY

CHELSEA HOUSE
NEW YORK, LONDON
1980

Cover design by Zimmerman Foyster Design

Copyright © 1980 by Chelsea House Publishers, a division of
Chelsea House Educational Communications, Inc.
All rights reserved
Printed and bound in the United States of America

Library of Congress Cataloging in Publication Data

Alcott, Louisa May, 1832-1888.
    Louisa May Alcott.

    (American men and women of letters)
    Reprint of the 1889 ed. published by Roberts
Brothers, Boston.
    Includes bibliographical references.
    1. Alcott, Louisa May, 1832-1888--Biography.
2. Novelists, American--19th century--Biography.
I. Cheney, Ednah Dow Littlehale, 1824-1904.
II. Series.
PS1018.A4 1980   813'.4   80-19285
ISBN 0-87754-162-0

Chelsea House Publishers
Harold Steinberg, Chairman & Publisher
Andrew E. Norman, President
A Division of Chelsea House Educational Communications, Inc.
70 West 40 Street, New York 10018

TO

MRS. ANNA B. PRATT,

THE SOLE SURVIVING SISTER OF LOUISA M. ALCOTT, AND HER
NEVER-FAILING HELP, COMFORTER, AND FRIEND
FROM BIRTH TO DEATH

𝕮𝖍𝖎𝖘 𝕸𝖊𝖒𝖔𝖎𝖗

IS RESPECTFULLY AND TENDERLY DEDICATED,

BY

EDNAH D. CHENEY.

JAMAICA PLAIN,
June, 1889.

CONTENTS

GENERAL INTRODUCTION, DANIEL AARON . . xi

INTRODUCTION, ANN DOUGLAS xiii

AUTHOR'S PREFACE 1889, EDNAH D. CHENEY . xxxi

CHAPTER.

I. GENEALOGY AND PARENTAGE 11

II. CHILDHOOD 16

III. FRUITLANDS 32

IV. THE SENTIMENTAL PERIOD 56

V. AUTHORSHIP 75

VI. THE YEAR OF GOOD LUCK 110

VII. "HOSPITAL SKETCHES" 136

VIII. EUROPE, AND "LITTLE WOMEN" 170

IX. EUROPE 204

X. FAMILY CHANGES 263

XI. LAST YEARS 329

XII. CONCLUSION 387

General Introduction

THE VISITABLE PAST
Daniel Aaron

THE TWENTY-FIVE BIOGRAPHIES of American worthies reissued in this Chelsea House series restore an all but forgotten chapter in the annals of American literary culture. Some of the authors of these volumes—journalists, scholars, writers, professional men—would be considered amateurs by today's standards, but they enjoyed certain advantages not open to their modern counterparts. In some cases they were blood relations or old friends of the men and women they wrote about, or at least near enough to them in time to catch the contemporary essence often missing in the more carefully researched and authoritative later studies of the same figures. Their leisurely, impressionistic accounts—sometimes as interesting for what is omitted as for what is emphasized—reveal a good deal about late Victorian assumptions, cultural and social, and about the vicissitudes of literary reputation.

Each volume in the series is introduced by a

recognized scholar who was encouraged to write an idiosyncratic appraisal of the biographer and his work. The introductions vary in emphasis and point of view, for the biographies are not of equal quality, nor are the writers memorialized equally appealing. Yet a kind of consensus is discernible in these random assessments: surprise at the insights still to be found in ostensibly unscientific and old-fashioned works; in some instances admiration for the solidity and liveliness of the biographer's prose and quality of mind; respect for the pioneer historians among them who made excellent use of the limited material at their disposal.

The volumes in this American Men and Women of Letters series contain none of the startling "private" and "personal" episodes modern readers have come to expect in biography, but they illuminate what Henry James called the "visitable past." As such, they are of particular value to all students of American cultural and intellectual history.

Cambridge, Massachusetts
Spring, 1980

INTRODUCTION
TO THE
CHELSEA HOUSE EDITION
Ann Douglas

EDNAH DOW CHENEY undertook to write the
life of Louisa May Alcott shortly after the latter's death in March of 1888. The choice of
biographer undoubtedly seemed then an apt
one, and the congruence of Cheney and Alcott
is still fascinating. By the late 1880s, Cheney's
credentials as a competent biographer in the
solid Victorian manner were impeccable. Like
many fine Victorian biographers, she was more
an appreciator than a critic. Her own original
desire to be an "author" had subsided into the
lowlier aim of being a "writer." Only gradually
had she consoled herself for her lack of literary
originality with the belief that a "reformer"
was an "artist" of sorts. A pragmatic inter-
preter of her more creative peers, Cheney approached biography as another act of service,
and her eulogistic books on her short-lived artist husband, Seth Cheney, and a number of talented women of her acquaintance are Victorian

biographical compilations still of much value
for modern scholars with interests quite foreign
to the biographer's. Despite Alcott's censorship
and destruction of much pertinent material,
Cheney provides copious extracts from what
evidence Alcott did leave behind her and lets
her "speak mainly for herself." Alcott was pre-
sumably in skillful and sympathetic hands.

The two women had much in common. Born
in 1824, eight years before Louisa May,
Cheney had grown up an intimate of the whole
Alcott family, particularly of Bronson, who
was at least half in love with her in the 1850s,
and in whose summer school for philosophers
she lectured on art in the early 1880s. She
knew and admired Louisa May's early idol and
lifelong friend, Ralph Waldo Emerson. Both
women moved all their lives in the Boston-
Concord circle usually described as "high-
minded." By the time Cheney memorialized
Alcott, she had already shown herself a leader
of reforms in which Alcott expressed lasting
interest: women's suffrage, medical care for
women, the rights of blacks (which included,
Cheney fully believed, intermarriage), education in general and the liberalization of New
England Calvinism.

On a more personal level, Alcott and Cheney
alike represent that curious mid-Victorian and

New England amalgam of patriarchal and matriarchal influences; strong women inspired and backed their effort at independence (a grandmother in Cheney's case, a mother in Alcott's), and male mentors defined its direction (Bronson Alcott, Theodore Parker, and Emerson in both instances). They admired the difficult and brilliant Margaret Fuller, high priestess of suffering and revolt in the New England imagination, and with special reason. Cheney and Alcott, like Fuller, had experienced feelings of shyness, of being misunderstood; they too had felt, as Cheney wrote of her youth, "constant antagonism to constituted authorities." Cheney married only briefly and bore but one child. Alcott stayed single and childless. By middle age, Cheney had lost her father, her husband, half her siblings; Alcott a sister, her mother, a much loved brother-in-law. Neither was a stranger to suffering.

Some of Alcott's contemporaries considered Cheney's view of Alcott too "sombre," yet the modern student of Alcott has reason to suspect that Cheney simply would not or could not face the unhappiness and conflict evident in the Alcott autobiographical material she herself presents. Cheney had outgrown or successfully suppressed and rechanneled her early rebelliousness. She belonged to the next-to-last

generation of Victorian women richly able to
convert unsatisfied personal needs into public
causes and ideals. In her youthful attempts at
fiction, Cheney was unable to create those
"bad characters" which constitute Alcott's
youthful specialty. Shortly before her death,
Cheney expressed her confidence in "the
stream of progress which has been flowing on
since the dawn of time," now reaching full tide
in the nineteenth, and, she prophecied on the
eve of World War I, the twentieth century.
Alcott was too constitutionally careless to look
ahead, but she evidently knew a great deal
more about anxiety than about the "hope" her
father and Cheney so amply shared. Louisa
May Alcott cared shockingly little about history and dismissed the European upheavals of
1870 as "little flurries"; her concern for reform
never even approached the then permissible
proportions.

Alcott, despite her early and lasting sympathy with abolitionism, her short-lived cou-
rageous work as a nurse in the Civil War, her
support of women's rights and liberal education, despite the dozens of diverting, didactic,
best-selling books she wrote for those whom
she called the "little folk," a series that began
with *Flower Fables* in 1855 and ended, with a
disconcerting floral continuity, in *A Garland*

for Girls in 1888, was not at heart a reformer. Very unlike Cheney, who ran a half-dozen organizations in her lifetime, Alcott seldom joined "societies," those quasi-institutional, semi-social hybrids of change and tradition so integral to the New England way. "Duty's child," Bronson Alcott called her; she could neither evade the charges "duty" levied on her life nor be reconciled to them. She never liked George Eliot; perhaps she resented the greater writer's complex exploration and troubled justification of female self-renunciation. Margaret Fuller understood with Eliot that "to renounce is to be chosen"; Alcott did not. Cheney's biography ostensibly records the difficulties and rewards of self-sacrifice in the interests of supporting a talented but indigent family. She even claims that Alcott's writings are perhaps the better because they were written for a purpose quite different from any aspiration to artistic excellence. It is painfully clear, however, that Alcott, the "children's friend," considered her life a failure.

As a child in the early 1840s, watching her father's utopian experiment at Harvard, Massachusetts, collapse, witnessing the near-disintegration of her parents' marriage amidst grim material destitution and psychological conflict, Louisa May consciously planned her life to

answer the needs of others. Her course was
innately problematic. How could she resolve
the tensions created by the mutual dependence
between herself and her mother, Abba May,
whose vehement, practical, loyal, moody temperament she shared? Or those springing from
her often uneasy relationship with her father,
the Transcendentalist philosopher-at-large *par
excellence,* whose astonishing capacities for
calm in the midst of worldly failure both enraged and awed his gifted and ambitious daughter? Her mother's suffering and her increasingly
overt pleas for her daughter's aid spurred
Louisa May to action; her father's placidity
questioned the value of such action. Bronson
Alcott benignly accepted as Louisa's due, and
his, the role reversal that brought her fame and
him freedom from financial care. But he had
seldom felt the financial care as care, and Abba,
disconcertingly, for all her complaints, adored
Bronson precisely for his "fidelity to the pursuit of truth"; the years of poverty with him,
she wrote, were "great years" for her soul.
Louisa May inevitably dunned her "brains" (as
she always referred to her talent) for their last
iota of money-making energy and regarded the
successful result with a mixture of pride and
scorn. Her feminism, one possible conscious
structure for her complicated ego, was faulty

from the start.

Alcott freely professed her desire to live the exciting life of a man, and her inability to fall in love with a member of the opposite sex. She preferred to be, as she put it, "a free spinster" paddling "my own canoe"; "liberty" was the best husband, she believed, for many women. Cheney equates Alcott's spinsterhood with her desire to support and remain near her original family. The actual situation was a different and ironic one. Alcott's deepest feminist impulse corresponded to a pragmatic fantasy of high-spirited autonomy. She believed most marriages were unhappy, that any man as a husband would surely bore her; yet she labored under a familial yoke as heavy as the matrimonial one that might have chafed her. "Shall never lead my own life" runs one of her many curtly despondent late journal entries. And she never quite did.

Where Cheney proudly defended American art and society, Alcott resented Concord, Boston, and sometimes the United States altogether, as stifling, small-minded, provincial. Her youngest sister, May (cast and devalued as Amy in *Little Women*), a gifted artist, got out of Concord relatively young and moved to Europe. There she acquired a husband much younger than herself and a self-directed, un-

profitable, but fulfilling career. Louisa May's
envy was just barely covered by her affectionate support (financial and emotional) of her
sibling's blithe determination to "lead her own
life." By her mid-thirties, Alcott's health was
broken by psychological and physiological
strains; she suffered from neuralgia, insomnia,
and finally meningitis. Ladies like Ednah
Cheney and her intimate friend Julia Ward
Howe, whose real careers began relatively late,
lived on until their eighties; and they were typi-
cal of their type and their time. Alcott's life, in
contrast, ended in her mid-fifties. She outlived
her mother by only eleven years, and died
within a few days of her father. Restless from
start to finish, unable to enjoy her life or to
alter it, she still vibrates in Cheney's pages, an
emblem of irritation and frustration.

Alcott, who had worked so hard for recognition and success, found "fame," when it
arrived in force after the publication of *Little
Women* in 1868, her "worst scrape"; she had
asked for bread, she complained, and received
"a stone in the shape of a pedestal." Fame
brought the celebrity-hunters she hated, and
little satisfaction; she was lauded for achievements she thought insignificant: "moral pap
for the young" was her trenchant description
of her output. Her father believed that Louisa

May could not accept her talent or its recognition. But perhaps she was infuriated less because she thought the tales for girls and boys that sold like hotcakes were bad (many of them, most notably *Little Women, An Old-Fashioned Girl* [1870], *Eight Cousins* [1875], and *Jo's Boys* [1886], were not), than because they were not the works she was best suited to write. Alcott firmly believed she had never had the leisure or the incentive to write a book, with the partial exception of her early novel *Moods* (1865) and the later *A Modern Mephistopheles* (1887), worthy of her talents. Unflaggingly productive, she seldom expressed herself.

Cheney has little to say about the "sensational" magazine tales full of incest, murder, drugs and passion that Alcott wrote literally as "pot-boilers" in the 1860s. Here Cheney apparently follows Alcott's lead. Alcott published her melodramatic fictions under pseudonyms; she stopped writing them as soon as she conquered the lucrative field of children's fiction in the late 1860s, and she steadfastly refused to identify or acknowledge them. They have only recently been identified and republished by Madeleine Stern. Yet Cheney breaks with Alcott in giving such chary praise to Alcott's own favorite works, *Moods* and *Modern Mephistopheles,* both of which drew heavily on the early sensational tales. When Cheney catches a trace of the former melodramatist at work —Alcott's vivid description, for example, of an insane girl's suicide in her semi-autobiographical novel *Work* (1873)—she dismisses the scene as a "blemish." She fails to note that *Work* is dotted with suicide attempts, not least among them the heroine's own.

Cheney does not see that Alcott's most interesting characters in the children's tales (Jo of *Little Women* and its sequels, to a lesser degree, Phoebe in *Eight Cousins* and *Rose In Bloom* [1876], and, last but not least, the wayward Dan of *Little Men* [1871] and *Jo's Boys*) are all imports into the world of domestic fiction from the earlier sensationalist writing. They are creatures of passion, all liable to error, and even, in Dan's case, to crime. Dan is the favorite "boy" of Jo Bhaer; she would rather save this most creative and violent of her protégées, we learn, than any of his less gifted and better-tempered mates at her eclectic boarding school for young people. With Jo's commitment to Dan, Alcott is making a last stand for her own deepest imaginative gifts. Usually, she "tames" (the word is hers, and one she uses frequently) her rebellious "little folk" by a fearful reversal of the movement of *Huck Finn,* a book Alcott significantly and strenuously was

to oppose. While Huck enters and flees a number of adult worlds, Alcott's children are increasingly under constant and multiplying
kindly adult surveillance. Rose of *Eight Cousins,* an orphan at the story's start, has nearly as
many aunts and uncles running her life as cousins to play with by its close. The peer pressure
of a gentler friend or twin aids the process;
quiet Beth dies in a benign haze of pain and
acquiescence, one critic has noted, so that Jo
can domesticate herself enough to marry.

But Dan, like Huck, finally lights out for
"the territory." Although he loves Bess, Amy
and Laurie's lovely spoiled daughter, he can't
have her or even approach her. His tainted past
(he's killed a man) forbids it, and he must go
back West and "help" the Indians. Yet his loss
is also a gain; for he leaves accompanied only
by "Mother Bhaer's" love—and his author's—
and he leaves unmarried. Alcott had not wanted to marry Jo off to anyone; she detested, she
asserted, the public pressure that forced her to
pair off her characters like animals entering
Noah's ark. In the late and flawed *Jo's Boys,*
the last of the March family sagas, Alcott, tired
as she clearly was, unable to acknowledge fully
what she was doing, nonetheless permitted a
character congenial to her own violent nature
to enter the solitary life of adventure she had

craved and sacrificed. Dan exits in one movement from Plumfield, the Marchs's kingdom,
and from Alcott's fictive domain, to places
mercifully unspecified. He escapes, in other
words, censorship—by this point a working
synonym for fiction in Alcott's unconscious
lexicon.

Alcott belonged by inclination and talent to
an Anglo-American literary tradition hardly
suitable, she herself reportedly remarked bit-
terly, to Bronson Alcott's daughter of Concord.
Little Women testifies to the devotion of the
Alcott girls to Dickens. It is clear from her
work that Alcott was drawn not simply to the
hilarious creator of Sairy Gamp and Mr.
Micawber, but also to the darker author of
the heavily plotted, sombre late masterpieces.
Alcott early expressed a fondness for the fierce
genius of Charlotte Brontë; as a young woman
she read Mrs. Gaskell's classic biography of
Brontë with avid interest. Among American
authors, Alcott's predilection again ran to ex-
plorers of the darker places of the human soul.
Much as she admired Emerson as a man, there
is little evidence that she was influenced by his
thinking or writing. She was instead a devotee
of an artist Emerson was never able to appreciate—his neighbor Nathaniel Hawthorne,
whose romances Alcott found "lurid" but

"true and strong." Alcott was deeply flattered
when Hawthorne's son Julian was widely believed to have written her anonymously published, very Hawthornian novel, *A Modern
Mephistopheles.*

In her various books for children, Alcott's
literary schizophrenia is evident. Her young
characters occasionally read the brilliantly
melodramatic Englishwoman Mary Elizabeth
Braddon, best known for *Lady Audley's Secret*
(1862), or the rampantly overwrought American, Mrs. E.D.E.N. Southworth (the "Mrs.
Northbury" whose work Jo March originally
imitates). But more often they praise Dinah
Mulock's sedate, plotless, over-moralizing,
popular *John Halifax, Gentleman* (1857), or
the works of the English High Church novelist
"dear Miss [Charlotte] Yonge," as one Alcott
character describes her, "with her nice large
families and their trials and their pious ways."
Alcott settled for sprightly, careless, slangy
children's versions of the domestic fiction of
Mulock and Yonge, but she devoted her best
efforts to her gloomy, "sensational" romances.
She rewrote *Moods* at least three times and
labored over *A Modern Mephistopheles;* she
sent off all her children's fiction, including
Little Women, in rough draft form. Only the
writing of the adult books, as well as the early

"sensational" tales for the penny press, threw Alcott into her famous "vortex" of nonstop creativity, writing for days on end without break for food or rest. After entering her forbidden, magical kingdom, she couldn't stop; perhaps, if she stopped, she couldn't start again. In a state of obsession, fittingly, she wrote about obsession.

This daughter of a Concord sage whose best advice to perplexed souls was "You ought to do nothing" or "Meantime, there is Providence" was fascinated, as her father realized and lamented, with "the will," with the machinations by which it distorts and destroys human life, with the calculated commitment to evil, with the very essence of plot. Bronson saw Louisa May as "demonic," and, if to be demonic is to study the mechanism of attention in its starkest, strongest form, she was. *Moods* and *A Modern Mephistopheles,* like the best of Alcott's early melodramas, "Behind the Mask," "V.V.," "Pauline's Passion and Punishment," "A Marble Woman," and "A Whisper in the Dark," detail the difficulty and danger of loving and being loved, the ease, even the pleasure of hating and being hated, the high art of scheming. Only in the anonymous, early, often brilliant magazine tales, however, was Alcott uncensored by self or society, and the results are startling.

Unlike Dickens, Hawthorne, Wilkie Collins, or Mary Elizabeth Braddon, her contemporaries in variants of the sensational genre, Alcott shows no interest in mystery or detection; for example, she unveils Jean Muir, the duplicitous heroine of "Behind a Mask," to the reader at once. She grants scant consideration to any character who might provide the conventional "good" foil to her damned souls. She is frank in her admiration of deceit—an admiration partly bred, perhaps, by the hypocrisy of what she called "poky" Concord but more profoundly rooted in her unconscious sense that the deceitful tactics of her characters were close kin to her own wickedly literal imaginative process. Deception in Alcott is a vigilante hunt conducted by the will against the emotions.

In "Behind A Mask," Jean Muir, who poses as a 19-year-old ingenue in order to win the affection of all the members of the rich family in which she serves as governess, is in reality a 30-year-old actress. She is fond of her drink, addicted to intrigue, on edge with the self-dislike that makes her declare herself "old, ugly, bad and lost," and at the same time exhilarated by the sense of her own skillfulness, her ability to imitate or use any emotion as a weapon in the cause of her own advancement, to bring off a "scene." She marries the wealthy uncle of her employer's family minutes before his now-alerted relatives plan to stop the match. Alcott, here riding high, cannot punish her heroine as she clearly deserves; it would be to discredit her own imaginative life. What fascinated and fueled Alcott, the future supplier of "wholesome" reading for America's young, the woman destined to write ever looser and lighter fare, was excitement itself.

As a girl, Alcott wrote, produced, and acted in overwrought dramas, collaborations with her sister Anna bearing titles like *Norna: or, the Witch's Curse* and *The Unloved Wife: or, Woman's Faith,* plays which rush frantically and awkwardly from emotional peak to emotional peak. In her mid-forties, she still occasionally took to the boards as an amateur actress and enjoyed it, but she was ever more tightly trapped in the role of her "real" identity. In her cheery autobiographical writings, she wove endless verbal variations on this personage: "the stern Livy" (the name she adopts in *Shawl Straps,* her 1872 account of a trip abroad), "dowager Livy," "the sombre spinster," and so on. Her tragedy was not that she outgrew or rejected these half-caricatured roles, but that she did not. "Queer" is a word Alcott uses in letters, journals, and in her children's fiction in reference to herself and many of her characters. The word's evasive admission of nonconformity, its lack of precision, its refusal to hunt down its own meaning, banned it from Alcott's highly purposeful "lurid" writing and made it a favored word in the three decades after she had largely abandoned the attempt to write "true and strong" fiction. "Queer" was Alcott's synonym for unexplored complexity.

It is impossible to judge to what degree Alcott's milieu and her turbulent, even self-destructive nature were responsible for her blockage. She remains a figure of gathering interest: the writer of powerful sensational stories and novels, the author of a young people's literature that, at its best, offers a crisply subversive tribute to female consolidated effort and felicity. Her quintessentially Victorian and troubled story is decipherable although never enunciated in Cheney's pages.

New York, New York
May, 1980

AUTHOR'S PREFACE
TO THE
1889 EDITION

———•———

LOUISA MAY ALCOTT is universally recognized as the greatest and most popular story-teller for children in her generation. She has known the way to the hearts of young people, not only in her own class, or even country, but in every condition of life, and in many foreign lands. Plato says, " Beware of those who teach fables to children ; " and it is impossible to estimate the influence which the popular writer of fiction has over the audience he wins to listen to his tales. The preacher, the teacher, the didactic writer find their audience in hours of strength, with critical faculties all alive, to question their propositions and refute their arguments. The novelist comes to us in the intervals of recreation and relaxation, and by his seductive powers of imagination and sentiment takes possession of the fancy and the heart before judgment and reason are aroused to defend the citadel. It well becomes us, then, who would guard young minds from subtle temptations, to study the character of those works which charm and delight the children.

Of no author can it be more truly said than of Louisa Alcott that her works are a revelation of herself. She rarely sought for the material of her stories in old chronicles, or foreign adventures. Her capital was her own life and experiences and those of others directly about her; and her own well-remembered girlish frolics and fancies were sure to find responsive enjoyment in the minds of other girls.

It is therefore impossible to understand Miss Alcott's works fully without a knowledge of her own life and experiences. By inheritance and education she had rich and peculiar gifts; and her life was one of rare advantages, as well as of trying difficulties. Herself of the most true and frank nature, she has given us the opportunity of knowing her without disguise; and it is thus that I shall try to portray her, showing what influences acted upon her through life, and how faithfully and fully she performed whatever duties circumstances laid upon her. Fortunately I can let her speak mainly for herself.

Miss Alcott revised her journals at different times during her later life, striking out what was too personal for other eyes than her own, and destroying a great deal which would doubtless have proved very interesting.

The small number of letters given will undoubtedly be a disappointment. Miss Alcott wished to
have most of her letters destroyed, and her sister
respected her wishes. She was not a voluminous
correspondent; she did not encourage many in-
timacies, and she seldom wrote letters except to
her family, unless in reference to some purpose
she had strongly at heart. Writing was her constant occupation, and she was not tempted to indulge in it as a recreation. Her letters are brief,
and strictly to the point, but always characteristic
in feeling and expression; and, even at the risk of
the repetition of matter contained in her journals
or her books, I shall give copious extracts from
such as have come into my hands.

E. D. C.

JAMAICA PLAIN, Mass., 1889.

LOUISA MAY ALCOTT.

CHAPTER I.

GENEALOGY AND PARENTAGE.

TO LOUISA MAY ALCOTT.

BY HER FATHER.

WHEN I remember with what buoyant heart,
  Midst war's alarms and woes of civil strife,
In youthful eagerness thou didst depart,
  At peril of thy safety, peace, and life,
To nurse the wounded soldier, swathe the dead, —
  How piercèd soon by fever's poisoned dart,
And brought unconscious home, with wildered head,
  Thou ever since 'mid langour and dull pain,
To conquer fortune, cherish kindred dear,
  Hast with grave studies vexed a sprightly brain,
In myriad households kindled love and cheer,
  Ne'er from thyself by Fame's loud trump beguiled,
Sounding in this and the farther hemisphere, —
  I press thee to my heart as Duty's faithful child.

LOUISA ALCOTT was the second child of Amos Bronson and Abba May Alcott. This name was spelled Alcocke in English history. About 1616 a coat-of-arms was granted to Thomas Alcocke of Silbertoft, in the county of Leicester. The device represents three cocks, emblematic of watchfulness; and the motto is *Semper Vigilans.*

The first of the name appearing in English history is John Alcocke of Beverley, Yorkshire, of whom Fuller gives an account in his Worthies of England.

Thomas and George Alcocke were the first of the name among the settlers in New England. The name is frequently found in the records of Dorchester and Roxbury, and has passed through successive changes to its present form.

The name of Bronson came from Mr. Alcott's maternal grandfather, the sturdy Capt. Amos Bronson of Plymouth, Conn. " His ancestors on both sides had been substantial people of respectable position in England, and were connected with the founders and governors of the chief New England colonies. At the time of Mr. Alcott's birth they had become simple farmers, reaping a scanty living from their small farms in Connecticut."

Amos Bronson Alcott, the father of Louisa, was born Nov. 29, 1799, at the foot of Spindle Hill, in the region called New Connecticut. He has himself given in simple verse the story of his quaint rustic life in his boyhood, and Louisa has reproduced it in her story of " Eli's Education " (in the Spinning-Wheel Stories), which gives a very true account of his youthful life and adventures. He derived his refined, gentle nature from his mother, who had faith in her son, and who lived to see him the accomplished scholar he had vowed to become in his boyhood. Although brought up in these rustic surroundings, his manners were always those of a true gentleman. The name of the little mountain town afterward became Wolcott, and Louisa records in her journal a pilgrimage made thither in after years.[1]

Louisa Alcott's mother was a daughter of Col. Joseph May of Boston. This family is so well known that it is hardly necessary to repeat its genealogy here.[2] She was a sister of Samuel J. May, for many years pastor of the Unitarian church at Syracuse, who was so tenderly beloved by men of all religious persuasions in his home, and so widely known and respected for his courage and zeal in the Antislavery cause, as well as for his many philanthropic labors.

Mrs. Alcott's mother was Dorothy Sewall, a descendant of that family already distinguished in the annals of the Massachusetts colony, and which has lost nothing of its reputation for ability and virtue in its latest representatives.[3]

Mrs. Alcott inherited in large measure the traits which distinguished her family. She was a woman of large stature, fine physique, and overflowing life. Her temper was as quick and warm as her affections, but she was full of broad unselfish generosity. Her untiring energies were constantly employed, not only for the benefit of her family, but for all

[1] For further particulars of the Alcott genealogy, see "New Connecticut," a poem by A. B. Alcott, published in 1887. I am also indebted to Mr. F. B. Sanborn's valuable paper read at the memorial service at Concord in 1888.

[2] For particulars of the genealogy of the May families, see "A Genealogy of the Descendants of John May," who came from England to Roxbury in America, 1640.

[3] For the Sewall family, see "Drake's History of Boston," or fuller accounts in the Sewall Papers published by the Massachusetts Historical Society.

around her. She had a fine mind, and if she did not have large opportunities for scholastic instruction, she always enjoyed the benefit of intellectual society and converse with noble minds. She loved expression in writing, and her letters are full of wit and humor, keen criticism, and noble moral sentiments. Marriage with an idealist, who had no means of support, brought her many trials and privations. She bore them heroically, never wavering in affection for her husband or in devotion to her children. If the quick, impatient temper sometimes relieved itself in hasty speech, the action was always large and unselfish.

It will be apparent from Louisa's life that she inherited the traits of both her parents, and that the uncommon powers of mind and heart that distinguished her were not accidental, but the accumulated result of the lives of generations of strong and noble men and women.

She was well born.

Mr. Alcott to Colonel May.

GERMANTOWN, Nov. 29, 1832.

DEAR SIR, — It is with great pleasure that I announce to you the *birth of a second daughter*. She was born at half-past 12 this morning, on my birthday (33), and is a very fine healthful child, much more so than Anna was at birth, — has a fine foundation for health and energy of character. Abba is very comfortable, and will soon be restored to the discharge of those domestic and maternal duties in which she takes so much delight, and in the performance of which she furnishes so excellent a model for imitation. Those only who have seen her in those relations, much as there is in her general character to admire and esteem, can form a true estimate of her personal worth and uncommon devotion of heart. She was formed for domestic sentiment rather than the gaze and heartlessness of what is falsely called "society." Abba inclines to call the babe *Louisa May*, — a name to her full of every association connected with amiable benevolence and exalted worth. I hope *its present possessor* may rise to equal attainment, and deserve a place in the estimation of society.

With Abba's and Anna's and Louisa's regards, allow me to assure you of the sincerity with which I am

Yours,

A. BRONSON ALCOTT.

The children who lived to maturity were —

ANNA BRONSON ALCOTT,
LOUISA MAY ALCOTT,
ELIZABETH SEWALL ALCOTT,
ABBA MAY ALCOTT.

CHAPTER II.

CHILDHOOD.

TO THE FIRST ROBIN.[1]

WELCOME, welcome, little stranger,
Fear no harm, and fear no danger;
We are glad to see you here,
For you sing "Sweet Spring is near."

Now the white snow melts away;
Now the flowers blossom gay:
Come dear bird and build your nest,
For we love our robin best.

LOUISA MAY ALCOTT.
CONCORD.

MR. ALCOTT had removed to Germantown, Penn, to take charge of a school, and here Louisa was born, Nov. 29, 1832. She was the second daughter, and was welcomed with the same pride and affection as her elder sister had been. We have this pleasant little glimpse of her when she was hardly a month old, from the pen of one of her mother's friends. Even at that extremely early age love saw the signs of more than usual intelligence, and friends as well as fond parents looked forward to a promising career.

[1] Written at eight years of age.

Extract from a Letter by Miss Donaldson.

GERMANTOWN, PENN., Dec. 16, 1832.

I HAVE a dear little pet in Mrs. Alcott's little Louisa. It is the prettiest, best little thing in the world. You will wonder to hear me call anything so young pretty, but it is really so in an uncommon degree; it has a fair complexion, dark bright eyes, long dark hair, a high fore-head, and altogether a countenance of more than usual intelligence.

The mother is such a delightful woman that it is a cordial to my heart whenever I go to see her. I went in to see her for a few moments the evening we received your letter, and I think I never saw her in better spirits; and truly, if goodness and integrity can insure felicity, she deserves to be happy.

The earliest anecdote remembered of Louisa is this: When the family went from Philadelphia to Boston by steamer, the two little girls were nicely dressed in clean nankeen frocks for the voyage; but they had not been long on board before the lively Louisa was missing, and after a long search she was brought up from the engine-room, where her eager curiosity had carried her, and where she was having a beautiful time, with " plenty of dirt."

The family removed to Boston in 1834, and Mr. Alcott opened his famous school in Masonic Temple. Louisa was too young to attend the school except as an occasional visitor; but she found plenty of interest and amusement for her-self in playing on the Common, making friends with every child she met, and on one occasion falling into the Frog Pond. She has given a very lively picture of this period of her life in " Poppy's Pranks," that vivacious young person being a picture of herself, not at all exaggerated.

The family lived successively in Front Street, Cottage Place, and Beach Street during the six succeeding years in Boston. They occasionally passed some weeks at Scituate during the summer, which the children heartily enjoyed.

Mrs. Hawthorne gives a little anecdote which shows how the child's heart was blossoming in this family sunshine: " One morning in Front Street, at the breakfast table, Louisa suddenly broke silence, with a sunny smile saying, ' I love everybody in *dis* whole world.' "

Two children were born during this residence in Boston. Elizabeth was named for Mr. Alcott's assistant in his school, — Miss E. P. Peabody, since so widely known and beloved by all friends of education. A boy was born only to die. The little body was laid reverently away in the lot of Colonel May in the old burial-ground on the Common, and the children were taught to speak with tenderness of their " baby brother."

When Louisa was about seven years old she made a visit to friends in Providence. Miss C. writes of her: " She is a beautiful little girl to look upon, and I love her affectionate manners. I think she is more like her mother than either of the others." As is usually the case, Louisa's journal, which she began at this early age, speaks more fully of her struggles and difficulties than of the bright, sunny moods which made her attractive. A little letter carefully printed and sent home during this visit is preserved. In it she says she is not happy; and she did have one trying experience there, to which she refers in " My Boys." Seeing some poor children who she thought were hungry, she took food from the house without asking permission, and carried it to them, and was afterward very much astonished and grieved at being reprimanded instead of praised for the deed. Miss C. says: " She has had several spells of feeling sad; but a walk or a talk soon dispels all gloom. She was half moody when she wrote her letter; but now she is gay as a lark. She loves to play out of doors, and sometimes she is not inclined to stay in when it is unpleasant." In her sketches of " My Boys " she describes two of her companions here, not forgetting the kindness of the one and the mischievousness of the other.

Although the family were quite comfortable during the time of Mr. Alcott's teaching in Boston, yet the children wearied of their extremely simple diet of plain boiled rice without sugar, and graham meal without butter or molasses. An old friend who could not eat the bountiful rations provided for her at the United States Hotel, used to save her piece of pie or cake for the Alcott children. Louisa often took it home to the others in a bandbox which she brought for the purpose.

This friend was absent in Europe many years, and returned to find the name of Louisa Alcott famous. When she met the authoress on the street she was eagerly greeted. "Why, I did not think you would remember me!" said the old lady.

" Do you think I shall ever forget that bandbox? " was the instant reply.

In 1840, Mr. Alcott's school having proved unsuccessful, the family removed to Concord, Mass., and took a cottage which is described in " Little Women " as " Meg's first home," although Anna never lived there after her marriage. It was a pleasant house, with a garden full of trees, and best of all a large barn, in which the children could have free range and act out all the plays with which their little heads were teeming. Of course it was a delightful change from the city for the children, and here they passed two very happy years, for they were too young to understand the cares which pressed upon the hearts of their parents. Life was full of interest. One cold morning they found in the garden a little half-starved bird; and having warmed and fed it, Louisa was inspired to write a pretty poem to " The Robin." The fond mother was so delighted that she said to her, " You will grow up a Shakspeare! " From the lessons of her father she had formed the habit of writing freely, but this is the first recorded instance of her attempting to express her feelings in verse.

From the influences of such parentage as I have described, the family life in which Louisa was brought up became wholly unique.

If the father had to give up his cherished projects of a school modelled after his ideas, he could at least conduct the education of his own children; and he did so with the most tender devotion. Even when they were infants he took a great deal of personal care of them, and loved to put the little ones to bed and use the " children's hour " to instil into their hearts lessons of love and wisdom. He was full of fun too, and would lie on the floor and frolic with them, making compasses of his long legs with which to draw letters and diagrams. No shade of fear mingled with the children's reverent recognition of his superior spiritual life. So their hearts lay open to him, and he was able to help them in their troubles.

He taught them much by writing; and we have many specimens of their lists of words to be spelled, written, and understood. The lessons at Scituate were often in the garden, and their father always drew their attention to Nature and her beautiful forms and meanings. Little symbolical pictures helped to illustrate his lessons, and he sometimes made drawings himself. Here is an example of lessons. A quaint little picture represents one child playing on a harp, another drawing an arrow. It is inscribed —

FOR LOUISA.

1840.

Two passions strong divide our life, —
Meek, gentle love, or boisterous strife.

Below the child playing the harp is —

Love, Music,
Concord.

Below the shooter is —

Anger, Arrow,
Discord.

Another leaflet is —

FOR LOUISA

1840.

Louisa loves —
What?
(*Softly.*)
Fun.
Have some then,
Father
says.
Christmas Eve, December, 1840.
Concordia.

————————

FOR ANNA.

1840.

Beauty or Duty, —
which
loves Anna best?
A
Question
from her
Father.
Christmas Eve,
December, 1840.
Concordia.

A letter beautifully printed by her father for
Louisa (1839) speaks to her of conscience, and she
adds to it this note: "L. began early, it seems, to
wrestle with her conscience." The children were

always required to keep their journals regularly, and although these were open to the inspection of father and mother, they were very frank, and really recorded their struggles and desires. The mother had the habit of writing little notes to the children when she wished to call their attention to any fault or peculiarity. Louisa preserved many of them, headed, —

[*Extracts* from letters from Mother, received during these early years. I preserve them to show the ever tender, watchful help she gave to the child who caused her the most anxiety, yet seemed to be the nearest to her heart till the end. — L. M. A.]

No. 1. — MY DEAR LITTLE GIRL, — Will you accept this doll from me on your seventh birthday? She will be a quiet playmate for my active Louisa for seven years more. Be a kind mamma, and love her for my sake.

YOUR MOTHER.

BEACH STREET, BOSTON, 1839.

From her Mother.

COTTAGE IN CONCORD.

DEAR DAUGHTER, — Your tenth birthday has arrived. May it be a happy one, and on each returning birthday may you feel new strength and resolution to be gentle with sisters, obedient to parents, loving to every one, and happy in yourself.

I give you the pencil-case I promised, for I have observed that you are fond of writing, and wish to encourage the habit.

Go on trying, dear, and each day it will be easier to be and do good. You must help yourself, for the cause of your little troubles is in yourself; and patience and courage only will make you what mother prays to see you, — her good and happy girl.

CONCORD, 1843.

DEAR LOUY, — I enclose a picture for you which I always liked very much, for I imagined that you might be just such an industrious daughter and I such a feeble but loving mother, looking to your labor for my daily bread.

Keep it for my sake and your own, for you and I always liked to be grouped together.

MOTHER.

The lines I wrote under the picture in my journal : —

TO MOTHER.

> I hope that soon, dear mother,
>   You and I may be
> In the quiet room my fancy
>   Has so often made for thee, —
>
> The pleasant, sunny chamber,
>   The cushioned easy-chair,
> The book laid for your reading,
>   The vase of flowers fair ;
>
> The desk beside the window
>   Where the sun shines warm and bright :
> And there in ease and quiet
>   The promised book you write ;
>
> While I sit close beside you,
>   Content at last to see
> That you can rest, dear mother,
>   And I can cherish thee.

[The dream came true, and for the last ten years of her life Marmee sat in peace, with every wish granted, even to the "grouping together;" for she died in my arms. — L. M. A.]

A passage in Louisa's story of "Little Men" (p. 268) describes one of their childish plays. They "made believe" their minds were little round rooms in which the soul lived, and in which good or bad things were preserved. This play was never forgotten in after life, and the girls often looked into their little rooms for comfort or guidance in trial or temptation.

Louisa was very fond of animals, as is abundantly shown in her stories. She never had the happiness of owning many pets, except cats, and these were the delight of the household. The children played all manner of plays with them, tended them in sickness, buried them with funeral honors, and Louisa has embalmed their memory in the story of " The Seven Black Cats " in " Aunt Jo's Scrap-Bag."

Dolls were an equal source of pleasure. The imaginative children hardly recognized them as manufactured articles, but endowed them with life and feeling. Louisa put her dolls through every experience of life; they were fed, educated, punished, rewarded, nursed, and even hung and buried, and then resurrected in her stories. The account of the " Sacrifice of the Dolls " to the exacting Kitty Mouse in " Little Men " delights all children by its mixture of pathetic earnestness and playfulness. It is taken from the experience of another family of children.

Miss Alcott twice says that she never went to any school but her father's; but there were some slight exceptions to this rule. She went a few months to a little district school in Still River Village. This was a genuine old-fashioned school,

from which she took the hint of the frolics in
"Under the Lilacs." Miss Ford also kept a little
school in Mr. Emerson's barn, to which the children went; and Mary Russell had a school, which
Louisa attended when eight or nine years old.
These circumstances, however, had small influence
in her education.

During this period of life in Concord, which was
so happy to the children, the mother's heart was
full of anxious care. She however entered into
all their childish pleasûres, and her watchful care
over their moral growth is shown by· her letters
and by Louisa's journals.

The youngest child, Abba May, who was born
in the cottage, became the pet of the family and
the special care of the oldest sister, Anna.

Louisa's childish journal gives us many hints
of this happy life. She revised these journals in
later years, adding significant comments which
are full of interest. She designed them to have
place in her autobiography, which she hoped to
write.

From three different sources — her journals, an
article written for publication, and a manuscript
prepared for a friend, — we give her own account
of these childish years. She has not followed the
order of events strictly, and it has not been possible, therefore, to avoid all repetition; but they
give the spirit of her early life, and clearly show
the kind of education she received from her father
and from the circumstances around her.

Sketch of Childhood, by herself.

ONE of my earliest recollections is of playing with books in my father's study, — building houses and bridges of the big dictionaries and diaries, looking at pictures, pretending to read, and scribbling on blank pages whenever pen or pencil could be found. Many of these first attempts at authorship still remain in Bacon's Essays, Plutarch's Lives, and other works of a serious nature, my infant taste being for solid literature, apparently.

On one occasion we built a high tower round baby Lizzie as she sat playing with her toys on the floor, and being attracted by something out-of-doors, forgot our little prisoner. A search was made, and patient baby at last discovered curled up and fast asleep in her dungeon cell, out of which she emerged so rosy and smiling after her nap that we were forgiven for our carelessness.

Another memory is of my fourth birthday, which was celebrated at my father's school-room in Masonic Temple. All the children were there. I wore a crown of flowers, and stood upon a table to dispense cakes to each child as the procession marched past. By some oversight the cakes fell short, and I saw that if I gave away the last one *I* should have none. As I was queen of the revel, I felt that I ought to have it, and held on to it tightly till my mother said, —

"It is always better to give away than to keep the nice things; so I know my Louy will not let the little friend go without."

The little friend received the dear plummy cake, and I a kiss and my first lesson in the sweetness of self-denial, — a lesson which my dear mother beautifully illustrated all her long and noble life.

Running away was one of the delights of my early

days; and I still enjoy sudden flights out of the nest to look about this very interesting world, and then go back to report.

On one of these occasions I passed a varied day with some Irish children, who hospitably shared their cold potatoes, salt-fish, and crusts with me as we revelled in the ash-heaps which then adorned the waste lands where the Albany Depot now stands. A trip to the Common cheered the afternoon, but as dusk set in and my friends deserted me, I felt that home was a nice place after all, and tried to find it. I dimly remember watching a lamp-lighter as I sat to rest on some doorsteps in Bedford Street, where a big dog welcomed me so kindly that I fell asleep with my head pillowed on his curly back, and was found there by the town-crier, whom my distracted parents had sent in search of me. His bell and procla-mation of the loss of "a little girl, six years old, in a pink frock, white hat, and new green shoes," woke me up, and a small voice answered out of the darkness, —

"Why, dat's me !"

Being with difficulty torn from my four-footed friend, I was carried to the crier's house, and there feasted sumptuously on bread-and-molasses in a tin plate with the alphabet round it. But my fun ended next day when I was tied to the arm of the sofa to repent at leisure.

I became an Abolitionist at a very early age, but have never been able to decide whether I was made so by seeing the portrait of George Thompson hidden under a bed in our house during the Garrison riot, and going to comfort "the poor man who had been good to the slaves," or because I was saved from drowning in the Frog Pond some years later by a colored boy. How-ever that may be, the conversion was genuine; and my greatest pride is in the fact that I lived to know the brave men and women who did so much for the cause, and that I had a very small share in the war which put an end to a great wrong.

Another recollection of her childhood was of a "contraband" hidden in the oven, which must have made her sense of the horrors of slavery very keen.

I never went to school except to my father or such governesses as from time to time came into the family. Schools then were not what they are now; so we had lessons each morning in the study. And very happy hours they were to us, for my father taught in the wise way which unfolds what lies in the child's nature, as a flower blooms, rather than crammed it, like a Strasburg goose, with more than it could digest. I never liked arithmetic nor grammar, and dodged those branches on all occasions; but reading, writing, composition, history, and geography I enjoyed, as well as the stories read to us with a skill peculiarly his own.

"Pilgrim's Progress," Krummacher's "Parables," Miss Edgeworth, and the best of the dear old fairy tales made the reading hour the pleasantest of our day. On Sundays we had a simple service of Bible stories, hymns, and conversation about the state of our little consciences and the conduct of our childish lives which never will be forgotten.

Walks each morning round the Common while in the city, and long tramps over hill and dale when our home was in the country, were a part of our education, as well as every sort of housework, — for which I have always been very grateful, since such knowledge makes one independent in these days of domestic tribulation with the "help" who are too often only hindrances.

Needle-work began early, and at ten my skilful sister made a linen shirt beautifully; while at twelve I set up as a doll's dressmaker, with my sign out and wonderful models in my window. All the children employed me, and my turbans were the rage at one time, to the great dismay of the neighbors' hens, who were hotly hunted down, that I might tweak out their downiest feathers to adorn the dolls' headgear.

Active exercise was my delight, from the time when a child of six I drove my hoop round the Common without stopping, to the days when I did my twenty miles in five hours and went to a party in the evening.

I always thought I must have been a deer or a horse in some former state, because it was such a joy to run. No boy could be my friend till I had beaten him in a race, and no girl if she refused to climb trees, leap fences, and be a tomboy.

My wise mother, anxious to give me a strong body to support a lively brain, turned me loose in the country and let me run wild, learning of Nature what no books can teach, and being led, — as those who truly love her seldom fail to be, —

"Through Nature up to Nature's God."

I remember running over the hills just at dawn one summer morning, and pausing to rest in the silent woods, saw, through an arch of trees, the sun rise over river, hill, and wide green meadows as I never saw it before.

Something born of the lovely hour, a happy mood, and the unfolding aspirations of a child's soul seemed to bring me very near to God; and in the hush of that morning hour I always felt that I "got religion," as the phrase goes. A new and vital sense of His presence, tender and sustaining as a father's arms, came to me then, never to change through forty years of life's vicissitudes, but to grow stronger for the sharp discipline of poverty and pain, sorrow and success.

Those Concord days were the happiest of my life, for we had charming playmates in the little Emersons, Channings, Hawthornes, and Goodwins, with the illustrious parents and their friends to enjoy our pranks and share our excursions.

Plays in the barn were a favorite amusement, and we dramatized the fairy tales in great style. Our giant came tumbling off a loft when Jack cut down the squash-vine running up a ladder to represent the immortal bean. Cinderella rolled away in a vast pumpkin, and a long black pudding was lowered by invisible hands to fasten itself on the nose of the woman who wasted her three wishes.

Pilgrims journeyed over the hill with scrip and staff and cockle-shells in their hats; fairies held their pretty revels among the whispering birches, and strawberry parties in the rustic arbor were honored by poets and philosophers, who fed us on their wit and wisdom while the little maids served more mortal food.

CHAPTER III.

FRUITLANDS.

MY KINGDOM.

A LITTLE kingdom I possess,
　　Where thoughts and feelings dwell,
And very hard I find the task
　　Of governing it well;
For passion tempts and troubles me,
　　A wayward will misleads,
And selfishness its shadow casts
　　On all my words and deeds.

How can I learn to rule myself,
　　To be the child I should,
Honest and brave, nor ever tire
　　Of trying to be good?
How can I keep a sunny soul
　　To shine along life's way?
How can I tune my little heart
　　To sweetly sing all day?

Dear Father, help me with the love
　　That casteth out my fear;
Teach me to lean on thee, and feel
　　That thou art very near,
That no temptation is unseen,
　　No childish grief too small,
Since thou, with patience infinite,
　　Doth soothe and comfort all.

I do not ask for any crown
　　But that which all may win,
Nor seek to conquer any world
　　Except the one within.
Be thou my guide until I find,
　　Led by a tender hand,
Thy happy kingdom in *myself*,
　　And dare to take command.

IN 1842 Mr. Alcott went to England. His mind was very much exercised at this time with plans for organized social life on a higher plane, and he found like-minded friends in England who gave him sympathy and encouragement. He had for some years advocated a strictly vegetarian diet, to which his family consented from deference to him; consequently the children never tasted meat till they came to maturity. On his return from England he was accompanied by friends who were ready to unite with him in the practical realization of their social theories. Mr. Lane resided for some months in the Alcott family at Concord, and gave instruction to the children. Although he does not appear to have won their hearts, they yet reaped much intellectual advantage from his lessons, as he was an accomplished scholar.

In 1843 this company of enthusiasts secured a farm in the town of Harvard, near Concord, which with trusting hope they named Fruitlands. Mrs. Alcott did not share in all the peculiar ideas of her husband and his friends, but she was so utterly devoted to him that she was ready to help him in carrying out his plans, however little they commended themselves to her better judgment.

She alludes very briefly to the experiment in her diary, for the experience was too bitter to dwell upon. She could not relieve her feelings by bringing out the comic side, as her daughter did. Louisa's account of this colony, as given in her story called " Transcendental Wild Oats," is very close to the facts; and the mingling of pathos and humor, the reverence and ridicule with which she

3

alternately treats the personages and the notions of those engaged in the scheme, make a rich and delightful tale. It was written many years later, and gives the picture as she looked back upon it, the absurdities coming out in strong relief, while she sees also the grand, misty outlines of the high thoughts so poorly realized. This story was published in the "Independent," Dec. 8, 1873, and may now be found in her collected works ("Silver Pitchers," p. 79).

Fortunately we have also her journal written at the time, which shows what education the experience of this strange life brought to the child of ten or eleven years old.

The following extract from Mr. Emerson proves that this plan of life looked fair and pleasing to his eye, although he was never tempted to join in it. He was evidently not unconscious of the inadequacy of the means adopted to the end proposed, but he rejoiced in any endeavor after high ideal life.

JULY, 8, 1843.

Journal. — The sun and the evening sky do not look calmer than Alcott and his family at Fruitlands. They seemed to have arrived at the fact, — to have got rid of the show, and so to be serene. Their manners and behavior in the house and in the field were those of superior men, — of men at rest. What had they to conceal? What had they to exhibit? And it seemed so high an attainment that I thought — as often before, so now more, because they had a fit home, or the picture was fitly framed — that these men ought to be maintained in their place by the country for its culture.

Young men and young maidens, old men and women, should visit them and be inspired. I think there is as much merit in beautiful manners as in hard work. I will not prejudge them successful. They look well in July; we will see them in December. I know they are better for themselves than as partners. One can easily see that they have yet to settle several things. Their saying that things are clear, and they sane, does not make them so. If they will in very deed be lovers, and not selfish; if they will serve the town of Harvard, and make their neighbors feel them as benefactors wherever they touch them, — they are as safe as the sun.[1]

Early Diary kept at Fruitlands, 1843.

Ten Years Old.

September 1*st.* — I rose at five and had my bath. I love cold water! Then we had our singing-lesson with Mr. Lane. After breakfast I washed dishes, and ran on the hill till nine, and had some thoughts, — it was so beautiful up there. Did my lessons, — wrote and spelt and did sums; and Mr. Lane read a story, " The Judicious Father ": How a rich girl told a poor girl not to look over the fence at the flowers, and was cross to her because she was unhappy. The father heard her do it, and made the girls change clothes. The poor one was glad to do it, and he told her to keep them. But the rich one was very sad; for she had to wear the old ones a week, and after that she was good to shabby girls. I liked it very much, and I shall be kind to poor people.

Father asked us what was God's noblest work. Anna said *men*, but I said *babies*. Men are often bad; babies

---

[1] Emerson in Concord. By Edward Waldo Emerson.

never are. We had a long talk, and I felt better after it, and *cleared up.*

We had bread and fruit for dinner. I read and walked and played till supper-time. We sung in the evening. As I went to bed the moon came up very brightly and looked at me. I felt sad because I have been cross to-day, and did not mind Mother. I cried, and then I felt better, and said that piece from Mrs. Sigourney, "I must not tease my mother." I get to sleep saying poetry, — I know a great deal.

Thursday, 14th. — Mr. Parker Pillsbury came, and we talked about the poor slaves. I had a music lesson with Miss F. I hate her, she is so fussy. I ran in the wind and played be a horse, and had a lovely time in the woods with Anna and Lizzie. We were fairies, and made gowns and paper wings. I " flied " the highest of all. In the evening they talked about travelling. I thought about Father going to England, and said this piece of poetry I found in Byron's poems : —

> " When I left thy shores, O Naxos,
>   Not a tear in sorrow fell ;
> Not a sigh or faltered accent
>   Told my bosom's struggling swell."

It rained when I went to bed, and made a pretty noise on the roof.

Sunday, 24th. — Father and Mr. Lane have gone to N. H. to preach. It was very lovely. . . . Anna and I got supper. In the eve I read " Vicar of Wakefield." I was cross to-day, and I cried when I went to bed. I made good resolutions, and felt better in my heart. If I only *kept* all I make, I should be the best girl in the world. But I don't, and so am very bad.

[Poor little sinner ! *She says the same at fifty.* — L. M. A.]

October 8th. — When I woke up, the first thought I got was, " It 's Mother's birthday : I must be very good." I ran and wished her a happy birthday, and gave her my kiss. After breakfast we gave her our presents. I had a moss cross and a piece of poetry for her.

We did not have any school, and played in the woods and got red leaves. In the evening we danced and sung, and I read a story about " Contentment." I wish I was rich, I was good, and we were all a happy family this day.

Thursday, 12th. — After lessons I ironed. We all went to the barn and husked corn. It was good fun. We worked till eight o'clock and had lamps. Mr. Russell came. Mother and Lizzie are going to Boston. I shall be very lonely without dear little Betty, and no one will be as good to me as mother. I read in Plutarch. I made a verse about sunset : —

> Softly doth the sun descend
>   To his couch behind the hill,
> Then, oh, then, I love to sit
>   On mossy banks beside the rill.

Anna thought it was very fine ; but I did n't like it very well.

Friday, Nov. 2nd. — Anna and I did the work. In the evening Mr. Lane asked us, " What is man?" These were our answers : A human being ; an animal with a mind ; a creature ; a body ; a soul and a mind. After a long talk we went to bed very tired.

[No wonder, after doing the work and worrying their little wits with such lessons. — L. M. A.]

A sample of the vegetarian wafers we used at Fruitlands : —

Vegetable diet
and sweet repose.
Animal food and
nightmare.

Pluck your body
from the orchard;
do not snatch it
from the shamble.

Without flesh diet
there could be no
blood-shedding war.

Apollo eats no
flesh and has no
beard; his voice is
melody itself.

Snuff is no less snuff
though accepted from
a gold box.

Tuesday, 20th. — I rose at five, and after breakfast washed the dishes, and then helped mother work. Miss F. is gone, and Anna in Boston with Cousin Louisa. I took care of Abby (May) in the afternoon. In the evening I made some pretty things for my dolly. Father and Mr. L. had a talk, and father asked us if *we* saw any reason for us to separate. Mother wanted to, she is so tired. I like it, but not the school part or Mr. L.

Eleven years old. *Thursday, 29th.* — It was Father's and my birthday. We had some nice presents. We played in the snow before school. Mother read " Rosamond " when we sewed. Father asked us in the eve what fault troubled us most. I said my bad temper.

I told mother I liked to have her write in my book. She said she would put in more, and she wrote this to help me : —

DEAR LOUY, — Your handwriting improves very fast. Take pains and do not be in a hurry. I like to have you make observations about our conversations and your own thoughts. It helps you to express them and to understand your little self. Remember, dear girl, that a diary should be an epitome of your life. May it be a record of pure thought and good actions, then you will indeed be the precious child of your loving mother.

December 10th. — I did my lessons, and walked in the afternoon. Father read to us in dear Pilgrim's Progress.

Mr. L. was in Boston, and we were glad. In the eve father and mother and Anna and I had a long talk. I was very unhappy, and we all cried. Anna and I cried in bed, and I prayed God to keep us all together.

[Little Lu began early to feel the family cares and peculiar trials. — L. M. A.]

I liked the verses Christian sung and will put them in : —

"This place has been our second stage,
  Here we have heard and seen
Those good things that from age to age
  To others hid have been.

"They move me for to watch and pray,
  To strive to be sincere,
To take my cross up day by day,
  And serve the Lord with fear."

[The appropriateness of the song at this time was much greater than the child saw. She never forgot this experience, and her little cross began to grow heavier from this hour. — L. M. A.]

CONCORD, *Sunday.* — We all went into the woods to get moss for the *arbor* Father is making for *Mr. Emerson.* I miss Anna so much. I made two verses for her : —

TO ANNA.

Sister, dear, when you are lonely,
  Longing for your distant home,
And the images of loved ones
  Warmly to your heart shall come,
Then, mid tender thoughts and fancies,
  Let one fond voice say to thee,
"Ever when your heart is heavy,
  Anna, dear, then think of me."

Think how we two have together
  Journeyed onward day by day,
Joys and sorrows ever sharing,
  While the swift years roll away.
Then may all the sunny hours
  Of our youth rise up to thee,
And when your heart is light and happy,
  Anna, dear, then think of me.

[Poetry began to flow about this time in a thin but copious stream. — L. M. A.]

Wednesday. — Read Martin Luther. A long letter
from Anna. She sends me a picture of Jenny Lind, the
great singer. She must be a happy girl. I should like
to be famous as she is. Anna is very happy; and I
don't miss her as much as I shall by and by in the
winter.

I wrote in my Imagination Book, and enjoyed it very
much. Life is pleasanter than it used to be, and I don't
care about dying any more. Had a splendid run, and
got a box of cones to burn. Sat and heard the pines
sing a long time. Read Miss Bremer's "Home" in the
eve. Had good dreams, and woke now and then to
think, and watch the moon. I had a pleasant time with
my mind, for it was happy.

[Moods began early. — L. M. A.]

January, 1845, *Friday.* — Did my lessons, and in the
P. M. mother read "Kenilworth" to us while we sewed.
It is splendid! I got angry and called Anna mean.
Father told me to look out the word in the Dic., and it
meant "base," "contemptible." I was so ashamed to
have called my dear sister that, and I cried over my bad
tongue and temper.

We have had a lovely day. All the trees were covered

with ice, and it shone like diamonds or fairy palaces. I
made a piece of poetry about winter : —

> The stormy winter's come at last,
>   With snow and rain and bitter blast;
> Ponds and brooks are frozen o'er,
>   We cannot sail there any more.

> The little birds are flown away
>   To warmer climes than ours ;
> They'll come no more till gentle May
>   Calls them back with flowers.

> Oh, then the darling birds will sing
>   From their neat nests in the trees.
> All creatures wake to welcome Spring,
>   And flowers dance in the breeze.

> With patience wait till winter is o'er,
>   And all lovely things return ;
> Of every season try the more
>   Some knowledge or virtue to learn.

[A moral is tacked on even to the early poems. —
L. M. A.]

I read " Philothea," [1] by Mrs. Child. I found this that
I liked in it. Plato said : —

" When I hear a note of music I can at once strike its
chord. Even as surely is there everlasting harmony between the soul of man and the invisible forms of creation.
If there were no innocent hearts there would be no white
lilies. . . . I often think flowers are the angel's alphabet

---

[1] " Philothea " was the delight of girls. The young Alcotts
made a dramatic version of it, which they acted under the trees.
Louisa made a magnificent Aspasia, which was a part much to her
fancy. Mrs. Child was a very dear friend of Mrs. Alcott, and her
daughters knew her well.

whereby they write on hills and fields mysterious and beautiful lessons for us to feel and learn."

[Well done, twelve-year-old! Plato the father's delight, had a charm for the little girl also. — L. M. A.]

Wednesday. — I am so cross I wish I had never been born.

Thursday. — Read the "Heart of Mid-Lothian," and had a very happy day. Miss Ford gave us a botany lesson in the woods. I am always good there. In the evening Miss Ford told us about the bones in our bodies, and how they get out of order. I must be careful of mine, I climb and jump and run so much.

I found this note from dear mother in my journal : —

MY DEAREST LOUY, — I often peep into your diary, hoping to see some record of more happy days. "Hope, and keep busy," dear daughter, and in all perplexity or trouble come freely to your

MOTHER.

DEAR MOTHER, — You *shall* see more happy days, and I *will* come to you with my worries, for you are the best woman in the world.　　　　L. M. A.

A Sample of our Lessons.

"What virtues do you wish more of ? " asks Mr. L. I answer : —

Patience,	Love,	Silence,
Obedience,	Generosity,	Perseverance,
Industry,	Respect,	Self-denial.

"What vices less of ? "

Idleness,	Wilfulness,	Vanity,
Impatience,	Impudence,	Pride,
Selfishness,	Activity.	Love of cats.

MR. L.   L.
SOCRATES.   ALCIBIADES.

How can you get what you need? By trying.
How do you try? By resolution and perseverance.
How gain love? By gentleness.
What is gentleness? Kindness, patience, and care for other people's feelings.
Who has it? Father and Anna.
Who means to have it? Louisa, if she can.

[She never got it. — L. M. A.]

Write a sentence about anything. "I hope it will rain; the garden needs it."
What are the elements of *hope?* Expectation, desire, faith.
What are the elements in *wish?* Desire.
What is the difference between faith and hope? "Faith can believe without seeing; hope is not sure, but tries to have faith when it desires."

No. 3.

What are the most valuable kinds of self-denial? Appetite, temper.
How is self-denial of temper known? If I control my temper, I am respectful and gentle, and every one sees it.
What is the result of this self-denial? Every one loves me, and I am happy.
Why use self-denial? For the good of myself and others.
How shall we learn this self-denial? By resolving, and then trying *hard*.
What then do you mean to do? To resolve and try.

[Here the record of these lessons ends, and poor little Alcibiades went to work and tried till fifty, but without any very great success, in spite of all the help Socrates and Plato gave her. — L. M. A.]

Tuesday. — More people coming to live with us; I wish we could be together, and no one else. I don't

see who is to clothe and feed us all, when we are so
poor now. I was very dismal, and then went to walk
and made a poem.

DESPONDENCY.

Silent and sad,
When all are glad,
And the earth is dressed in flowers;
When the gay birds sing
Till the forests ring,
As they rest in woodland bowers.

Oh, why these tears,
And these idle fears
For what may come to-morrow?
The birds find food
From God so good,
And the flowers know no sorrow.

If He clothes these
And the leafy trees,
Will He not cherish thee?
Why doubt His care;
It is everywhere,
Though the way we may not see.

Then why be sad
When all are glad,
And the world is full of flowers?
With the gay birds sing,
Make life all Spring,
And smile through the darkest hours.

Louisa Alcott grew up so naturally in a healthy
religious atmosphere that she breathed and worked
in it without analysis or question. She had not

suffered from ecclesiastical tyranny or sectarian bigotry, and needed not to expend any time or strength in combating them. She does not appear to have suffered from doubt or questioning, but to have gone on her way fighting all the real evils that were presented to her, trusting in a sure power of right, and confident of victory.

CONCORD, *Thursday.* — I had an early run in the woods before the dew was off the grass. The moss was like velvet, and as I ran under the arches of yellow and red leaves I sang for joy, my heart was so bright and the world so beautiful. I stopped at the end of the walk and saw the sunshine out over the wide " Virginia meadows."

It seemed like going through a dark life or grave into heaven beyond. A very strange and solemn feeling came over me as I stood there, with no sound but the rustle of the pines, no one near me, and the sun so glorious, as for me alone. It seemed as if I *felt* God as I never did before, and I prayed in my heart that I might keep that happy sense of nearness all my life.

[I have, for I most sincerely think that the little girl "got religion " that day in the wood when dear mother Nature led her to God. — L. M. A., 1885.]

One of Louisa's strongest desires at this time was for a room of her own, where she might have the solitude she craved to dream her dreams and work out her fancies. These sweet little notes and an extract from her journal show how this desire was felt and gratified.

DEAREST MOTHER, — I have tried to be more contented, and I think I have been more so. I have been thinking about my little room, which I suppose I never shall have. I should want to be there about all the time, and I should go there and sing and think.

> But I 'll be contented
> 　With what I have got;
> Of folly repented,
> 　Then sweet is my lot.

From your trying daughter,

LOUY.

MY DEAR LOUISA, — Your note gave me so much delight that I cannot close my eyes without first thanking you, dear, for making me so happy, and blessing God who gave you this tender love for your mother.

I have observed all day your patience with baby, your obedience to me, and your kindness to all.

Go on "trying," my child; God will give you strength and courage, and help you fill each day with words and deeds of love. I shall lay this on your pillow, put a warm kiss on your lips, and say a little prayer over you in your sleep.

MOTHER.

MY LOUY, — I was grieved at your selfish behavior this morning, but also greatly pleased to find you bore so meekly Father's reproof for it. That is the way, dear; if you find you are wrong, take the discipline sweetly, and do so no more. It is not to be expected that children should always do right; but oh, how lovely to see a child penitent and patient when the passion is over.

I thought a little prayer as I looked at you, and said in my heart, "Dear God, sustain my child in this moment of trial, that no hasty word, no cruel look, no angry action may add to her fault." And you were helped. I know that you will have a happy day after the storm and the gentle shower; keep quiet, read, walk, but do not talk much till all is peace again.

MOTHER.

HILLSIDE, CONCORD.

DEAR, — I am glad you put your heart in the right place; for I am sure all true strength comes from above. Continue to feel that God is *near* you, dear child, and He never will forsake you in a weak moment. Write me always when you feel that I can help you; for, though God is near, Mother never forgets you, and your refuge is her arms.

Patience, dear, will give us content, if nothing else. Be assured the little room you long for will come, if it is necessary to your peace and well-being. Till then try to be happy with the good things you have. They are many, — more perhaps than we deserve, after our frequent complaints and discontent.

Be cheerful, my Louy, and all will be gayer for your laugh, and all good and lovely things will be given to you when you deserve them.

I am a busy woman, but never can forget the calls of my children.

MOTHER.

DEAREST, — I am sure you have lived very near to God *to-day*, you have been so good and happy. Let each day be like this, and life will become a sweet song for you and all who love you, — none so much as your

MOTHER.

Thirteen Years Old.

HILLSIDE.

March, 1846. — I have at last got the little room I have wanted so long, and am very happy about it. It does me good to be alone, and Mother has made it very pretty and neat for me. My work-basket and desk are by the window, and my closet is full of dried herbs that smell very nice. The door that opens into the garden will be very pretty in summer, and I can run off to the woods when I like.

I have made a plan for my life, as I am in my teens, and no more a child. I am old for my age, and don't care much for girl's things. People think I 'm wild and queer; but Mother understands and helps me. I have not told any one about my plan; but I 'm going to *be* good. I 've made so many resolutions, and written sad notes, and cried over my sins, and it does n't seem to do any good ! Now I 'm going to *work really*, for I feel a true desire to improve, and be a help and comfort, not a care and sorrow, to my dear mother.

Fifteen Years Old.

Sunday, Oct. 9, 1847. — I have been reading to-day Bettine's correspondence with Goethe.

She calls herself a child, and writes about the lovely things she saw and heard, and felt and did. I liked it much.

[First taste of Goethe. Three years later R. W. E. gave me "Wilhelm Meister," and from that day Goethe has been my chief idol. — L. M. A., 1885.]

The experiment at Fruitlands was (outwardly) an utter failure, and had exhausted Mr. Alcott's resources of mind, body, and estate. Louisa has not exaggerated the collapse which followed. But the brave, loving mother could not give way to despondency, for she had her young to care for. After a few days Mr. Alcott rose from his despair, and listened to her counsel. They lived a short time at Still River, and then returned to Concord; but not to the happy little cottage.

Mr. Alcott sought such work as he could find to do with his hands; but it was scanty and insufficient. Mrs. Alcott subdued her proud heart to the necessity of seeking help from friends. They had a few rooms in the house of a kind neighbor, who welcomed them to her house, in addition to her own large family; and there they struggled with the poverty which Louisa for the first time fully realized.

Yet her journal says little of the hardships they endured, but is full of her mental and moral struggles. It was characteristic of this family that they never were conquered by their surroundings. Mr. Alcott might retire into sad and silent musing, Mrs. Alcott's warm, quick temper, might burst out into flame, the children might be quarrelsome or noisy; but their ideal of life always remained high, fresh, and ennobling. Their souls always " knew their destiny divine," and believed that they would find fitting expression in life some time. " Chill penury " could not repress " their noble rage," nor freeze " the genial current" of their souls.

The children escaped from the privations of daily life into a world of romance, and in the plays in the old barn revelled in luxury and splendor. This dramatic tendency was very strong in Louisa, and she never outgrew it. It took various shapes and colors, and at one time threatened to dominate her life.

The education of the children was certainly des-

4

ultory and insufficient; but it was inspiring, and brought out their powers. They learned to feel and to think justly, and to express their thoughts and feelings freely and forcibly, if they did not know well the rules of grammar and rhetoric. Mr. Alcott always loved the study of language, and became a master of it; while Mrs. Alcott had a rich and well-chosen vocabulary, gained from the intelligent companions of her youth and the best literature, which she read freely. Mr. Alcott made great use of the study of language in his teaching, and often employed the definition of a word to convey a lesson or a rebuke. The children were encouraged, and even required, to keep their journals regularly, and to write letters. Their efforts at poetry or the drama were not laughed at, but treasured by their parents as indications of progress. Mr. Alcott's records of his own theory and practice in the education of children are full of valuable suggestion, and much yet remains buried in his journals. The girls had full freedom to act out their natures, with little fear of ridicule or criticism. An innate sense of dignity and modesty kept them from abusing this liberty; and perhaps nowhere in the world could it have been more safely indulged than in the simple life of Concord, whose very atmosphere seemed then filled with a spiritual presence which made life free, pure, and serene.

Louisa gives this interesting anecdote of their life at that time: —

People wondered at our frolics, but enjoyed them, and droll stories are still told of the adventures of those days.

Mr. Emerson and Margaret Fuller were visiting my parents one afternoon, and the conversation having turned to the ever interesting subject of education, Miss Fuller said : —

"Well, Mr. Alcott, you have been able to carry out your methods in your own family, and I should like to see your model children."

She did in a few moments, for as the guests stood on the door-steps a wild uproar approached, and round the corner of the house came a wheelbarrow holding baby May arrayed as a queen; I was the horse, bitted and bridled, and driven by my elder sister Anna; while Lizzie played dog, and barked as loud as her gentle voice permitted.

All were shouting and wild with fun, which, however, came to a sudden end as we espied the stately group before us; for my foot tripped, and down we all went in a laughing heap; while my mother put a climax to the joke by saying, with a dramatic wave of the hand, —

"Here are the model children, Miss Fuller."

They were undoubtedly very satisfactory to Miss Fuller, who partook largely of the educational views of that time, and who loved to tell anecdotes of this family. One of the sisters writes in her diary: " She *said* prayers; but I think my resolutions to be good are prayers."

In 1841 Colonel May, Mrs. Alcott's father, died and left her a small amount of property. Mrs. Alcott decided to purchase with this a house in Concord, and the addition of five hundred dollars from Mr. Emerson, who was always the good Providence of the family, enabled her in 1845 to buy the place in Concord known as Hillside. This house is on the road to Lexington, about one third of a mile from Mr. Emerson's home. It was afterward occupied by Mr. Hawthorne.

In this house the girlish life of Louisa was passed, which she has represented so fully in "Little Women," and of which she speaks in her journal as the happiest time of her life. Yet she was not unmindful of the anxiety of her parents; and the determined purpose to retrieve the fortunes of the family and to give to her mother the comfort and ease which she had never known in her married life became the constant motive of her conduct. It is in the light of this purpose alone that her character and her subsequent career can be fully understood. She naturally thought of teaching as her work, and had for a short time a little school in the barn for Mr. Emerson's children and others.

It was indeed a great comfort to be sure of the house over their heads, but there were still six mouths to be fed, six bodies to be clothed, and four young, eager minds to be educated. Concord offered very little opportunity for such work as either Mr. or Mrs. Alcott could do, and at last even the mother's brave heart broke down. She was painfully anxious about the support of her household. A friend passing through Concord called upon her, and Mrs. Alcott could not hide the traces of tears on her face. "Abby Alcott, what does this mean?" said the visitor, with determined kindness. The poor mother opened her heart to her friend, and told the story of their privations and sufferings.

"Come to Boston, and I will find you employment," said the friend.

The family removed to Boston in 1848, and Mrs. Alcott became a visitor to the poor in the employ of one or more benevolent societies, and finally kept an intelligence office. Her whole heart went into her work; and the children, as well as the mother, learned many valuable lessons from it. Her reports of her work are said to have been very interesting, and full of valuable suggestion.

Mr. Alcott began to hold conversations in West Street. He attracted a small circle of thoughtful men and women about him, who delighted in the height of his aspirations and the originality of his thoughts. It was congenial occupation for him, and thus added to the happiness of the family, though very little to its pecuniary resources. His price of admission was small, and he freely invited any one who would enjoy the meetings although unable to pay for them. He was a great and helpful influence to young minds. Besides the morally pure and spiritually elevated atmosphere of thought to which they were introduced by him, they found a great intellectual advantage in the acquaintance with ancient poets and philosophers, into whose life he had entered sympathetically. His peculiar theories of temperament and diet never failed to call out discussion and opposition. One of my earliest recollections of Louisa is on one of these occasions, when he was emphasizing his doctrine that a vegetable diet would produce unruffled sweetness of temper and disposition. I heard a voice behind me saying to her neighbor: "I don't know about that. I 've never eaten any meat, and I 'm awful cross and irritable very often."

On her fourteenth birthday her mother wrote her the following poem, with a present of a pen. It was a prophetic gift, and well used by the receiver.

> Oh, may this pen your muse inspire,
>   When wrapt in pure poetic fire,
> To write some sweet, some thrilling verse;
>   A song of love or sorrow's lay,
> Or duty's clear but tedious way
>   In brighter hope rehearse.
> Oh, let your strain be soft and high,
>   Of crosses here, of crowns beyond the sky;
> Truth guide your pen, inspire your theme,
>   And from each note joy's music stream.

[Original, I think. I have tried to obey. — L. M. A., 1885.]

In a sketch written for a friend, Louisa gives this account of the parents' influence on the children: —

When cautious friends asked mother how she dared to have such outcasts among her girls, she always answered, with an expression of confidence which did much to keep us safe, "I can trust my daughters, and this is the best way to teach them how to shun these sins and comfort these sorrows. They cannot escape the knowledge of them; better gain this under their father's roof and their mother's care, and so be protected by these experiences when their turn comes to face the world and its temptations." Once we carried our breakfast to a starving family; once lent our whole dinner to a neighbor suddenly taken unprepared by distinguished guests. Another time, one snowy Saturday night, when our wood was very low, a poor child came to beg a little, as the baby was

sick and the father on a spree with all his wages. My
mother hesitated at first, as we also had a baby. Very
cold weather was upon us, and a Sunday to be got
through before more wood could be had. My father
said, "Give half our stock, and trust in Providence; the
weather will moderate, or wood will come." Mother
laughed, and answered in her cheery way, "Well, their
need is greater than ours, and if our half gives out we
can go to bed and tell stories." So a generous half went
to the poor neighbor, and a little later in the eve, while
the storm still raged and we were about to cover our fire
to keep it, a knock came, and a farmer who usually supplied us appeared, saying anxiously, "I started for Boston
with a load of wood, but it drifts so I want to go home.
Would n't you like to have me drop the wood here; it
would accommodate me, and you need n't hurry about
paying for it." "Yes," said Father; and as the man went
off he turned to Mother with a look that much impressed
us children with his gifts as a seer, "Did n't I tell you
wood would come if the weather did not moderate?"
Mother's motto was "Hope, and keep busy," and one
of her sayings, "Cast your bread upon the waters, and
after many days it will come back buttered."

CHAPTER IV.

THE SENTIMENTAL PERIOD.

A SONG FROM THE SUDS.

QUEEN of my tub, I merrily sing,
　　While the white foam rises high,
And sturdily wash, and rinse, and wring,
　　And fasten the clothes to dry;
Then out in the free fresh air they swing,
　　Under the sunny sky.

I wish we could wash from our hearts and our souls
　　The stains of the week away,
And let water and air by their magic make
　　Ourselves as pure as they;
Then on the earth there would be indeed
　　A glorious washing-day !

Along the path of a useful life
　　Will heart's-ease ever bloom;
The busy mind has no time to think
　　Of sorrow, or care, or gloom;
And anxious thoughts may be swept away
　　As we busily wield a broom.

I am glad a task to me is given
　　To labor at day by day;
For it brings me health, and strength, and hope,
　　And I cheerfully learn to say, —
" Head, you may think; heart, you may feel;
　　But hand, you shall work alway ! "

THE period of free, happy childhood was neces-
sarily short, and at about the age of fifteen
Louisa Alcott began to feel the pressure of thoughts
and duties which made life a more solemn matter.

In spite of the overflowing fun which appears in her books, her nature was very serious, and she could not cast aside care lightly. So many varying tendencies existed in her character that she must have struggled with many doubts and questions before finding the true path. But she always kept the pole-star of right strictly in view, and never failed in truth to that duty which seemed to her nearest and most imperative. If she erred in judgment, she did not err in conscientious fidelity.

Her mother's rules for her guidance were —

> Rule yourself.
> Love your neighbor.
> Do the duty which lies nearest you.

She never lost sight of these instructions.

I will introduce this period in her own words, as written later for the use of a friend.

My romantic period began at fifteen, when I fell to writing poetry, keeping a heart-journal, and wandering by moonlight instead of sleeping quietly. About that time, in browsing over Mr. Emerson's library, I found Goethe's " Correspondence with a Child," and at once was fired with a desire to be a Bettine, making my father's friend my Goethe. So I wrote letters to him, but never sent them; sat in a tall cherry-tree at midnight, singing to the moon till the owls scared me to bed ; left wild flowers on the doorstep of my " Master," and sung Mignon's song under his window in very bad German.

Not till many years later did I tell *my* Goethe of this early romance and the part he played in it. He was much amused, and begged for his letters, kindly saying he felt honored to be so worshipped. The letters were burnt long ago, but Emerson remained my " Master ' while he lived, doing more for me, — as for many another, — than he knew, by the simple beauty of his life, the truth and wisdom of his books, the example of a great, good man, untempted and unspoiled by the world which he made better while in it, and left richer and nobler when he went.

The trials of life began about this time, and happy childhood ended. One of the most memorable days of my life is a certain gloomy November afternoon, when we had been holding a family council as to ways and means. In summer we lived much as the birds did, on our fruit and bread and milk ; the sun was our fire, the sky our roof, and Nature's plenty made us forget that such a thing as poverty existed.

In 1850 she heads her diary " The Sentimental Period." She was then seventeen years old, but her diary gives no hint of the sentimental notions that often fill the heads of young girls at that period. The experiences of Jo with her charming young neighbor in " Little Women " do not represent hers at all.

One bit of romance was suggested by Goethe's " Correspondence with a Child." It may be difficult for readers of to-day to understand the fascination which this book exercised upon young minds of the last generation, yet it is certain that it led more than one young girl to form an ideal attachment to a man far older than herself, but full of nobility and intellectual greatness. Theodore Parker said of letters addressed to him by a young New Hampshire girl, " They are as good as Bettine's without the lies." This mingling of idealism and hero-worship was strongly characteristic of that transcendental period when women, having little solid education and less industrial employment, were full of noble aspirations and longings for fuller and freer life, which must find expression in some way.

The young woman of to-day, wearing waterproof and india-rubber boots, skating, driving, and bicycling, studying chemistry in the laboratory, exhibiting her pictures in open competition, adopting a profession without opposition, and living single without fear of reproach, has less time for fancies and more regard for facts.

Miss Alcott was safe in choosing her idol. Worship of Emerson could only refine and elevate her thoughts, and her intimate acquaintance with his beautiful home chastened her idolatry into pure reverent friendship which never failed her. She kept her worship to herself, and never sent him the letters in which she poured out the longings and raptures which filled her girlish heart.

Her diary, which was revised by herself in later years, tells the story of this period quite fully. The details may seem trifling, but they help to illustrate this important formative period of her life.

Journal.

THE SENTIMENTAL PERIOD.

Boston, *May,* 1850. — So long a time has passed since I kept a journal that I hardly know how to begin. Since coming to the city I don't seem to have thought much,

for the bustle and dirt and change send all lovely images
and restful feelings away.   Among my hills and woods I
had fine free times alone, and though my thoughts were
silly, I daresay, they helped to keep me happy and good.
I see now what Nature did for me, and my " romantic
tastes," as people called that love of solitude and out-of-
door life, taught me much.

This summer, like the last, we shall spend in a large
house (Uncle May's, Atkinson Street), with many comforts about us which we shall enjoy, and in the autumn I
hope I shall have something to show that the time has
not been wasted.   Seventeen years have I lived, and yet
so little do I know, and so much remains to be done
before I begin to be what I desire, — a truly good and
useful woman.

In looking over our journals, Father says, " Anna's is
about other people, Louisa's about herself."   That is
true, for I don't *talk* about myself ; yet must always
think of the wilful, moody girl I try to manage, and in
my journal I write of her to see how she gets on.   Anna
is so good she need not take care of herself, and can
enjoy other people.   If I look in my glass, I try to keep
down vanity about my long hair, my well-shaped head,
and my good nose.   In the street I try not to covet
fine things.   My quick tongue is always getting me into
trouble, and my moodiness makes it hard to be cheerful
when I think how poor we are, how much worry it is
to live, and how many things I long to do I never can.

So every day is a battle, and I 'm so tired I don't
want to live ; only it 's cowardly to die till you have done
something.

I can't talk to any one but Mother about my troubles,
and she has so many now to bear I try not to add any
more.   I know God is always ready to hear, but heaven 's

so far away in the city, and I so heavy I can't fly up to find Him.

FAITH.

Written in the diary.

Oh, when the heart is full of fears
　And the way seems dim to heaven,
When the sorrow and the care of years
　Peace from the heart has driven, —
Then, through the mist of falling tears,
　Look up and be forgiven.

Forgiven for the lack of faith
　That made all dark to thee,
Let conscience o'er thy wayward soul
　Have fullest mastery :
Hope on, fight on, and thou shalt win
　A noble victory.

Though thou art weary and forlorn,
　Let not thy heart's peace go ;
Though the riches of this world are gone,
　And thy lot is care and woe,
Faint not, but journey hourly on :
　True wealth is not below.

Through all the darkness still look up:
　Let virtue be thy guide ;
Take thy draught from sorrow's cup,
　Yet trustfully abide ;
Let not temptation vanquish thee,
　And the Father will provide.

[We had small-pox in the family this summer, caught from some poor immigrants whom mother took into our garden and fed one day. We girls had it lightly, but Father and Mother were very ill, and we had a curious time of exile, danger, and trouble. No doctors, and all got well. — L. M. A.]

July, 1850. — Anna is gone to L. after the varioloid. She is to help Mrs. —— with her baby. I had to take A.'s school of twenty in Canton Street. I like it better than I thought, though it's very hard to be patient with the children sometimes. They seem happy, and learn fast ; so I am encouraged, though at first it was very hard, and I missed Anna so much I used to cry over my dinner and be very blue. I guess this is the teaching I need ; for as a *school-marm* I must behave myself and guard my tongue and temper carefully, and set an example of sweet manners.

I found one of mother's notes in my journal, so like those she used to write me when she had more time. It always encourages me ; and I wish some one would write as helpfully to her, for she needs cheering up with all the care she has. I often think what a hard life she has had since she married, — so full of wandering and all sorts of worry ! so different from her early easy days, the youngest and most petted of her family. I think she is a very brave, good woman ; and my dream is to have a lovely, quiet home for her, with no debts or troubles to burden her. But I'm afraid she will be in heaven before I can do it. Anna, too, she is feeble and homesick, and I miss her dreadfully ; for she is my conscience, always true and just and good. She must have a good time in a nice little home of her own some day, as we often plan. But waiting is so *hard !*

August, 1850. — School is hard work, and I feel as though I should like to run away from it. But my children get on ; so I travel up every day, and do my best.

I get very little time to write or think ; for my working days have begun, and when school is over Anna wants me ; so I have no quiet. I think a little solitude every day is good for me. In the quiet I see my faults, and try to mend them; but, deary me, I don't get on at all.

I used to imagine my mind a room in confusion, and I was to put it in order; so I swept out useless thoughts and dusted foolish fancies away, and furnished it with good resolutions and began again. But cobwebs get in. I 'm not a good housekeeper, and never get my room in nice order. I once wrote a poem about it when I was fourteen, and called it " My Little Kingdom." It is still hard to rule it, and always will be I think.

Reading Miss Bremer and Hawthorne. The " Scarlet Letter " is my favorite. Mother likes Miss B. better, as more wholesome. I fancy " lurid " things, if true and strong also.

Anna wants to be an actress, and so do I. We could make plenty of money perhaps, and it is a very gay life. Mother says we are too young, and must wait. A. acts often splendidly. I like tragic plays, and shall be a Siddons if I can. We get up fine ones, and make harps, castles, armor, dresses, water-falls, and thunder, and have great fun.

It was at this period of her life that she was violently attacked by a mania for the stage, and the greater part of her leisure time was given to writing and enacting dramas. Her older sister, Anna, had the same taste, and assisted her in carrying out all her plans. A family of great talent with whom they were intimate joined with them, and their mother always allowed them to have all the private theatricals they wished to perform.

Some of these early plays are preserved in manuscripts as she wrote them. They are written in

stilted, melodramatic style, full of highstrung sentiments of loyalty, honor and devotion, with the
most improbable incidents and violent devices, and
without a touch of common life or the slightest
flavor of humor.   The idea of self-sacrifice always
comes into them; but they are thoroughly girlish.
It is so that girls dream and feel before they know
life at all.   Their hearts are full of vague, restless
longings, and they seek some vent for the repressed
energies of their natures away from the prosaic realities of the present.   While Louisa sat sewing
the tedious seams of her daily task what a relief it
was to let her imagination run riot among the
wildest and most exciting scenes.   Of course she
had a " Bandit's Bride " among her plays.   " The
Captive of Castile; or, The Moorish Maiden's
Vow," is preserved entire, and is a good specimen
of these girlish efforts.   It is full of surprises
and concealments, and the denouement is as unnatural as could well be imagined.   The dialogue
is often bright and forcible, and the sentiments
always lofty, and we have no doubt it seemed very
grand to the youthful audience.   It is taken from
her reading, with no touch of her own life in it.   This
is not the same play described with such a ludicrous
finale in " Little Women," although the heroine
bears the same favorite name of Zara.   Her own
early amusement was, however, fully in her mind
when she wrote that scene, which is true to fact.

A friend and relative of the family living in Roxbury, Dr. Windship, was much interested in the
development of Louisa's dramatic talent.   The
girls always enjoyed delightful visits at his house.

He tried to help the young dramatist to public suc
cess, and writes to her mother: —

I have offered to Mr. Barry of the Boston Theatre
Louisa's " Prima Donnas." He is very much pleased
with it just as it is, and will bring it out this season in
good style. He thinks it will have a fine run.

Mrs. Barry and Mrs. Wood consented to take
the principal characters. But from some difficulty
in the arrangements "The Rival Prima Donnas"
was not produced. One great pleasure was gained,
however, as Mr. Barry gave her a free pass to the
theatre, which proved a source of constant refreshment and delight.

Of course Louisa was eager to go on to the stage
herself. She had indeed extraordinary dramatic
power, and could at any time quickly transform
herself into Hamlet, and recite a scene with tragic
effect. But the careful mother knew better than
the girl the trials and dangers of the profession,
and dissuaded her from it. She also knew how
little such youthful facility of expression indicates the power which will make a great actress.
Louisa has reproduced her dramatic experience in
" Work," which gives a picture faithful in spirit
and in many of its details to this phase of her life.
She here indicates a knowledge of her own limi-
tation of talent. " Christie's gala" was a part quite
after her own heart.

A farce, called " Nat Batchelor's Pleasure Trip;
or, The Trials of a Good-natured Man," was brought
out at the Howard Athenaeum. The papers of the
day said of it: " It is a creditable first attempt at

5

dramatic composition, and received frequent applause." Another critic says: "It proved a full success." This performance, however, took place in 1860,— a later period than that of which I am now speaking.

An incident which occurred at this representation probably suggested scenes which recur in "Work" and other of Miss Alcott's stories.

Quite a hit was made by a little girl, a Miss Jones, who, having to speak but a few lines, spoke them so well that upon her exit she received the rare compliment of an enthusiastic recall from the audience, despite the fact that "some necessary question of the play was then to be considered." For the time being she certainly was the sensation of the piece.

Miss Alcott had in Dr. Windship a kind and judicious helper in her dramatic undertakings, with whom she kept up a correspondence under the names of Beaumont and Fletcher.

In 1851 Louisa had an experience which she has reproduced in her story called "How I Went Out to Service." Her mother's work among the poor of Boston led to her being applied to for employment, and at one time she kept a regular intelligence office. A gentleman came to her seeking a companion for his aged father and sister, who was to do only light work, and to be treated with the greatest respect and kindness. As Mrs. Alcott did not readily think of any who would fill the place, the impulsive Louisa suggested, "Why could n't I go, Mother ?" She went, and had two months of disappointment and painful experience which she never forgot. She wrote out the story which was published later, called " How I Went Out to Service."

The story has an important lesson for those who condemn severely young girls who prefer the more independent life of the factory or shop to what is considered the safety and comfort of service in families. If a girl like Louisa Alcott, belonging to a well-known, highly esteemed family, and herself commanding respect by her abilities and character, could be treated with such indignity by a family in which no one would have feared to place her, how much may not a poor unfriended girl be called upon to endure!

Journal.

1851. — We went to a meeting, and heard splendid speaking from Phillips, Channing, and others. People were much excited, and cheered " Shadrack and liberty," groaned for " Webster and slavery," and made a great noise. I felt ready to do anything, — fight or work, hoot or cry, — and laid plans to free Simms. I shall be horribly ashamed of my country if this thing happens and the slave is taken back.

[He was. — L. M. A.]

1852. — *High Street, Boston.* — After the small-pox summer, we went to a house in High Street. Mother opened an intelligence office, which grew out of her city missionary work and a desire to find places for good girls. It was not fit work for her, but it paid ; and she always did what came to her in the way of duty or charity, and let pride, taste, and comfort suffer for love's sake.

Anna and I taught ; Lizzie was our little housekeeper, — our angel in a cellar kitchen ; May went to school ; father wrote and talked when he could get classes or conversations.   Our poor little home had much love and happiness in it, and was a shelter for lost girls, abused wives, friendless children, and weak or wicked men. Father and Mother had no money to give, but gave them time, sympathy, help ; and if blessings would make them rich, they would be millionnaires.   This is practical Christianity.

My first story was printed, and $5 paid for it.   It was written in Concord when I was sixteen.   Great rubbish ! Read it aloud to sisters, and when they praised it, not knowing the author, I proudly announced her name.

Made a resolution to read fewer novels, and those only of the best.   List of books I like : —

> Carlyle's French Revolution and Miscellanies.
> Hero and Hero-Worship.
> Goethe's poems, plays, and novels.
> Plutarch's Lives.
> Madame Guion.
> Paradise Lost and Comus.
> Schiller's Plays.
> Madame de Staël.
> Bettine.
> Louis XIV.
> Jane Eyre.
> Hypatia.
> Philothea.
> Uncle Tom's Cabin.
> Emerson's Poems.

In " Little Women " (p. 174), she has told a story which has usually been supposed to represent her first success in literature ; but she has transferred the incident from her sister to her own representative, Jo. It was the quiet Anna who had secretly written a story and fastened it inside of a newspaper. She read it to her mother and sisters, as described in the book, and was very much delighted with their approbation and astonishment.

1853. — In January I started a little school, — E. W., W. A., two L's, two H's, — about a dozen in our parlor. In May, when my school closed, I went to L. as second girl. I needed the change, could do the wash, and was glad to earn my $2 a week. Home in October with $34 for my wages. After two days' rest, began school again with ten children. Anna went to Syracuse to teach; Father to the West to try his luck, — so poor, so hopeful, so serene. God be with him ! Mother had several boarders, and May got on well at school. Betty was still the home bird, and had a little romance with C.

Pleasant letters from Father and Anna. A hard year. Summer distasteful and lonely ; winter tiresome with school and people I did n't like. I miss Anna, my one bosom friend and comforter.

1854. — *Pinckney Street.* — I have neglected my journal for months, so must write it up. School for me month after month. Mother busy with boarders and sewing. Father doing as well as a philosopher can in a money-loving world. Anna at S.

I earned a good deal by sewing in the evening when my day's work was done.

In February Father came home. Paid his way, but no more. A dramatic scene when he arrived in the night. We were waked by hearing the bell. Mother flew down, crying " My husband ! " We rushed after, and five white figures embraced the half-frozen wanderer who came in hungry, tired, cold, and disappointed, but smiling bravely and as serene as ever. We fed and warmed and brooded over him, longing to ask if he had made any money ; but no one did till little May said, after he had told all the pleasant things, " Well, did people pay you ? " Then, with a queer look, he opened his pocket-book and showed one dollar, saying with a smile that made our eyes fill, " Only that ! My overcoat was stolen, and I had to buy a shawl. Many promises were not képt, and travelling is costly ; but I have opened the way, and another year shall do better."

I shall never forget how beautifully Mother answered him, though the dear, hopeful soul had built much on his success ; but with a beaming face she kissed him, saying, " I call that doing *very well*. Since you are safely home, dear, we don't ask anything more."

Anna and I choked down our tears, and took a little lesson in real love which we never forgot, nor the look that the tired man and the tender woman gave one another. It was half tragic and comic, for Father was very dirty and sleepy, and Mother in a big nightcap and funny old jacket.

[I began to see the strong contrasts and the fun and follies in every-day life about this time. — L. M. A.]

Anna came home in March. Kept our school all summer. I got " Flower Fables " ready to print.

Louisa also tried service with a relative in the country for a short time, but teaching, sewing, and writing were her principal occupations during this residence in Boston.

These seven years, from Louisa's sixteenth to her twenty-third year, might be called an apprentice-ship to life. She tried various paths, and learned to know herself and the world about her, although she was not even yet certain of success in the way which finally opened before her and led her so successfully to the accomplishment of her life-purpose. She tried teaching, without satisfaction to herself or perhaps to others. The kind of education she had herself received fitted her admirably to understand and influence children, but not to carry on the routine of a school. Sewing was her resource when nothing else offered, but it is almost pitiful to think of her as confined to such work when great powers were lying dormant in her mind. Still, Margaret Fuller said that a year of enforced quiet in the country devoted mainly to sewing was very useful to her, since she reviewed and examined the treasures laid up in her memory; and doubtless Louisa Alcott thought out many a story which afterward delighted the world while her fingers busily plied the needle. Yet it was a great deliverancè when she first found that the products of her brain would bring in the needed money for family support.

L. in Boston to A. in Syracuse.

THURSDAY, 27th.

DEAREST NAN, — I was so glad to hear from you, and hear that all were well.

I am grubbing away as usual, trying to get money enough to buy Mother a nice warm shawl. I have eleven dollars, all my own earnings, — five for a story, and four for the pile of sewing I did for the ladies of Dr. Gray's society, to give him as a present.

. . . I got a crimson ribbon for a bonnet for May, and

I took my straw and fixed it nicely with some little duds I had.   Her old one has haunted me all winter, and I want her to look neat.   She is so graceful and pretty and loves beauty so much, it is hard for her to be poor and wear other people's ugly things.   You and I have learned not to mind *much*; but when I think of her I long to dash out and buy the finest hat the limited sum of ten dollars can procure.   She says so sweetly in one of her letters: "It is hard sometimes to see other people have so many nice things and I so few; but I try not to be envious, but contented with my poor clothes, and cheerful about it." I hope the little dear will like the bonnet and the frills I made her and some bows I fixed over from bright ribbons L. W. threw away.   I get half my rarities from her rag-bag, and she does n't know her own rags when fixed over.   I hope I shall live to see the dear child in silk and lace, with plenty of pictures and " bottles of cream," Europe, and all she longs for.

For our good little Betty, who is wearing all the old gowns we left, I shall soon be able to buy a new one, and send it with my blessing to the cheerful saint.   She writes me the funniest notes, and tries to keep the old folks warm and make the lonely house in the snowbanks cosey and bright.

To Father I shall send new neckties and some paper; then he will be happy, and can keep on with the beloved diaries though the heavens fall.

Don't laugh at my plans; I 'll carry them out, if I go to service to do it.   Seeing so much money flying about, I long to honestly get a little and make my dear family more comfortable.   I feel weak-minded when I think of all they need and the little I can do.

Now about you : Keep the money you have earned by so many tears and sacrifices, and clothe yourself; for it makes me mad to know that my good little lass is going round in shabby things, and being looked down upon by people who are not worthy to touch her patched shoes or the hem of her ragged old gowns. Make yourself tidy, and if any is left over send it to Mother; for there are always many things needed at home, though they won't tell us. I only wish I too by any amount of weeping and homesickness could earn as much. But my mite won't come amiss; and if tears can add to its value, I 've shed my quart, — first, over the book not coming out; for that was a sad blow, and I waited so long it was dreadful when my castle in the air came tumbling about my ears. Pride made me laugh in public; but I wailed in private, and no one knew it. The folks at home think I rather enjoyed it, for I wrote a jolly letter. But my visit was spoiled; and now I 'm digging away for dear life, that I may not have come entirely in vain. I did n't mean to groan about it; but my lass and I must tell some one our trials, and so it becomes easy to confide in one another. I never let Mother know how unhappy you were in S. till Uncle wrote.

My doings are not much this week. I sent a little tale to the " Gazette," and Clapp asked H. W. if five dollars would be enough. Cousin H. said yes, and gave it to me, with kind words and a nice parcel of paper, saying in his funny way, " Now, Lu, the door is open, go in and win." So I shall try to do it. Then cousin L. W. said Mr. B. had got my play, and told her that if Mrs. B. liked it as well, it must be clever, and if it did n't cost too much, he would bring it out by and by. Say nothing about it yet. Dr. W. tells me Mr. F. is very sick; so the farce cannot be acted yet. But the Doctor is set on its coming out, and we have fun about it. H. W. takes me often to the theatre when L. is done with me. I read to her all the P. M. often, as she is poorly, and in that way I pay my debt to them.

I 'm writing another story for Clapp. I want more fives, and mean to have them too.

Uncle wrote that you were Dr. W.'s pet teacher, and every one loved you dearly. But if you are not well, don't stay. Come home, and be cuddled by your old   LU.

CHAPTER V.

AUTHORSHIP.

OUR ANGEL IN THE HOUSE.

SITTING patient in the shadow
   Till the blessed light shall come,
A serene and saintly presence
   Sanctifies our troubled home.
Earthly joys and hopes and sorrows
   Break like ripples on the strand
Of the deep and solemn river,
   Where her willing feet now stand.

O my sister, passing from me
   Out of human care and strife,
Leave me as a gift those virtues
   Which have beautified your life.
Dear, bequeath me that great patience
   Which has power to sustain
A cheerful, uncomplaining spirit
   In its prison-house of pain.

Give me — for I need it sorely —
   Of that courage, wise and sweet,
Which has made the path of duty
   Green beneath your willing feet.
Give me that unselfish nature
   That with charity divine
Can pardon wrong for love's dear sake, —
   Meek heart, forgive me mine !

Thus our parting daily loseth
   Something of its bitter pain,
And while learning this hard lesson
   My great loss becomes my gain ;

For the touch of grief will render
　My wild nature more serene,
Give to life new aspirations,
　A new trust in the unseen.

Henceforth safe across the river
　I shall see forevermore
A beloved household spirit
　　Waiting for me on the shore;
Hope and faith, born of my sorrow,
　Guardian angels shall become;
And the sister gone before me
　By their hands shall lead me home.

WHEN only twenty-two years old Miss Alcott
began her career of authorship by launch-
ing a little flower bark, which floated gaily on the
stream.　She had always written poems, plays, and
stories for her own and her friends' pleasure, and
now she gathered up some tales she had written
for Mr. Emerson's daughter, and published them
under the name of " Flower Fables."　She received
the small amount of thirty-two dollars for the book;
but it gave her the great satisfaction of having
earned it by work that she loved, and which she
could do well.　She began to have applications for
stories from the papers; but as yet sewing and
teaching paid better than writing.　While she sewed
her brain was busy with plans of poems, plays, and
tales, which she made use of at a later period.

The following letter to her mother shows how
closely she associated her with this early success: —

20 PINCKNEY STREET, BOSTON, Dec. 25, 1854.
(With " Flower Fables.")

DEAR MOTHER, — Into your Christmas stocking I
have put my " first-born," knowing that you will accept

it with all its faults (for grandmothers are always kind), and look upon it merely as an earnest of what I may yet do ; for, with so much to cheer me on, I hope to pass in time from fairies and fables to men and realities.

Whatever beauty or poetry is to be found in my little book is owing to your interest in and encouragement of all my efforts from the first to the last ; and if ever I do anything to be proud of, my greatest happiness will be that I can thank you for that, as I may do for all the good there is in me ; and I shall be content to write if it gives you pleasure.

> Jo is fussing about ;
> My lamp is going out.

To dear mother, with many kind wishes for a happy New Year and merry Christmas.
I am ever your loving daughter
LOUY.

This letter shows that she had already begun to see that she must study not only fairies and fancies, but men and realities; and she now began to observe life, not in books, but as it went on around her. In the intense excitement of the anti-slavery struggles of that period she might well learn how full of dramatic situations and the elements of both tragedy and comedy real human life is. She says: " I began to see the strong contrasts and fun and frolic in every day life about this time." She also considered her reading, and tried to make it more thorough and profitable; and she did not " waste even *ink* on poems and fancies," but planned stories, that everything might help toward her great object of earning support for her family.

In June, 1855, Miss Alcott went to Walpole, N. H., where she had a free life among the hills for a few months. It must have been a great refreshment to her after the winter's work in the city. In July the family followed her thither, and occupied a small house. The country life and joy soon began to find expression, and she wrote a little story called " King Goldenrod," which she says " ought to be fresh and true," as written at that beautiful time and place. But this pleasant country life was for a short season only; and in chill November she set out for the city, with brave heart and scanty outfit, to seek her fortune once more. While still continuing to sew as a means of livelihood, she began to try a great variety of literary ventures. She wrote notices of books for the papers, and at one time got five dollars for a story, besides twelve dollars for sewing. The following year the publishers began to find out the value of her work, and to call for more stories. Even her poems were accepted. Little Nell was then the favorite heroine of Dickens, and Louisa's poem on that subject was published in the " Courier." Although she at first enjoyed the beautiful scenery of Walpole, she found the dull little town did not offer her the opportunities for work that she needed; and leaving her family there, she came down to Boston to seek her fortune, and went to the well-known boarding-house of Mrs. David Reed on Chauncey Street. The happy home which she had here during the winter is represented as Mrs. Kirke's house in " Little Women," and Jo's garret is the sky-parlor in which she lived and wrote. She had a rich winter, hearing many of the finest lectures, and enjoying her free pass to the theatre. One of her greatest helps, however, was the friendship of Theodore Parker, who took great interest in her struggles, and wisely strengthened and encouraged her. She loved to go to his Sunday evening receptions, and sit quietly watching the varied company who collected there; and a word or pressure of the hand from her host was enough to cheer her for the whole week. She has gratefully recorded this influence in her sketch of Mr. Power in "Work;" but she has not given to that delineation the striking personality of her subject which we should have expected of her. She then perhaps looked up to him too much to take note of the rich elements of wit and humor in his nature, and has painted him wholly seriously, and with a colorless brush.

Journal.
Twenty-two Years Old.

PINCKNEY STREET, BOSTON, *Jan.* 1, 1855. — The principal event of the winter is the appearance of my book " Flower Fables." An edition of sixteen hundred. It has sold very well, and people seem to like it. I feel quite proud that the little tales that I wrote for Ellen E. when I was sixteen should now bring money and fame.

I will put in some of the notices as "varieties." Mothers are always foolish over their first-born.

Miss Wealthy Stevens paid for the book, and I received $32.

[A pleasing contrast to the receipts of six months only in 1886, being $8000 for the sale of books, and no new one; but I was prouder over the $32 than the $8000. — L. M. A., 1886.]

April, 1855. — I am in the garret with my papers round me, and a pile of apples to eat while I write my journal, plan stories, and enjoy the patter of rain on the roof, in peace and quiet.

[Jo in the garret. — L. M. A.]

Being behindhand, as usual, I 'll make note of the main events up to date, for I don't waste ink in poetry and pages of rubbish now. I 've begun to *live,* and have no time for sentimental musing.

In October I began my school ; Father talked, Mother looked after her boarders, and tried to help everybody. Anna was in Syracuse teaching Mrs. S——'s children.

My book came out ; and people began to think that topsey-turvey Louisa would amount to something after all, since she could do so well as housemaid, teacher, seamstress, and story-teller. Perhaps she may.

In February I wrote a story for which C. paid $5, and asked for more.

In March I wrote a farce for W. Warren, and Dr. W. offered it to him ; but W. W. was too busy.

Also began another tale, but found little time to work on it, with school, sewing, and house-work. My winter's earnings are, —

School, one quarter	$50
Sewing	$50
Stories	$20

if I am ever paid.

A busy and a pleasant winter, because, though hard at times, I do seem to be getting on a little ; and that encourages me.

Have heard Lowell and Hedge lecture, acted in plays, and thanks to our rag-money and good cousin H., have been to the theatre several times, — always my great joy.

Summer plans are yet unsettled. Father wants to go to England : not a wise idea, I think. We shall probably stay here, and A. and I go into the country as governesses. It 's a queer way to live, but dramatic, and I rather like it ; for we never know what is to come next. We are real " Micawbers," and always " ready for a spring."

I have planned another Christmas book, and hope to be able to write it.

1855. — Cousin L. W. asks me to pass the summer at Walpole with her. If I can get no teaching, I shall go ; for I long for the hills, and can write my fairy tales there.

I delivered my burlesque lecture on " Woman, and Her Position ; by Oronthy Bluggage," last evening at Deacon G.'s. Had a merry time, and was asked by Mr. W. to do it at H. for money. Read " Hamlet " at our club, — my favorite play. Saw Mrs. W. H. Smith about the farce ; says she will do it at her benefit.

May. — Father went to C. to talk with Mr. Emerson about the England trip. I am to go to Walpole. I have made my own gowns, and had money enough to fit up the girls. So glad to be independent.

[I wonder if $40 fitted up the whole family. Perhaps so, as my wardrobe was made up of old clothes from cousins and friends. — L. M. A.]

WALPOLE, N. H., *June,* 1855. — Pleasant journey and a kind welcome. Lovely place, high among the hills. So glad to run and skip in the woods and up the splendid ravine. Shall write here, I know.

Helped cousin L. in her garden ; and the smell of the fresh earth and the touch of green leaves did me good.

Mr. T. came and praised my first book, so I felt much
inspired to go and do another. I remember him at
Scituate years ago, when he was a young ship-builder and
I a curly-haired hoyden of five or six.

Up at five, and had a lovely run in the ravine, seeing
the woods wake. Planned a little tale which ought to be
fresh and true, as it came at that hour and place, —
" King Goldenrod." Have lively days, — writing in
A. M., driving in P. M., and fun in eve. My visit is doing
me much good.

July, 1855. — Read " Hyperion." On the 16th the
family came to live in Mr. W.'s house rent free. No
better plan offered, and we were all tired of the city.
Here Father can have a garden ; Mother can rest and be
near her good niece ; the children have freedom and fine
air ; and A. and I can go from here to our teaching,
wherever it may be.

Busy and happy times as we settle in the little house
in the lane near by my dear ravine, — plays, picnics,
pleasant people, and good neighbors. Fanny Kemble
came up, Mrs. Kirkland and others, and Dr. Bellows
is the gayest of the gay. We acted the " Jacobite,"
" Rivals," and " Bonnycastles," to an audience of a hundred, and were noticed in the Boston papers. H. T.
was our manager, and Dr. B., D. D., our dramatic direc-
tor. Anna was the star, her acting being really very
fine. I did " Mrs. Malaprop," " Widow Pottle," and the
old ladies.

Finished fairy book in September. Anna had an offer
from Dr. Wilbur of Syracuse to teach at the great idiot
asylum. She disliked it, but decided to go. Poor dear !
so beauty-loving, timid, and tender. It is a hard trial ;
but she is so self-sacrificing she tries to like it because it
is duty.

October. — A. to Syracuse. May illustrated my book, and tales called " Christmas Elves." Better than " Flower Fables." Now I must try to sell it.

[Innocent Louisa, to think that a Christmas book could be sold in October. — L. M. A.]

November. — Decided to seek my fortune; so, with my little trunk of home-made clothes, $20 earned by stories sent to the " Gazette," and my MSS., I set forth with Mother's blessing one rainy day in the dullest month in the year.

[My birth-month; always to be a memorable one. — L. M. A.]

Found it too late to do anything with the book, so put it away and tried for teaching, sewing, or any honest work. Won't go home to sit idle while I have a head and pair of hands.

December. — H. and L. W. very kind, and my dear cousins the Sewalls take me in. I sew for Mollie and others, and write stories. C. gave me books to notice. Heard Thackeray. Anxious times; Anna very home-sick. Walpole very cold and dull now the summer butterflies have gone. Got $5 for a tale and $12 for sewing; sent home a Christmas-box to cheer the dear souls in the snow-banks.

January, 1856. — C. paid $6 for " A Sister's Trial," gave me more books to notice, and wants more tales.

[Should think he would at that price. — L. M. A.]

Sewed for L. W. Sewall and others. Mr. J. M. Field took my farce to Mobile to bring out; Mr. Barry of the Boston Theatre has the play.

Heard Curtis lecture. Began a book for summer, — " Beach Bubbles." Mr. F. of the " Courier " printed a

poem of mine on " Little Nell."   Got $10 for " Bertha,"
and saw great yellow placards stuck up announcing it.
Acted at the W.'s.

March. — Got $10 for " Genevieve."   Prices go up,
as people like the tales and ask who wrote them.   Finished " Twelve Bubbles."   Sewed a great deal, and got
very tired ; one job for Mr. G. of a dozen pillow-cases,
one dozen sheets, six fine cambric neckties, and two
dozen handkerchiefs, at which I had to work all one
night to get them done, as they were a gift to him.   I
got only $4.

Sewing won't make my fortune ; but I can plan my
stories while I work, and then scribble 'em down on
Sundays.

Poem on " Little Paul ; " Curtis's lecture on " Dickens "
made it go well.   Hear Emerson on " England."

May. — Anna came on her way home, sick and worn
out ; the work was too much for her.   We had some
happy days visiting about.   Could not dispose of B. B.
in book form, but C. took them for his paper.   Mr. Field
died, so the farce fell through there.   Altered the play
for Mrs. Barrow to bring out next winter.

June, 1856. — Home, to find dear Betty very ill with
scarlet-fever caught from some poor children Mother
nursed when they fell sick, living over a cellar where
pigs had been kept.   The landlord (a deacon) would
not clean the place till Mother threatened to sue him
for allowing a nuisance.   Too late to save two of the
poor babies or Lizzie and May from the fever.

[L. never recovered, but died of it two years later. —
L. M. A.]

An anxious time.   I nursed, did house-work, and wrote
a story a month through the summer.

Dr. Bellows and Father had Sunday eve conversations.

October. — Pleasant letters from Father, who went on a tour to N. Y., Philadelphia, and Boston.

Made plans to go to Boston for the winter, as there is nothing to do here, and there I can support myself and help the family. C. offers 10 dollars a month, and perhaps more. L. W., M. S., and others, have plenty of sewing; the play *may* come out, and Mrs. R. will give me a sky-parlor for $3 a week, with fire and board. I sew for her also.

If I can get A. L. to governess I shall be all right.

I was born with a boy's spirit under my bib and tucker. I *can't wait* when I *can work;* so I took my little talent in my hand and forced the world again, braver than before and wiser for my failures.

[Jo in N. Y. — L. M. A.]

I don't often pray in words; but when I set out that day with all my worldly goods in the little old trunk, my own earnings ($25) in my pocket, and much hope and resolution in my soul, my heart was very full, and I said to the Lord, "Help us all, and keep us for one another," as I never said it before, while I looked back at the dear faces watching me, so full of love and hope and faith.

Journal.

Boston, *November,* 1856. *Mrs. David Reed's.* — I find my little room up in the attic very cosey, and a house full of boarders very amusing to study. Mrs. Reed very kind. Fly round and take C. his stories. Go to see Mrs. L. about A. Don't want me. A blow, but I cheer up and hunt for sewing. Go to hear Parker, and he does me good. Asks me to come Sunday evenings to his house. I did go there, and met Phillips, Garrison, Hedge, and other great men, and sit in my corner weekly, staring and enjoying myself.

When I went Mr. Parker said, " God bless you, Louisa ;
come again ; " and the grasp of his hand gave me courage to face another anxious week.

November 3d. — Wrote all the morning.   In the P. M.
went to see the Sumner reception as he comes home
after the Brooks affair.   I saw him pass up Beacon
Street, pale and feeble, but smiling and bowing.   I
rushed to Hancock Street, and was in time to see him
bring his proud old mother to the window when the
crowd gave three cheers for her.   I cheered too, and
was very much excited.   Mr. Parker met him somewhere
before the ceremony began, and the above P. cheered
like a boy ; and Sumner laughed and nodded as his friend
pranced and shouted, bareheaded and beaming.

My kind cousin, L. W., got tickets for a course of lectures on "Italian Literature," and seeing my old cloak sent
me a new one, with other needful and pretty things such
as girls love to have.   I shall never forget how kind she
has always been to me.

November 5th. — Went with H. W. to see Manager
Barry about the everlasting play which is always coming
out but never comes.   We went all over the great new
theatre, and I danced a jig on the immense stage.   Mr.
B. was very kind, and gave me a pass to come whenever
I liked.   This was such richness I did n't care if the play
was burnt on the spot, and went home full of joy.   In
the eve I saw La Grange as Norma, and felt as if I
knew all about that place.   Quite stage-struck, and imagined myself in her place, with white robes and oak-leaf
crown.

November 6th. — Sewed happily on my job of twelve
sheets for H. W., and put lots of good will into the work
after his kindness to me.

Walked to Roxbury to see cousin Dr. W. about the

play and tell the fine news. Rode home in the new cars, and found them very nice.

In the eve went to teach at Warren Street Chapel Charity School. I'll help as I am helped, if I can. Mother says no one so poor he can't do a little for some one poorer yet.

Sunday. — Heard Parker on "Individuality of Character," and liked it much. In the eve I went to his house. Mrs. Howe was there, and Sumner and others. I sat in my usual corner, but Mr. P. came up and said, in that cordial way cf his, "Well, child, how goes it?" "Pretty well, sir." "That's brave;" and with his warm hand-shake he went on, leaving me both proud and happy, though I have my trials. He is like a great fire where all can come and be warmed and comforted. Bless him!

Had a talk at tea about him, and fought for him when W. R. said he was not a Christian. He is my *sort;* for though he may lack reverence for other people's God, he works bravely for his own, and turns his back on no one who needs help, as some of the pious do.

Monday, 14*th.* — May came full of expectation and joy to visit good aunt B. and study drawing. We walked about and had a good home talk, then my girl went off to Auntie's to begin what I hope will be a pleasant and profitable winter. She needs help to develop her talent, and I can't give it to her.

Went to see Forrest as Othello. It is funny to see how attentive all the once cool gentlemen are to Miss Alcott now she has a pass to the new theatre.

November 29*th.* — My birthday. Felt forlorn so far from home. Wrote all day. Seem to be getting on slowly, so should be contented. To a little party at the B.'s in the eve. May looked very pretty, and seemed to be a favorite. The boys teased me about being an authoress, and I said I 'd be famous yet. Will if I can, but something else may be better for me.

Found a pretty pin from Father and a nice letter when I got home. Mr. H. brought them with letters from Mother and Betty, so I went to bed happy.

December. — Busy with Christmas and New Year's tales. Heard a good lecture by E. P. Whipple on "Courage." Thought I needed it, being rather tired of living like a spider, — spinning my brains out for money.

Wrote a story, "The Cross on the Church Tower," suggested by the tower before my window.

Called on Mrs. L., and she asked me to come and teach A. for three hours each day. Just what I wanted ; and the children's welcome was very pretty and comforting to "Our Olly," as they call me.

Now board is all safe, and something over for home, if stories and sewing fail. I don't do much, but can send little comforts to Mother and Betty, and keep May neat.

December 18*th.* — Begin with A. L., in Beacon Street. I taught C. when we lived in High Street, A. in Pinckney Street, and now Al. ; so I seem to be an institution and a success, since I can start the boy, teach one girl, and take care of the little invalid. It is hard work, but I can do it ; and am glad to sit in a large, fine room part of each day, after my sky-parlor, which has nothing pretty in it, and only the gray tower and blue sky outside as I sit at the window writing. I love luxury, but freedom and independence better.

To her Father, written from Mrs. Reed's.

BOSTON, Nov. 29, 1856.

DEAREST FATHER, — Your little parcel was very welcome to me as I sat alone in my room, with snow falling fast outside, and a few tears in (for birthdays are dismal times to me) ; and the fine letter, the pretty gift, and, most of all, the loving thought so kindly taken for your old absent daughter, made the cold, dark day as warm and bright as summer to me.

And now, with the birthday pin upon my bosom, many thanks on my lips, and a whole heart full of love for its giver, I will tell you a little about my doings, stupid as they will seem after your own grand proceedings. How I wish I could be with you, enjoying what I have always longed for, — fine people, fine amusements, and fine books. But as I can't, I am glad you are ; for I love to see your name first among the lecturers, to hear it kindly spoken of in papers and inquired about by good people here, — to say nothing of the delight and pride I take in seeing you at last filling the place you are so fitted for, and which you have waited for so long and patiently. If the New Yorkers raise a statue to the modern Plato, it will be a wise and highly creditable action.

    `.`   `.`   `.`   `.`   `.`   `.`   `.`   `.`

I am very well and very happy. Things go smoothly, and I think I shall come out right, and prove that though an *Alcott* I *can* support myself. I like the independent feeling ; and though not an easy life, it is a free one, and I enjoy it. I can't do much with my hands ; so I will make a battering-ram of my head and make a way through this rough-and-tumble world. I have very pleasant lectures to amuse my evenings, — Professor Gajani on " Italian Reformers," the Mercantile Library course, Whipple, Beecher, and others, and, best of all, a free pass at the Boston Theatre. I saw Mr. Barry, and he gave it to me with many kind speeches, and promises to bring out the play very soon. I hope he will.

My farce is in the hands of Mrs. W. H. Smith, who

acts at Laura Keene's theatre in New York. She took it, saying she would bring it out there. If you see or hear anything about it, let me know. I want something doing. My mornings are spent in writing. C. takes one a month, and I am to see Mr. B., who may take some of my wares.

In the afternoons I walk and visit my hundred relations, who are all kind and friendly, and seem interested in our various successes.

Sunday evenings I go to Parker's parlor, and there meet Phillips, Garrison, Scherb, Sanborn, and many other pleasant people. All talk, and I sit in a corner listening, and wishing a certain placid gray-haired gentleman was there talking too. Mrs. Parker calls on me, reads my stories, and is very good to me. Theodore asks Louisa "how her worthy parents do," and is otherwise very friendly to the large, bashful girl who adorns his parlor steadily.

Abby is preparing for a busy and, I hope, a profitable winter. She has music lessons already, French and drawing in store, and, if her eyes hold out, will keep her word and become what none of us can be, "an accomplished Alcott." Now, dear Father, I shall hope to hear from you occasionally, and will gladly answer all epistles from the Plato whose parlor parish is becoming quite famous. I got the "Tribune," but not the letter, and shall look it up. I have been meaning to write, but did not know where you were.

Good-by, and a happy birthday from your ever loving child, LOUISA.

Journal.

Twenty-four Years Old.

January, 1857. — Had my first new silk dress from good little L. W., — very fine ; and I felt as if all the

Hancocks and Quincys beheld me as I went to two parties in it on New Year's eve.

A busy, happy month, — taught, wrote, sewed, read aloud to the "little mother," and went often to the theatre ; heard good lectures ; and enjoyed my Parker evenings very much.

Father came to see me on his way home; little money; had had a good time, and was asked to come again. Why don't rich people who enjoy his talk pay for it? Philosophers are always poor, and too modest to pass round their own hats.

Sent by him a good bundle to the poor Forlornites among the ten-foot drifts in W.

February. — Ran home as a valentine on the 14th.

March. — Have several irons in the fire now, and try to keep 'em all hot.

April. — May did a crayon head of Mother with Mrs. Murdock; very good likeness. All of us as proud as peacocks of our "little Raphael."

Heard Mrs. Butler read ; very fine.

May. — Left the L.'s with my thirty-three dollars, glad to rest. May went home with her picture, happy in her winter's work and success.

Father had three talks at W. F. Channing's. Good company, — Emerson, Mrs. Howe, and the rest.

Saw young Booth in Brutus, and liked him better than his father; went about and rested after my labors; glad to be with Father, who enjoyed Boston and friends.

Home on the 10th, passing Sunday at the Emerson's. I have done what I planned, — supported myself, written eight stories, taught four months, earned a hundred dollars, and sent money home.

June. — All happy together. My dear Nan was with me, and we had good times. Betty was feeble, but seemed to cheer up for a time. The long, cold, lonely winter has been too hard for the frail creature, and we are all anxious about her. I fear she may slip away; for she never seemed to care much for this world beyond home.

So gradually the day seemed to be coming to which Louisa had long looked forward. She found that she could be independent, could help her family, and even indulge some of her own tastes.

About this time Miss Alcott mentions a young friend who died in her arms, and speaks of going to console the sister in her loneliness. This shows how warmly her heart beat for others while her head was so busy with her ambitious plans. She speaks also of the hint of a new story called " The Cost of an Idea." She never lost sight of this plan, but did not carry it out. Her father's life and character were in her mind, and she longed to portray the conflict between his high ideal and the practical difficulties of his life; but it was an impossible subject. The Fruitlands episode was told in " Transcendental Wild Oats," and his early life in " Elis's Education." But although her admiration and affection for him are abundantly shown in her journals, she never perhaps understood him so thoroughly that she could adequately portray his personality; neither could she do justice to all related to him without trenching upon the privacy due to sacred feelings.

A great shadow fell over Louisa's heart and life from the increasing illness of her dear younger sister Elizabeth. This young girl was tenderly beloved by all the family, and was indeed as pure, refined,

and holy as she is represented as Beth in " Little
Women." Her decay was very gradual, and she
was so patient and sweet that the sad time of anxiety was a very precious one in remembrance.

This sickness added to the pecuniary burdens of
the family, and eight years afterward Louisa paid
the bill of the physician who attended her sister.

In October, 1857, the family removed again to
Concord, and Louisa remained at home to assist in
the care of the beloved invalid. They lived a few
months in a part of a house which they hired until
the Orchard House, which they had bought, was
ready for them. Here the dear sister's life came
to a close.

This was the first break in the household, and
the mother's heart never fully recovered from it.
Louisa accepted death with strong, sweet wisdom.
It never seemed to have any terror for her.

In July they took possession of the Orchard
House, which was hereafter the permanent residence of the family. This was a picturesque old
house on the side of a hill, with an orchard of ap-
ple-trees. It was not far from Mr. Emerson's, and
within walking distance of the village, yet very
quiet and rural. Mr. Alcott had his library, and
was always very happy there; but Louisa's heart
never clung to it.

The engagement of the elder sister was a very
exciting event to Louisa, who did not like having
the old sisterly relation broken in upon; but everything was so genuine and true in the love of the
newly betrothed pair that she could not help ac-
cepting the change as a blessing to her sister and

taking the new brother into her heart. The entries in her journal show that the picture she has drawn in " Little Women " of this noble man is from life, and not exaggerated.

Louisa went to Boston for a visit, and again had hopes of going on to the stage; but an accident prevented it; and she returned to Concord and her writing, working off her disappointment in a story called " Only an Actress."

Among her experiences at this time was an offer of marriage, about which she consulted her mother, telling her that she did not care for the lover very much. The wise mother saved her from the impulse to self-sacrifice, which might have led her to accept a position which would have given help to the family.

Although this was not the only instance of offers of marriage, more or less advantageous, made to her, Louisa had no inclination toward matrimony. Her heart was bound up in her family, and she could hardly contemplate her own interests as separate from theirs. She loved activity, freedom, and independence. She could not cherish illusions tenderly; and she always said that she got tired of everybody, and felt sure that she should of her husband if she married. She never wished to make her heroines marry, and the love story is the part of her books for which she cared least. She yielded to the desire of the public, who will not accept life without a recognition of this great joy in it. Still it must be acknowledged that she has sometimes painted very sweet and natural love scenes, although more often in quaint and homely guise than in the fashion of ancient romance.

"King of Clubs and Queen of Hearts" is very prettily told; and "Mrs. Todger's Teapot" is true to that quiet, earnest affection which does not pass away with youth.

The writing went on, and she received five, six, or ten dollars apiece for her stories; but she did not yet venture to give up the sewing and teaching, which was still the sure reliance.

Her younger sister now began to exercise her talent, and illustrated a little book of Louisa's called "Christmas Elves," which she says is better than "Flower Fables."

Journal.

Read Charlotte Brontë's life. A very interesting, but sad one. So full of talent; and after working long, just as success, love, and happiness come, she dies.

Wonder if I shall ever be famous enough for people to care to read my story and struggles. I can't be a C. B., but I may do a little something yet.

July. — Grandma Alcott came to visit us. A sweet old lady; and I am glad to know her, and see where Father got his nature. Eighty-four; yet very smart, industrious, and wise. A house needs a grandma in it.

As we sat talking over Father's boyhood, I never realized so plainly before how much he has done for himself. His early life sounded like a pretty old romance, and Mother added the love passages.

I got a hint for a story; and some day will do it, and call it "The Cost of an Idea." Spindle Hill, Temple School, Fruitlands, Boston, and Concord, would make fine chapters. The trials and triumphs of the Pathetic Family would make a capital book; may I live to do it.

August. — A sad, anxious month. Betty worse; Mother

takes her to the seashore. Father decides to go back to Concord ; he is never happy far from Emerson, the one true friend who loves and understands and helps him.

September. — An old house near R. W. E.'s is bought with Mother's money, and we propose to move. Mother in Boston with poor Betty, who is failing fast. Anna and I have a hard time breaking up.

October. — Move to Concord. Take half a house in town till spring, when the old one is to be made ready.

Find dear Betty a shadow, but sweet and patient always. Fit up a nice room for her, and hope home and love and care may keep her.

People kind and friendly, and the old place looks pleasant, though I never want to live in it.

November. — Father goes West, taking Grandma home. We settle down to our winter, whatever it is to be. Lizzie seems better, and we have some plays. Sanborn's school makes things lively, and we act a good deal.

Twenty-five this month. I feel my quarter of a century rather heavy on my shoulders just now. I lead two lives. One seems gay with plays, etc., the other very sad, — in Betty's room ; for though she wishes us to act, and loves to see us get ready, the shadow is there, and Mother and I see it. Betty loves to have me with her ; and I am with her at night, for Mother needs rest. Betty says she feels " strong " when I am near. So glad to be of use.

December. — Some fine plays for charity.

January, 1858. — Lizzie much worse ; Dr. G. says there is no hope. A hard thing to hear ; but if she is only to suffer, I pray she may go soon. She was glad to know she was to " get well," as she called it, and we tried to bear it bravely for her sake. We gave up plays ; Father came home ; and Anna took the housekeeping, so that Mother and I could devote ourselves to her. Sad, quiet days in her room, and strange nights keeping up the fire and watching the dear little shadow try to wile away the long sleepless hours without troubling me. She sews, reads, sings softly, and lies looking at the fire, — so sweet and patient and so worn, my heart is broken to see the change. I wrote some lines one night on "Our Angel in the House."

[Jo and Beth. — L. M. A.]

February. — A mild month; Betty very comfortable, and we hope a little.

Dear Betty is slipping away, and every hour is too precious to waste, so I 'll keep my lamentations over Nan's• [affairs] till this duty is over.

Lizzie makes little things, and drops them out of windows to the school-children, smiling to see their surprise. In the night she tells me to be Mrs. Gamp, when I give her her lunch, and tries to be gay that I may keep up. Dear little saint! I shall be better all my life for these sad hours with you.

March 14*th.* — My dear Beth died at three this morning, after two years of patient pain. Last week she put her work away, saying the needle was "too heavy," and having given us her few possessions, made ready for the parting in her own simple, quiet way. For two days she suffered much, begging for ether, though its effect was gone. Tuesday she lay in Father's arms, and called us round her, smiling contentedly as she said, "All here!" I think she bid us good-by then, as she held our hands and kissed us tenderly. Saturday she slept, and at midnight became unconscious, quietly breathing her life away till three; then, with one last look of the beautiful eyes, she was gone.

A curious thing happened, and I will tell it here, for

Dr. G. said it was a fact. A few moments after the last breath came, as Mother and I sat silently watching the shadow fall on the dear little face, I saw a light mist rise from the body, and float up and vanish in the air. Mother's eyes followed mine, and when I said, "What did you see?" she described the same light mist. Dr. G. said it was the life departing visibly.

For the last time we dressed her in her usual cap and gown, and laid her on her bed, — at rest at last. What she had suffered was seen in the face; for at twenty-three she looked like a woman of forty, so worn was she, and all her pretty hair gone.

On Monday Dr. Huntington read the Chapel service, and we sang her favorite hymn. Mr. Emerson, Henry Thoreau, Sanborn, and John Pratt, carried her out of the old home to the new one at Sleepy Hollow chosen by herself. So the first break comes, and I know what death means, — a liberator for her, a teacher for us.

April. — Came to occupy one wing of Hawthorne's house (once ours) while the new one was being repaired. Father, Mother, and I kept house together; May being in Boston, Anna at Pratt Farm, and, for the first time, Lizzie absent. I don't miss her as I expected to do, for she seems nearer and dearer than before; and I am glad to know she is safe from pain and age in some world where her innocent soul must be happy.

Death never seemed terrible to me, and now is beautiful; so I cannot fear it, but find it friendly and wonderful.

May. — A lonely month with all the girls gone, and Father and Mother absorbed in the old house, which I don't care about, not liking Concord.

On the 7th of April, Anna came walking in to tell us she was engaged to John Pratt; so another sister is gone.

J. is a model son and brother, — a true man, — full of fine possibilities, but so modest one does not see it at once. He is handsome, healthy, and happy; just home from the West, and so full of love he is pleasant to look at.

I moaned in private over my great loss, and said I 'd never forgive J. for taking Anna from me; but I shall if he makes her happy, and turn to little May for my comfort.

[Now that John is dead, I can truly say we all had cause to bless the day he came into the family; for we gained a son and brother, and Anna the best husband ever known.

For ten years he made her home a little heaven of love and peace; and when he died he left her the legacy of a beautiful life, and an honest name to his little sons. — L. M. A., 1873.]

June. — The girls came home, and I went to visit L. W. in Boston. Saw Charlotte Cushman, and had a stage-struck fit. Dr. W. asked Barry to let me act at his theatre, and he agreed. I was to do Widow Pottle, as the dress was a good disguise and I knew the part well. It was all a secret, and I had hopes of trying a new life; the old one being so changed now, I felt as if I must find interest in something absorbing. But Mr. B. broke his leg, so I had to give it up; and when it was known, the dear, respectable relations were horrified at the idea. I 'll try again by-and-by, and see if I have the gift. Perhaps it is acting, not writing, I 'm meant for. Nature must have a vent somehow.

July. — Went into the new house and began to settle. Father is happy; Mother glad to be at rest; Anna is in bliss with her gentle John; and May busy over her pictures. I have plans simmering, but must sweep and dust and wash my dish-pans a while longer till I see my way.

Worked off my stage fever in writing a story, and felt better; also a moral tale, and got twenty-five dollars, which pieced up our summer gowns and bonnets all round. The inside of my head can at least cover the outside.

August. — Much company to see the new house. All seem to be glad that the wandering family is anchored at last. We won't move again for twenty years if I can help it. The old people need an abiding place; and now that death and love have taken two of us away, I can, I hope, soon manage to care for the remaining four.

The weeklies will all take stories; and I can simmer novels while I do my housework, so see my way to a little money, and perhaps more by-and-by if I ever make a hit.

Probably owing to the excitement of grief for her sister's death, and sympathy in Anna's happy betrothal, Louisa became in October more discouraged than she had ever been, and went to Boston in search of work. As she walked over the mill-dam the running stream brought the thought of the River of Death, which would end all troubles. It was but a momentary impulse; and the brave young heart rallied to the thought, "There is work for me, and I'll have it!" Her journal narrates how Mr. Parker helped her through this period of anxiety. She was all ready to go to Lancaster, to hard drudgery at sewing, when her old place as governess was again offered to her, and her own support was assured.

October. — Went to Boston on my usual hunt for employment, as I am not needed at home and seem to be the only bread-winner just now.

· · · · · · · · ·

My fit of despair was soon over, for it seemed so cowardly to run away before the battle was over I

could n't do it. So I said firmly, "There *is* work for
me, and I 'll have it," and went home resolved to take
Fate by the throat and shake a living out of her.

Sunday Mr. Parker preached a sermon on "Laborious
Young Women." Just what I needed; for it said:
"Trust your fellow-beings, and let them help you.
Don't be too proud to ask, and accept the humblest
work till you can find the task you want."

"I will," said I, and went to Mr. P.'s. He was out;
but I told Mrs. P. my wants, and she kindly said Theodore and Hannah would be sure to have something for
me. As I went home I met Mrs. L., who had not
wanted me, as Alice went to school. She asked if I was
engaged, and said A. did not do well, and she thought
perhaps they would like me back. I was rejoiced, and
went home feeling that the tide had begun to turn.
Next day came Miss H. S. to offer me a place at the
Girls' Reform School at Lancaster, to sew ten hours
a day, make and mend. I said I 'd go, as I could do
anything with a needle; but added, if Mrs. L. wants me
I 'd rather do that.

"Of course you had. Take it if it comes, and if not,
try my work." I promised and waited. That eve, when
my bag was packed and all was ready for Lancaster,
came a note from Mrs. L. offering the old salary and the
old place. I sang for joy, and next day early posted off
to Miss S. She was glad and shook hands, saying, "It
was a test, my dear, and you stood it. When I told
Mr. P. that you would go, he said, 'That is a true girl;
Louisa will succeed.'"

I was very proud and happy; for these things are
tests of character as well as courage, and I covet the
respect of such true people as Mr. P. and Miss S.

So away to my little girl with a bright heart! for with

tales, and sewing for Mary, which pays my board, there I am fixed for the winter and my cares over. Thank the Lord!

She now found publishers eager for her stories, and went on writing for them. She was encouraged by E. P. Whipple's praise of "Mark Field's Mistake," and by earning thirty dollars, most of which she sent home.

Journal.

Earned thirty dollars; sent twenty home. Heard Curtis, Parker, Higginson, and Mrs. Dall lecture. See Booth's Hamlet, and my ideal done at last.

My twenty-sixth birthday on the 29th. Some sweet letters from home, and a ring of A.'s and J.'s hair as a peace-offering. A quiet day, with many thoughts and memories.

The past year has brought us the first death and betrothal, — two events that change my life. I can see that these experiences have taken a deep hold, and changed or developed me. Lizzie helps me spiritually, and a little success makes me more self-reliant. Now that Mother is too tired to be wearied with my moods, I have to manage them alone, and am learning that work of head and hand is my salvation when disappointment or weariness burden and darken my soul.

In my sorrow I think I instinctively came nearer to God, and found comfort in the knowledge that he was sure to help when nothing else could.

A great grief has taught me more than any minister, and when feeling most alone I find refuge in the Almighty Friend. If this is experiencing religion I have done it; but I think it is only the lesson one must learn as it comes, and I am glad to know it.

After my fit of despair I seem to be braver and more cheerful, and grub away with a good heart. Hope it will last, for I need all the courage and comfort I can get.

I feel as if I could write better now, — more truly of things I have felt and therefore *know.* I hope I shall yet do my great book, for that seems to be my work, and I am growing up to it. I even think of trying the "Atlantic." There's ambition for you! I'm sure some of the stories are very flat. If Mr. L. takes the one Father carried to him, I shall think I can do something.

December. — Father started on his tour West full of hope. Dear man! How happy he will be if people will only listen to and *pay* for his wisdom.

May came to B. and stayed with me while she took drawing lessons. Christmas at home. Write an Indian story.

January, 1859. — Send a parcel home to Marmee and Nan.

Mother very ill. Home to nurse her for a week. Wonder if I ought not to be a nurse, as I seem to have a gift for it. Lizzie, L. W., and Mother all say so ; and I like it. If I couldn't write or act I'd try it. May yet. $21 from L.; $15 home.

. . . .

Some day I'll do my best, and get well paid for it.

[$3,000 for a short serial in 1876. True prophet. — L. M. A.]

Wrote a sequel to "Mark Field." Had a queer time over it, getting up at night to write it, being too full to sleep.

March. — "Mark" was a success, and much praised. So I found the divine afflatus did descend. Busy life teaching, writing, sewing, getting all I can from lectures, books, and good people. Life is my college. May I graduate well, and earn some honors !

April. — May went home after a happy winter at the School of Design, where she did finely, and was pro-nounced full of promise. Mr. T. said good things of her, and we were very proud. No doubt now what she is to be, if we can only keep her along.

I went home also, being done with A., who went out of town early. Won't teach any more if I can help it; don't like it; and if I can get writing enough can do much better.

I have done more than I hoped. Supported myself, helped May, and sent something home. Not borrowed a penny, and had only five dollars given me. So my third campaign ends well.

May. — Took care of L. W., who was ill. Walked from C. to B. one day, twenty miles, in five hours, and went to a party in the evening. Not very tired. Well done for a vegetable production!

June. — Took two children to board and teach. A busy month, as Anna was in B.

September. — Great State Encampment here. Town full of soldiers, with military fuss and feathers. I like a camp, and long for a war, to see how it all seems. I can't fight, but I can nurse.

[Prophetic again. — L. M. A.]

October, 1859. — May did a fine copy of Emerson's Endymion [1] for me.

Mother sixty. God bless the dear, brave woman!

Good news of Parker in Florence, — my beloved minister and friend. To him and R. W. E. I owe much of my education. May I be a worthy pupil of such men!

November. — Hurrah! My story was accepted; and Lowell asked if it was not a translation from the German,

---

[1] A fine bas-relief owned by Mr. Emerson.

it was so unlike most tales. I felt much set up, and my fifty dollars will be very happy money. People seem to think it a great thing to get into the "Atlantic;" but I 've not been pegging away all these years in vain, and may yet have books and publishers and a fortune of my own. Success has gone to my head, and I wander a little. Twenty-seven years old, and very happy.

The Harper's Ferry tragedy makes this a memorable month. Glad I have lived to see the Antislavery movement and this last heroic act in it. Wish I could do my part in it.

December, 1859. — The execution of Saint John the Just took place on the second. A meeting at the hall, and all Concord was there. Emerson, Thoreau, Father, and Sanborn spoke, and all were full of reverence and admiration for the martyr.

I made some verses on it, and sent them to the "Liberator."

A sickness of Mrs. Alcott through which she nursed her makes Louisa question whether nursing is not her true vocation. She had an opportunity to try it later.

Much interest attaches to this period of Louisa's work, when she dashed off sensational stories as fast as they were wanted, from the account which she has given of it in "Little Women." She has concentrated into one short period there the work and the feelings of a much longer time. She certainly did let her fancy run riot in these tales, and they were as sensational as the penny papers desired. She had a passion for wild, adventurous life, and even for lurid passion and melodramatic action, which she could indulge to the utmost in these stories. Louisa was always a creature of moods; and it was a great relief to work off certain feelings by the safe vent of imaginary persons and scenes in a story. She had no one to guide or criticise her; and the fact that these gambols of fancy brought the much-needed money, and were, as she truly called them, "pot boilers," certainly did not discourage her from indulging in them. She is probably right in calling most of them "trash and rubbish," for she was yet an unformed girl, and had not studied herself or life very deeply; but her own severe condemnation of them in "Little Women" might give a false idea. The stories are never coarse or immoral. They give a lurid, unnatural picture of life, but sin is not made captivating or immorality attractive. There is often a severe moral enforced. They did not give poison to her readers, only over-seasoned unnatural food, which might destroy the relish for wholesome mental nourishment.

We are inclined to ask, What did Louisa herself get out of this wild, Walpurgis-Night ride among ghosts and goblins, letting her fancy run riot, and indulging every mood as it rose? Did it not give her the dash and freedom in writing which we find in all her books, a command of language, and a recognition of the glow and force of life? She finds life no mere commonplace drudgery, but full of great possibilities. Did it not also give her an interest in all the wild fancies and dreams of girls, all the longing for adventure of boys, and make her hopeful even of the veriest young scamps that they would work off the turbulent energies of youth safely if activities were wisely provided for them?

No writer for children ever was so fully recognized as understanding them. They never felt that she stood on a pinnacle of wisdom to censure them, but came right down into their midst to work and play with them, and at the same time to show them the path out of the tangled thickets, and to help them to see light in their gloomiest despair.

Yet she unquestionably recognized that she was not doing the best work of which she was capable; and she looked forward still to the books she was to write, as well as the fortune she was to make. She did not like any reference to these sensational stories in after life, although she sometimes re-used plots or incidents in them; and she was very unwilling to have them republished.

Boston Bulletin, — Ninth Issue.

SUNDAY EVE, November, 1858.

MY BLESSED NAN, — Having finished my story, I can refresh my soul by a scribble to you, though I have nothing to tell of much interest.

Mrs. L. is to pay me my " celery " each month, as she likes to settle all bills in that way; so yesterday she put $20.85 into my willing hands, and gave me Saturday P. M. for a holiday. This unexpected $20, with the $10 for my story (if I get it) and $5 for sewing, will give me the immense sum of $35. I shall get a second-hand carpet for the little parlor, a bonnet for you, and some shoes and stockings for myself, as three times round the Common in cold weather conduces to chilblains, owing to stockings with a profusion of toe, but no heel, and shoes with plenty of heel, but a paucity of toe. The prejudices of society demand that my feet be covered in the houses of the rich and great; so I shall hose and shoe myself, and if any of my fortune is left, will invest it in the Alcott Sinking Fund, the Micawber R. R., and the Skimpole three per cents.

Tell me how much carpet you need, and T. S. will find me a good one. In December I shall have another $20; so let me know what is wanting, and don't live on "five pounds of rice and a couple of quarts of split peas" all winter, I beg.

How did you like "Mark Field's Mistake"? I don't know whether it is good or bad; but it will keep the pot boiling, and I ask no more. I wanted to go and see if "Hope's Treasures" was accepted, but was afeared. M. and H. both appeared; but one fell asleep, and the other forgot to remember; so I still wait like Patience on a hard chair, smiling at an inkstand. Miss K. asked me to go to see Booth for the last time on Saturday. Upon that ravishing thought I brooded all the week very merrily, and I danced, sang, and clashed my cymbals daily. Saturday A. M. Miss K. sent word she couldn't go, and from my pinnacle of joy I was precipitated into an abyss of woe. While in said abyss Mrs. L. put the $20 into my hands. That was a moment of awful trial. Every one of those dollars cried aloud, "What, ho! Come hither, and be happy!" But eight cold feet on a straw carpet marched to and fro so pathetically that I locked up the tempting fiend, and fell to sewing, as a Saturday treat!

But, lo! virtue was rewarded. Mrs. H. came flying in, and took me to the Museum to see "Gold" and "Lend Me Five Shillings." Warren, in an orange tie, red coat, white satin vest, and scarlet ribbons on his ankles, was the funniest creature you ever saw; and I laughed till I cried, — which was better for me than the melancholy Dane, I dare say.

I 'm disgusted with this letter; for I always begin trying to be proper and neat; but my pen will not keep in order, and ink has a tendency to splash when used copiously and with rapidity. I have to be so moral and so dignified nowadays that the jocosity of my nature will gush out when it gets a chance, and the consequences are, as you see, rubbish. But you like it; so let's be merry while we may, for to-morrow is Monday, and the weekly grind begins again.

CHAPTER VI.

THE YEAR OF GOOD LUCK.

THE CHILDREN'S SONG.

Tune. — "Wait for the Wagon."

THE world lies fair about us, and a friendly sky above;
Our lives are full of sunshine, our homes are full of love;
Few cares or sorrows sadden the beauty of our day;
We gather simple pleasures like daisies by the way.

> *Chorus.* — Oh! sing with cheery voices,
> Like robins on the tree;
> For little lads and lasses
> As blithe of heart should be.

The village is our fairyland: its good men are our kings;
And wandering through its by-ways our busy minds find wings.
The school-room is our garden, and we the flowers there,
And kind hands tend and water us that we may blossom fair.

> *Chorus.* — Oh! dance in airy circles,
> Like fairies on the lee;
> For little lads and lasses
> As light of foot should be.

There's the Shepherd of the sheepfold; the Father of the vines;
The Hermit of blue Walden; the Poet of the pines;
And a Friend who comes among us, with counsels wise and mild,
With snow upon his forehead, yet at heart a very child.

> *Chorus.* — Oh! smile as smiles the river,
> Slow rippling to the sea;
> For little lads and lasses
> As full of peace should be.

There's not a cloud in heaven but drops its silent dew;
No violet in the meadow but blesses with its blue;
No happy child in Concord who may not do its part
To make the great world better by innocence of heart.
          Chorus. — Oh! blossom in the sunshine
                    Beneath the village tree;
                    For little lads and lasses
                    Are the fairest flowers we see.

AFTER such long and hard struggles, it is pleasant to find the diary for 1860 headed "A Year of Good Luck." The appointment of Mr. Alcott as Superintendent of Schools in Concord was a great happiness to the family. It was a recognition of his character and ability, and gave him congenial occupation and some small pecuniary compensation.

Louisa was writing for the "Atlantic," and receiving better pay for her work; Anna was happy; and May absorbed in her art.

In the summer Miss Alcott had an experience in caring for a young friend during a temporary fit of insanity, which she has partially reproduced in the touching picture of Helen in the story of "Work." It is a powerful lesson; but it is almost cruelly enforced, and is an artistic blemish in the book. While the great problem of heredity should be studied and its lessons enforced, it is yet a mystery, whose laws are not understood; and it is not wise to paint its possible effects in the lurid light of excited imagination, which may too often bring about the very evils which a wise and temperate caution might prevent. For the physician and teacher such investigations are important; but they are dangerous to the young and sensitive.

The following unusually long letter gives a pleasing picture of the family life at this time : —

To Mrs. Bond.

APPLE SLUMP, Sept. 17, 1860.

DEAR AUNTIE, — I consider this a practical illustration of one of Mother's naughty amended sayings, " Cast your bread upon the waters, and after many days it will return buttered ; " and this " rule of three " don't " puzzle me," as the other did ; for my venerable raiment went away with one if not two feet in the grave, and came back in the guise of three stout angels, having been resurrection-ized by the spirit who lives on the other side of a Charles River Jordan. Thank you very much, and be sure the dreams I dream in them will be pleasant ones ; for, whether you sewed them or not, I know they bring some of the Auntie influence in their strength, softness, and warmth ; and, though a Vandal, I think any prayers I may say in them will be the better for the affectionate recollections that will clothe me with the putting on of these friendly gowns, while my belief in both heavenly and earthly providences will be amazingly strengthened by the knowledge of some lives here, whose beauty renders it impossible to doubt the existence of the life hereafter.

We were very glad to hear that the Papa was better ; for when paternal " Richards " ain't " themselves," everybody knows the anxious state of the domestic realms.

I hope Georgie (last name disremembered) has recovered from the anguish of discontented teeth and berry-seeds, and that " the Mama " was as much benefited by the trip as the other parties were, barring the horse perhaps.

This amiable town is convulsed just now with a gymnastic fever, which shows itself with great violence in all the schools, and young societies generally. Dr. Lewis has "inoculated us for the disease," and it has "taken finely;" for every one has become a perambulating windmill, with all its four sails going as if a wind had set in; and the most virulent cases present the phenomena of black eyes and excoriation of the knobby parts of the frame, to say nothing of sprains and breakage of vessels looming in the future.

The City Fathers approve of it; and the city sons and daughters intend to show that Concord has as much muscle as brain, and be ready for another Concord fight, if Louis Napoleon sees fit to covet this famous land of Emerson, Hawthorne, Thoreau, Alcott, & Co. Abby and I are among the pioneers; and the delicate vegetable productions clash their cymbals in private, when the beef-eating young ladies faint away and become superfluous *dumb belles.*

Saturday we had J. G. Whittier, Charlotte Cushman, Miss Stebbins the sculptress, and Mr. Stuart, conductor of the underground railroad of this charming free country. So you see our humble place of abode is perking up; and when the " great authoress and artist " are fairly out of the shell, we shall be an honor to our country and terror to the foe, — provided good fortune don't addle or bad fortune smash us.

Father continues to stir up the schools like a mild pudding-stick, Mother to sing Hebron among her pots and pans, Anna and the Prince Consort to bill and coo in the little dove-cot, Oranthy Bluggage to launch chips on the Atlantic and make a gigantic blot of herself in working the vessel, Abby to teach the fine arts and play propriety for the family, and the old house to put its best foot foremost and hoot at the idea of ever returning to the chaos from which it came.

8

This is a condensed history of " the pathetic family," which is also a " happy family," owing to the prevalence of friends and lots of kindness in the original packages, " which are always arriving " when the " Widow Cruise's oil-bottle " begins to give out.

You know I never *could* do anything in a neat and proper manner ; so you will receive this topsy-turvy note as you do its writer, and with love to all from all, believe her, dear auntie,

Ever lovingly yours,

L. M. A.

This characteristic letter not only shows Louisa's affectionate feelings and gives a picture of her life, but indicates that " The Pathetic Family," which was the foundation of " Little Women," was already shaping itself in her mind.

Mr. Alcott's career as Superintendent of Schools was a gratifying success, and is still remembered by friends of education in the town. The year closed with a school festival, for which Louisa wrote a poem, and in which she took hearty delight.

In 1861 war was declared with the South. The Alcotts were all alive with patriotic enthusiasm, and Louisa took an active part in fitting off the boys for the army. But she also found time for much reading. Mr. Alcott, in his sonnet, uses the expression about Louisa —

" Hast with grave studies vexed a lively brain."

He may possibly have referred to this period, though she could never properly be called a student.

She was a rapid, intelligent reader, and her taste was severe and keen. From her childhood she had browsed in her father's library, full of the works of ancient philosophers and quaint English poets, and had imbibed from them great thoughts and noble sentiments; but her reading, like all her education, was immethodical. Occasionally she would lay out courses of reading, which she pursued for a time; but in general she followed the cravings of a healthy appetite for knowledge, reading what came in her way. Later in life she often read light literature in abundance, to drown the sensations of pain, and to pass away the hours of invalidism.

She read French easily, and learned to speak it when abroad; she also studied German, but did not acquire equal facility in that tongue. Of ancient languages she had no knowledge. History could not fail to interest such a student of life, and she loved Nature too well not to enjoy the revelations of science when brought to her notice; but she had never time to give to a thorough study of either.

In her journal at this time she speaks of her religious feelings, which the experiences of grief and despair and reviving hope had deepened. Louisa Alcott's was a truly religious soul; she always lived in the consciousness of a Higher Power sustaining and blessing her, whose presence was revealed to her through Nature, through the inspired words of great thinkers and the deep experiences of her own heart. She never held her life as an isolated possession which she was free to use for her own enjoyment or glory. Her father truly called her " Duty's faithful child," and her life was consecrated to the duty she recognized as specially hers. But for outward forms and rites of religion she cared little ; her home was sacred to her, and she found her best life there. She loved Theodore Parker, and found great strength and help from his preaching, and afterward liked to listen to Dr. Bartol ; but she never joined any church. The Bible was not her favorite reading, though her father had read it much to her in her childhood, with his own peculiar charm of interpretation. Pilgrim's Progress was one of the few religious books which became dear to her in the same way.

Her sister Anna was married in May ; this was of course a great event in the family. While fully rejoicing in her sister's happiness, Louisa felt her loss as a constant companion and confidant. The journal gives a sufficient description of the event. Her strong affection for her brother-in-law appears in " Little Women " and in " Jo's Boys." About this time her farce was brought out at the Howard Athenæum.

The story-writing continued, as it helped to pay the expenses of the family ; but the continuous, hurried work had begun to affect her health, and she occasionally suffered from illness.

In the summer of 1861 Miss Alcott began to write her first novel, entitled " Moods ; " this proved to be the least successful of her books, and yet like many an unfortunate child, it was the dearest to the mother's heart. It was not written for money, but for its own sake, and she was possessed by the plot and the characters. Warwick represented her ideal of a hero, while her sister preferred the type of the amiable Moor; yet there is far less of her outward self revealed in this than in her other stories. It is full of her thoughts and fancies, but not of her life. The wilful, moody, charming Sylvia does not affect us like the stormy Jo, who is a real presence to us, and whom we take to our hearts in spite of her faults. The men are such as she found in books, but had never known herself, and, carefully as she has drawn them, have not the individuality of Laurie and Professor Bhaer. The action takes place in an unreal world; and though there are many pretty scenes, they have not the real flavor of New England life. The principal incident, of a young girl going up the river on a picnic-voyage for some days with her brother and two other young men, was so contrary to common ideas of decorum, that the motive hardly seems sufficient for the staid sister's consent ; but in the simple, innocent life which the Alcotts lived in Concord such scruples were little felt.

Miss Alcott did not lay stress upon the marriage question as the principal feature of the book; she cared more to describe the wilful moods of a young girl, full of good feelings, and longing for a rich and noble life, but not established in convictions and principles. She meant to represent much of her own nature in Sylvia, for she was always a creature of moods, which her family learned to recognize and respect. But how unlike was the discipline of family work and love, which saved Louisa from fatal caprices and fitful gusts of fancy called passion, to the lot of the wealthy and admired Sylvia. Miss Alcott says that the incidents of the marriage, although not drawn from life, were so close to an actual case that the wife asked her how she had known her secret; but such realism is a poor justification in art. It is that which becomes true to the imagination and heart through its vivid personation of character which is accepted, not the bare facts. The great question of the transcendental period was truth to the inward life instead of the outward law. But in " Moods " the marriage question is not stated strongly; it does not reach down to this central principle. It is only in tragedy that such a double relation could be endured, when the situation is compelled by fate, — the fate of character and overpowering circumstances, — and when there is no happy solution possible. But Sylvia's position is made only by her own weakness, and the love which stands in opposition to outward duty has no right of existence. If her love for Warwick *could* be overcome, there was no question of her duty; and when she accepts Faith's criticism of him, it is clear that it is a much lighter spell than love which has fascinated her. We do not accept the catastrophe which sacrifices a splendid life to make a comfortable solution of the practical difficulty, and to allow Sylvia to accept a happy home without a thorough regeneration of heart and mind. But these were the natural mistakes of youth and inexperience;

Louisa had known but little of such struggles. Love and marriage were rather uninteresting themes to her, and she had not yet found her true power.

Still the book has great literary merit. It is well written, in a more finished style than any of her other work, except "Modern Mephistopheles," and the dialogue is vigorous and sprightly. In spite of her careful revision and pruning, there is something left of youthful gush in it, and this perhaps touched the heart of young girls, who found in Sylvia's troubles with herself a reflection of their own.

The "golden wedding" scenes have some of her usual freedom and vivacity. She is at home with a troop of mothers and babies and noisy boys. But the "golden wedding" was a new importation from Germany, and not at home in the New England farmhouse. Why might it not have been a true wedding or a harvest feast?

Louisa never lost her interest in this early work, though it was the most unlucky of books, and subjected to severe handling. It was sent to and fro from publisher to author, each one suggesting some change. Redpath sent it back as being too long. Ticknor found it very interesting, but could not use it then. Loring liked it, but wanted it shorter. She condensed and altered until her author's spirit rebelled, and she declared she would change it no more.

After her other books had made her famous, "Moods" was again brought forward and republished as it was originally written. It met with warmer welcome than before, and a cheap edition was published in England to supply the popular demand.

Miss Alcott learned the first painful lesson of over-work on this book. She was possessed by it, and for three weeks labored so constantly that she felt the physical effects keenly. Fortunately new household tasks (for the daughters of John Brown came to board with them), and the enthusiasm of the time, changed the current of her thoughts.

Journal.

February, 1860. — Mr. —— won't have " M. L.," as it is antislavery, and the dear South must not be offended. Got a carpet with my $50, and wild Louisa's head kept the feet of the family warm.

March. — Wrote " A Modern Cinderella," with Nan for the heroine and John for the hero.

Made my first ball dress for May, and she was the finest girl at the party. My tall, blond, graceful girl ! I was proud of her.

Wrote a song for the school festival, and heard it sung by four hundred happy children. Father got up the affair, and such a pretty affair was never seen in Concord before. He said, " We spend much on our cattle and flower shows ; let us each spring have a show of our children, and begrudge nothing for their culture." All liked it but the old fogies who want things as they were in the ark.

April. — Made two riding habits, and May and I had some fine rides. Both needed exercise, and this was good for us. So one of our dreams came true, and we really did " dash away on horseback."

Sanborn was nearly kidnapped for being a friend of John Brown ; but his sister and A. W. rescued him when he was handcuffed, and the scamps drove off. Great ferment in town. A meeting and general flurry.

Had a funny lover who met me in the cars, and said he lost his heart at once. Handsome man of forty. A Southerner, and very demonstrative and gushing, called and wished to pay his addresses ; and being told I did n't wish to see him, retired, to write letters and haunt the road with his hat off, while the girls laughed and had great fun over Jo's lover. He went at last, and peace reigned. My adorers are all queer.

Sent "Cinderella" to the "Atlantic," and it was accepted. Began "By the River," and thought that this was certainly to be a lucky year ; for after ten years hard climbing I had reached a good perch on the ladder, and could look more hopefully into the future, while my paper boats sailed gaily over the Atlantic.

May. — Meg's wedding.

My farce was acted, and I went to see it. Not very well done ; but I sat in a box, and the good Doctor handed up a bouquet to the author, and made as much as he could of a small affair.

Saw Anna's honeymoon home at Chelsea, — a little cottage in a blooming apple-orchard. Pretty place, simple and sweet. God bless it !

The dear girl was married on the 23d, the same day as Mother's wedding. A lovely day ; the house full of sunshine, flowers, friends, and happiness. Uncle S. J. May married them, with no fuss, but much love ; and we all stood round her. She in her silver-gray silk, with lilies of the valley (John's flower) in her bosom and hair. We in gray thin stuff and roses, — sackcloth, I called it, and ashes of roses ; for I mourn the loss of my Nan, and am not comforted. We have had a little feast, sent by good Mrs. Judge Shaw ; then the old folks danced round the bridal pair on the lawn in the German fashion, making a pretty picture to remember, under our Revolutionary elm.

Then, with tears and kisses, our dear girl, in her little white bonnet, went happily away with her good John; and we ended our first wedding. Mr. Emerson kissed her; and I thought that honor would make even matrimony endurable, for he is the god of my idolatry, and has been for years.

June. — To Boston to the memorial meeting for Mr. Parker, which was very beautiful, and proved how much he was beloved.   Music Hall was full of flowers and sunshine, and hundreds of faces, both sad and proud, as the various speakers told the life of love and labor which makes Theodore Parker's memory so rich a legacy to Boston.   I was very glad to have known so good a man, and been called "friend" by him.

Saw Nan in her nest, where she and her mate live like a pair of turtle doves.   Very sweet and pretty, but I'd rather be a free spinster and paddle my own canoe.

August. — "Moods."   Genius burned so fiercely that for four weeks I wrote all day and planned nearly all night, being quite possessed by my work.   I was perfectly happy, and seemed to have no wants.   Finished the book, or a rough draught of it, and put it away to settle.   Mr. Emerson offered to read it when Mother told him it was "Moods" and had one of his sayings for motto.

Daresay nothing will ever come of it; but it *had* to be done, and I'm the richer for a new experience.

September. — Received $75 of Ticknor for "Cinderella," and feel very rich.   Emerson praised it, and people wrote to me about it and patted me on the head.   Paid bills, and began to simmer another.

October. — I went to B. and saw the Prince of Wales trot over the Common with his train at a review. A yellow-haired laddie very like his mother. Fanny W. and I nodded and waved as he passed, and he openly winked his boyish eye at us; for Fanny, with her yellow curls and wild waving, looked rather rowdy, and the poor little prince wanted some fun. We laughed, and thought that we had been more distinguished by the saucy wink than by a stately bow. Boys are always jolly, — even princes.

Read Richter, and enjoyed him very much.

Mother went to see Uncle S. J. May, and I was house-keeper. Gave my mind to it so energetically that I dreamed dip-toast, talked apple-sauce, thought pies, and wept drop-cakes. Read my book to Nan, who came up to cheer me in my struggles; and she laughed and cried over it and said it was "good." So I felt encouraged, and will touch it up when duty no longer orders me to make a burnt-offering of myself.

November. — Father sixty-one; L. aged twenty-eight. Our birthday. Gave Father a ream of paper, and he gave me Emerson's picture; so both were happy.

Wrote little, being busy with visitors. The John Brown Association asked me for a poem, which I wrote.

Kind Miss R. sent May $30 for lessons, so she went to B. to take some of Johnstone. She is one of the fortunate ones, and gets what she wants easily. I have to grub for my help, or go without it. Good for me, doubt-less, or it would n't be so; so cheer up, Louisa, and grind away!

December. — More luck for May. She wanted to go to Syracuse and teach, and Dr. W. sends for her, thanks to Uncle S. J. May. I sew like a steam-engine for a week, and get her ready. On the 17th go to B. and see our youngest start on her first little flight alone into the world, full of hope and courage. May all go well with her!

Mr. Emerson invited me to his class when they meet to talk on Genius; a great honor, as all the learned ladies go.

Sent "Debby's Debit" to the "Atlantic," and they took it. Asked to the John Brown meeting, but had no "good gown," so did n't go; but my "pome" did, and came out in the paper. Not good. I 'm a better patriot than poet, and could n't say what I felt.

A quiet Christmas; no presents but apples and flowers. No merry-making; for Nan and May were gone, and Betty under the snow. But we are used to hard times, and, as Mother says, "while there is a famine in Kansas we must n't ask for sugar-plums."

All the philosophy in our house is not in the study; a good deal is in the kitchen, where a fine old lady thinks high thoughts and does kind deeds while she cooks and scrubs.

January, 1861. — Twenty-eight; received thirteen New Year's gifts. A most uncommon fit of generosity seemed to seize people on my behalf, and I was blessed with all manner of nice things, from a gold and ivory pen to a mince-pie and a bonnet.

Wrote on a new book — "Success" ["Work"] — till Mother fell ill, when I corked up my inkstand and turned nurse. The dear woman was very ill, but rose up like a phœnix from her ashes after what she gayly called "the irrepressible conflict between sickness and the May constitution."

Father had four talks at Emerson's; good people came, and he enjoyed them much; made $30. R. W. E. probably put in $20. He has a sweet way of bestowing gifts on the table under a book or behind a candle-stick, when he thinks Father wants a little money, and no one will help him earn. A true friend is this tender and illustrious man.

Wrote a tale and put it away, — to be sent when "Debby" comes out. "F. T." appeared, and I got a dress, having mended my six-year old silk till it is more patch and tear than gown. Made the claret merino myself, and enjoyed it, as I do anything bought with my "head-money."

February. — Another turn at "Moods," which I remodelled. From the 2d to the 25th I sat writing, with a run at dusk; could not sleep, and for three days was so full of it I could not stop to get up. Mother made me a green silk cap with a red bow, to match the old green and red party wrap, which I wore as a "glory cloak." Thus arrayed I sat in groves of manuscripts, "living for immortality," as May said. Mother wandered in and out with cordial cups of tea, worried because I could n't eat. Father thought it fine, and brought his reddest apples and hardest cider for my Pegasus to feed upon. All sorts of fun was going on; but I did n't care if the world returned to chaos if I and my inkstand only "lit" in the same place.

It was very pleasant and queer while it lasted; but after three weeks of it I found that my mind was too rampant for my body, as my head was dizzy, legs shaky, and no sleep would come. So I dropped the pen, and took long walks, cold baths, and had Nan up to frolic with me. Read all I had done to my family; and Father said : " Emerson must see this. Where did you get your metaphysics?" Mother pronounced it wonderful, and Anna laughed and cried, as she always does, over my works, saying, "My dear, I 'm proud of you."

So I had a good time, even if it never comes to any

thing; for it was worth something to have my three dearest sit up till midnight listening with wide-open eyes to Lu's first novel.

I planned it some time ago, and have had it in my mind ever so long; but now it begins to take shape.

Father had his usual school festival, and Emerson asked me to write a song, which I did. On the 16th the schools all met in the hall (four hundred), — a pretty posy bed, with a border of proud parents and friends. Some of the fogies objected to the names Phillips and John Brown. But Emerson said: " Give it up? No, no; *I* will read it." Which he did, to my great contentment; for when the great man of the town says " Do it," the thing is done. So the choir warbled, and the Alcotts were uplifted in their vain minds.

Father was in glory, like a happy shepherd with a large flock of sportive lambs; for all did something. Each school had· its badge, — one pink ribbons, one green shoulder-knots, and one wreaths of pop-corn on the curly pates. One school to whom Father had read Pilgrim's Progress told the story, one child after the other popping up to say his or her part; and at the end a little tot walked forward, saying with a pretty air of wonder, — " And behold it was all a dream."

When all was over, and Father about to dismiss them, F. H., a tall, handsome lad came to him, and looking up confidingly to the benign old face, asked " our dear friend Mr. Alcott to accept of Pilgrim's Progress and George Herbert's Poems from the children of Concord, as a token of their love and respect."

Father was much touched and surprised, and blushed and stammered like a boy, hugging the fine books while the children cheered till the roof rung.

His report was much admired, and a thousand copies

printed to supply the demand ; for it was a new thing to have a report, neither dry nor dull ; and teachers were glad of the hints given, making education a part ,of religion, not a mere bread-making grind for teacher and an irksome cram for children.

April. — War declared with the South, and our Concord company went to Washington. A busy time getting them ready, and a sad day seeing them off ; for in a little town like this we all seem like one family in times like these. At the station the scene was very dramatic, as the brave boys went away perhaps never to come back again.

I 've often longed to see a war, and now I have my wish. I long to be a man ; but as I can't fight, I will content myself with working for those who can.

Sewed a good deal getting May's summer things in order, as she sent for me to make and mend and buy and send her outfit.

Stories simmered in my brain, demanding to be writ ; but I let them simmer, knowing that the longer the divine afflatus was bottled up the better it would be.

John Brown's daughters came to board, and upset my plans of rest and writing when the report and the sewing were done. I had my fit of woe up garret on the fat rag-bag, and then put my papers away, and fell to work at housekeeping. I think disappointment must be good for me, I get so much of it ; and the constant thumping Fate gives me may be a mellowing process ; so I shall be a ripe and sweet old pippin before I die.

May. — Spent our May-day working for our men, — three hundred women all sewing together at the hall for two days.

May will not return to S. after her vacation in July ; and being a lucky puss, just as she wants something to do,

F. B. S. needs a drawing teacher in his school and offers her the place.

Nan found that I was wearing all the old clothes she and May left; so the two dear souls clubbed together and got me some new ones; and the great parcel, with a loving letter, came to me as a beautiful surprise.

Nan and John walked up from Cambridge for a day, and we all walked back. Took a sail to the forts, and saw our men on guard there. Felt very martial and Joan-of-Arc-y as I stood on the walls with the flag flying over me and cannon all about.

June. — Read a good deal; grubbed in my garden, and made the old house pretty for May. Enjoyed Carlyle's French Revolution very much. His earthquaky style suits me.

"Charles Auchester" is charming, — a sort of fairy tale for grown people. Dear old "Evelina," as a change, was pleasant. Emerson recommended Hodson's India, and I got it, and liked it; also read Sir Thomas More's Life. I read Fielding's "Amelia," and thought it coarse and queer. The heroine having "her lovely nose smashed all to bits falling from a post shay" was a new idea. What some one says of Richardson applies to Fielding, "The virtues of his heroes are the vices of decent men."

July. — Spent a month at the White Mountains with L. W., — a lovely time, and it did me much good. Mountains are restful and uplifting to my mind. Lived in the woods, and revelled in brooks, birds, pines, and peace.

August. — May came home very tired, but satisfied with her first attempt, which has been very successful in every way. She is quite a belle now, and much improved, — a tall blond lass, full of grace and spirit.

September. — Ticknor sent $50. Wrote a story for C., as Plato needs new shirts, and Minerva a pair of boots, and Hebe a fall hat.

October. — All together on Marmee's birthday. Sewing and knitting for " our boys " all the time. It seems as if a few energetic women could carry on the war better than the men do it so far.

A week with Nan in the dove-cot. As happy as ever.

November and *December.* — Wrote, read, sewed, and wanted something to do.

In 1862, at the suggestion of Miss Peabody, Miss Alcott opened a Kindergarten school; but it was not successful, and she took a final leave of the teacher's profession, and returned to her writing, which she found to be her true calling. She wrote much; for " brain was lively, and work paid for readily." Besides the occasional stories in papers and magazines, her most important labor was the preparation of the story called "Work," or, as she originally named it, "Success." This story however was not published until ten years later. Here she took the road that was later to lead to fame and fortune, by writing from her own experience of life. Christie is Louisa herself under very thin disguise; and all her own experiences, as servant, governess, companion, seamstress, and actress are brought in to give vividness to the picture; while many other persons may be recognized as models for her skilful portraiture. The book has always been deservedly popular.

9

January, 1862. — E. P. Peabody wanted me to open a Kindergarten, and Mr. Barnard gave a room at the Warren Street Chapel. Don't like to teach, but take what comes; so when Mr. F. offered $40 to fit up with, twelve pupils, and his patronage, I began.

Saw many great people, and found them no bigger than the rest of the world, — often not half so good as some humble soul who made no noise. I learned a good deal in my way, and am not half so much impressed by society as before I got a peep at it. Having known Emerson, Parker, Phillips, and that set of really great and good men and women living for the world's work and service of God, the mere show people seem rather small and silly, though they shine well, and feel that they are stars.

February. — Visited about, as my school did not bring enough to pay board and the assistant I was made to have, though I did n't want her.

Went to lectures; saw Booth at the Goulds', — a handsome, shy man, glooming in a corner.

Very tired of this wandering life and distasteful work; but kept my word and tugged on.

Hate to visit people who only ask me to help amuse others, and often longed for a crust in a garret with freedom and a pen. I never knew before what insolent things a hostess can do, nor what false positions poverty can push one into.

April. — Went to and from C. every day that I might be at home. Forty miles a day is dull work; but I have my dear people at night, and am not a beggar.

Wrote " King of Clubs," — $30. The school having no real foundation (as the people who sent did n't care for Kindergartens, and Miss P. wanted me to take pupils for nothing, to try the new system), I gave it up, as I

could do much better at something else. May took my
place for a month, that I might keep my part of the bargain; and I cleaned house, and wrote a story which
made more than all my months of teaching. They ended
in a wasted winter and a debt of $40, — to be paid if I
sell my hair to do it.

May. — School finished for me, and I paid Miss N.
by giving her all the furniture, and leaving her to do as
she liked; while I went back to my writing, which pays
much better, though Mr. F. did say, "Stick to your teaching; you can't write." Being wilful, I said, "I won't
teach; and I can write, and I'll prove it."

Saw Miss Rebecca Harding, author of "Margret
Howth," which has made a stir, and is very good. A
handsome, fresh, quiet woman, who says she never had
any troubles, though she writes about woes. I told her
I had had lots of troubles; so I write jolly tales; and we
wondered why we each did so.

June, July, August. — Wrote a tale for B., and he lost
it, and would n't pay.

Wrote two tales for L. I enjoy romancing to suit myself; and though my tales are silly, they are not bad;
and my sinners always have a good spot somewhere. I
hope it is good drill for fancy and language, for I can do
it fast; and Mr. L. says my tales are so "dramatic, vivid,
and full of plot," they are just what he wants.

September, October. — Sewing Bees and Lint Picks for
"our boys" kept us busy, and the prospect of the first
grandchild rejoiced the hearts of the family.

Wrote much; for brain was lively, and work paid for
readily. Rewrote the last story, and sent it to L., who
wants more than I can send him. So, between blue
flannel jackets for "our boys" and dainty slips for Louisa
Caroline or John B., Jr., as the case may be, I reel off

my " thrilling" tales, and mess up my work in a queer but interesting way.

War news bad. Anxious faces, beating hearts, and busy minds.

I like the stir in the air, and long for battle like a war-horse when he smells powder. The blood of the Mays is up !

After Anna's Marriage.

SUNDAY MORN, 1860.

MRS. PRATT :

MY DEAR MADAM, — The news of the town is as follows, and I present it in the usual journalesque style of correspondence. After the bridal train had departed, the mourners withdrew to their respective homes ; and the bereaved family solaced their woe by washing dishes for two hours and bolting the remains of the funeral baked meats. At four, having got settled down, we were all routed up by the appearance of a long procession of children filing down our lane, headed by the Misses H. and R. Father rushed into the cellar, and appeared with a large basket of apples, which went the rounds with much effect. The light infantry formed in a semi-circle, and was watered by the matron and maids. It was really a pretty sight, these seventy children loaded with wreaths and flowers, standing under the elm in the sunshine, singing in full chorus the song I wrote for them. It was a neat little compliment to the superintendent and his daughter, who was glad to find that her " pome " was a favorite among the " lads and lasses " who sang it " with cheery voices, like robins on the tree."

Father put the finishing stroke to the spectacle by going off at full speed, hoppity-skip, and all the babes followed in a whirl of rapture at the idea. He led them up and down and round and round till they were tired ;

then they fell into order, and with a farewell song marched away, seventy of the happiest little ones I ever wish to see. We subsided, and fell into our beds with the new thought " Annie is married and gone " for a lullaby, which was not very effective in its results with all parties.

Thursday we set our house in order, and at two the rush began. It had gone abroad that Mr. M. and Mrs. Captain Brown were to adorn the scene, so many people coolly came who were not invited, and who had no business here. People sewed and jabbered till Mrs. Brown, with Watson Brown's widow and baby came ; then a levee took place. The two pale women sat silent and serene through the clatter ; and the bright-eyed, handsome baby received the homage of the multitude like a little king, bearing the kisses and praises with the utmost dignity. He is named Frederick Watson Brown, after his murdered uncle and father, and is a fair, heroic-looking baby, with a fine head, and serious eyes that look about him as if saying, " I am a Brown ! Are these friends or enemies ? " I wanted to cry once at the little scene the unconscious baby made. Some one caught and kissed him rudely ; he did n't cry, but looked troubled, and rolled his great eyes anxiously about for some familiar face to reassure him with its smile. His mother was not there ; but though many hands were stretched to him, he turned to Grandma Bridge, and putting out his little arms to her as if she was a refuge, laughed and crowed as he had not done before when she danced him on her knee. The old lady looked delighted ; and Freddy patted the kind face, and cooed like a lawful descendant of that pair of ancient turtle doves.

When he was safe back in the study, playing alone at his mother's feet, C. and I went and worshipped in our own way at the shrine of John Brown's grandson, kissing

him as if he were a little saint, and feeling highly honored when he sucked our fingers, or walked on us with
his honest little red shoes, much the worse for wear.

Well, the baby fascinated me so that I forgot a raging
headache and forty gabbling women all in full clack. Mrs.
Brown, Sen., is a tall, stout woman, plain, but with a
strong, good face, and a natural dignity that showed she
was something better than a " lady," though she *did*
drink out of her saucer and used the plainest speech.

The younger woman had such a patient, heart-broken
face, it was a whole Harper's Ferry tragedy in a look.
When we got your letter, Mother and I ran into the study
to read it. Mother read aloud; for there were only C., A.,
I, and Mrs. Brown, Jr., in the room. As she read the
words that were a poem in their simplicity and happiness,
the poor young widow sat with tears rolling down her
face; for I suppose it brought back her own wedding-
day, not two years ago, and all the while she cried the
baby laughed and crowed at her feet as if there was no
trouble in the world.

The preparations had been made for twenty at the utmost; so when forty souls with the usual complement of
bodies appeared, we grew desperate, and our neat little
supper turned out a regular " tea fight." A., C., B., and
I rushed like comets to and fro trying to fill the multitude that would eat fast and drink like sponges. I filled
a big plate with all I could lay hands on, and with two
cups of tea, strong enough for a dozen, charged upon Mr.
E. and Uncle S., telling them to eat, drink, and be merry,
for a famine was at hand. They cuddled into a corner;
and then, feeling that my mission was accomplished, I let
the hungry *wait* and the thirsty *moan* for tea, while I
picked out and helped the regular Antislavery set.

We got through it; but it was an awful hour; and

Mother wandered in her mind, utterly lost in a grove of teapots; while B. pervaded the neighborhood demanding hot water, and we girls sowed cake broadcast through the land.

When the plates were empty and the teapots dry, people wiped their mouths and confessed at last that they had done. A conversation followed, in which Grandpa B. and E. P. P. held forth, and Uncle and Father mildly upset the world, and made a new one in which every one desired to take a place. Dr. B., Mr. B., T., etc., appeared, and the rattle continued till nine, when some Solomon suggested that the Alcotts must be tired, and every one departed but C. and S. We had a polka by Mother and Uncle, the lancers by C. and B., and an *étude* by S., after which scrabblings of feast appeared, and we "drained the dregs of every cup," all cakes and pies we gobbled up, etc.; then peace fell upon us and our remains were interred decently.

CHAPTER VII.

HOSPITAL SKETCHES.

THOREAU'S FLUTE.

WE sighing said, "Our Pan is dead;
His pipe hangs mute beside the river
Around it wistful sunbeams quiver,
But Music's airy voice is fled.
Spring mourns as for untimely frost;
The bluebird chants a requiem;
The willow-blossom waits for him; —
The Genius of the wood is lost."

Then from the flute, untouched by hands,
There came a low, harmonious breath:
"For such as he there is no death; —
His life the eternal life commands;
Above man's aims his nature rose.
The wisdom of a just content
Made one small spot a continent,
And tuned to poetry life's prose.

"Haunting the hills, the stream, the wild,
Swallow and aster, lake and pine, —
To him grew human or divine, —
Fit mates for this large-hearted child.
Such homage Nature ne'er forgets,
And yearly on the coverlid
'Neath which her darling lieth hid
Will write his name in violets.

"To him no vain regrets belong
Whose soul, that finer instrument,
Gave to the world no poor lament,
But wood-notes ever sweet and strong.
O lonely friend! he still will be
A potent presence, though unseen, —
Steadfast, sagacious, and serene;
Seek not for him — he is with thee."

MISS ALCOTT could not help feeling deeply the excitement of the hour when the war broke out. Her father had been one of the earliest Abolitionists, having joined the Antislavery Society with Garrison, and she well remembered the fugitive slave whom her mother had hidden in the oven. Now this feeling could be united with her patriotic zeal and her strong love of active life, and it was inevitable that she should long to share personally in the dangers and excitement of the war.

Louisa had always been the nurse in the family, and had by nature the magnetic power which encourages and helps the feeble and suffering; therefore, since no other way of serving the cause opened to her, it was most like her to take her own life in her hands and join the corps of devoted nurses. She was accepted, and went to Washington. Her journal gives an account of her situation in the Union Hospital at Georgetown. It was a small hospital, much inferior in its appointments to those which were afterward arranged. Although Louisa had never been very ill up to that time, and thought herself exceptionally strong, yet she had not the rugged constitution fit to bear the labors and exposures of such a position; and the healthful habits of outdoor life and simple food to which she had always been accustomed made the conditions of the crowded, ill-ventilated hospital peculiarly perilous to her. She says, " I was never ill before this time, and never well afterward."

But with all its hardships, Miss Alcott found in the hospital the varied and intense human life she had longed to know. Her great heart went out to all the men, black or white, the Virginia blacksmith and the rough Michigander. She even tried to befriend the one solitary rebel who had got left behind, and who was taken into the hospital to the disgust of some of the men; but he was impervious to all kindness, and she could find nothing in him for sympathy or romance to fasten upon.

Miss Alcott remained in the hospital only about six weeks. Yet this short period had a very strong influence, both for good and evil, on her future life. The severe attack of fever which drove her from her post left her with shattered nerves and weakened constitution, and she never again knew the fulness of life and health which she had before. The chamber in her quiet home at Concord was evermore haunted by the fearful visions of delirium, and she could not regain there the peace she needed for work. But the experience of life, the observation of men under the excitement of war, the way in which they met the great conqueror Death, the revelations of heroism and love, and sometimes of bitterness and hate, brought her a deeper insight into human life than she ever had before, and gave to her writings greater reality.

Louisa constantly wrote to the family of her experiences, and these letters were so interesting that she was persuaded to publish them in the "Commonwealth" newspaper. They attracted great attention, and first made her widely and favorably known to a higher public than that which had read her stories.

These letters were published by James Redpath

in book form, and Miss Alcott received $200 for
the book, — a welcome sum to her at that time.
The sketches are almost a literal reproduction of
her letters to her family; but as they have been
so extensively read, and are accessible to every
one, I shall give in preference to them extracts
from her journal kept at the hospital. Other
stories growing out of her experience in the hospital, or more remotely connected with it, have
been published in the same volume in later editions. "My Contraband" is one of the most dramatic and powerful stories she ever wrote. She
portrays the intensity of hatred in a noble nature, — hatred justified by the provocation, and
yet restrained from fatal execution by the highest
suggestions of religion. This story called forth a
letter of commendation and frank criticism from
Col. T. W. Higginson, which was very encouraging
to the young writer.

The beautiful lines on Thoreau's flute, the most
perfect of her poems, excepting the exquisite tribute to her mother, were first composed in the
watches of the night in the hospital, and afterwards recalled during the tedious days of conva-
lescence at Concord. This poem was printed in
the "Atlantic," and brought her a welcome ten-
dollar bill.

"Hospital Sketches" were hastily written, and
with little regard to literary execution, but they
are fresh and original, and, still more, they are
true, and they appeared at just the time the public
wanted them. Every heart was longing to hear
not only from field and camp, but from the hospi-

tals, where sons and brothers were tenderly cared for. The generous, hopeful spirit with which Miss Alcott entered into the work was recognized as that which animated the brave corps of women who answered so promptly to their country's call, and every loyal and loving heart vibrated in unison with the strings she touched so skilfully.

Journal kept at the Hospital, Georgetown, D. C., 1862.

November. — Thirty years old. Decided to go to Washington as nurse if I could find a place. Help needed, and I love nursing, and *must* let out my pent-up energy in some new way. Winter is always a hard and a dull time, and if I am away there is one less to feed and warm and worry over.

I want new experiences, and am sure to get 'em if I go. So I've sent in my name, and bide my time writing tales, to leave all snug behind me, and mending up my old clothes, — for nurses don't need nice things, thank Heaven!

December. — On the 11th I received a note from Miss H. M. Stevenson telling me to start for Georgetown next day to fill a place in the Union Hotel Hospital. Mrs. Ropes of Boston was matron, and Miss Kendall of Plymouth was a nurse there, and though a hard place, help was needed. I was ready, and when my commander said "March!" I marched. Packed my trunk, and reported in B. that same evening.

We had all been full of courage till the last moment came; then we all broke down. I realized that I had taken my life in my hand, and might never see them all again. I said, "Shall I stay, Mother?" as I hugged her

close. " No, go ! and the Lord be with you ! " answered
the Spartan woman ; and till I turned the corner she
bravely smiled and waved her wet handkerchief on the
door-step. Shall I ever see that dear old face again?

So I set forth in the December twilight, with May and
Julian Hawthorne as escort, feeling as if I was the son of
the house going to war.

Friday, the 12th, was a very memorable day, spent in
running all over Boston to get my pass, etc., calling for
parcels, getting a tooth filled, and buying a veil, — my
only purchase. A. C. gave me some old clothes ; the
dear Sewalls money for myself and boys, lots of love
and help ; and at 5 P. M., saying " good-by " to a group
of tearful faces at the station, I started on my long journey, full of hope and sorrow, courage and plans.

A most interesting journey into a new world full of
stirring sights and sounds, new adventures, and an ever-
growing sense of the great task I had undertaken.

I said my prayers as I went rushing through the country white with tents, all alive with patriotism, and already
red with blood.

A solemn time, but I 'm glad to live in it ; and am
sure· it will do me good whether I come out alive or
dead.

All went well, and I got to Georgetown one evening
very tired. Was kindly welcomed, slept in my narrow
bed with two other room-mates, and on the morrow began my new life by seeing a poor man die at dawn, and
sitting all day between a boy with pneumonia and a man
shot through the lungs. A strange day, but I did my
best ; and when I put mother's little black shawl round
the boy while he sat up panting for breath, he smiled
and said, " You are real motherly, ma'am." I felt as if
I was getting on. The man only lay and stared with his

big black eyes, and made me very nervous. But all were
well behaved; and I sat looking at the twenty strong
faces as they looked back at me, — the only new thing
they had to amuse them, — hoping that I looked "motherly" to them; for my thirty years made me feel old,
and the suffering round me made me long to comfort
every one.

January, 1863. *Union Hotel Hospital, Georgetown,
D. C.* — I never began the year in a stranger place
than this : five hundred miles from home, alone, among
strangers, doing painful duties all day long, and leading
a life of constant excitement in this great house, surrounded by three or four hundred men in all stages of
suffering, disease, and death. Though often homesick,
heartsick, and worn out, I like it, find real pleasure in
comforting, tending, and cheering these poor souls who
seem to love me, to feel my sympathy though unspoken,
and acknowledge my hearty good-will, in spite of the
ignorance, awkwardness, and bashfulness which I cannot
help showing in so new and trying a situation. The men
are docile, respectful, and affectionate, with but few exceptions; truly lovable and manly many of them. John
Sulie, a Virginia blacksmith, is the prince of patients;
and though what we call a common man in education
and condition, to me is all I could expect or ask from
the first gentleman in the land. Under his plain speech
and unpolished manner I seem to see a noble character,
a heart as warm and tender as a woman's, a nature fresh
and frank as any child's. He is about thirty, I think,
tall and handsome, mortally wounded, and dying royally
without reproach, repining, or remorse. Mrs. Ropes
and myself love him, and feel indignant that such a man
should be so early lost; for though he might never dis-
tinguish himself before the world, his influence and ex-

ample cannot be without effect, for real goodness is never wasted.

Monday, 4th. — I shall record the events of a day as a sample of the days I spend : —

Up at six, dress by gaslight, run through my ward and throw up the windows, though the men grumble and shiver ; but the air is bad enough to breed a pestilence ; and as no notice is taken of our frequent appeals for better ventilation, I must do what I can. Poke up the fire, add blankets, joke, coax, and command ; but continue to open doors and windows as if life depended upon it. Mine does, and doubtless many another, for a more perfect pestilence-box than this house I never saw, — cold, damp, dirty, full of vile odors from wounds, kitchens, wash-rooms, and stables. No competent head, male or female, to right matters, and a jumble of good, bad, and indifferent nurses, surgeons, and attendants, to complicate the chaos still more.

After this unwelcome progress through my stifling ward, I go to breakfast with what appetite I may ; find the uninvitable fried beef, salt butter, husky bread, and washy coffee ; listen to the clack of eight women and a dozen men, — the first silly, stupid, or possessed of one idea ; the last absorbed with their breakfast and themselves to a degree that is both ludicrous and provoking, for all the dishes are ordered down the table *full* and returned *empty;* the conversation is entirely among themselves, and each announces his opinion with an air of importance that frequently causes me to choke in my cup, or bolt my meals with undignified speed lest a laugh betray to these famous beings that a "chiel's amang them takin' notes."

Till noon I trot, trot, giving out rations, cutting up food for helpless "boys," washing faces, teaching my attendants how beds are made or floors are swept, dressing wounds, taking Dr. F. P.'s orders (privately wishing all the time that he would be more gentle with my big babies), dusting tables, sewing bandages, keeping my tray tidy, rushing up and down after pillows, bed-linen, sponges, books, and directions, till it seems as if I would joyfully pay down all I possess for fifteen minutes' rest. At twelve the big bell rings, and up comes dinner for the boys, who are always ready for it and never entirely satisfied. Soup, meat, potatoes, and bread is the bill of fare. Charley Thayer, the attendant, travels up and down the room serving out the rations, saving little for himself, yet always thoughtful of his mates, and patient as a woman with their helplessness. When dinner is over, some sleep, many read, and others want letters written. This I like to do, for they put in such odd things, and express their ideas so comically, I have great fun interiorly, while as grave as possible exteriorly. A few of the men word their paragraphs well and make excellent letters. John's was the best of all I wrote. The answering of letters from friends after some one had died is the saddest and hardest duty a nurse has to do.

Supper at five sets every one to running that can run; and when that flurry is over, all settle down for the evening amusements, which consist of newspapers, gossip, the doctor's last round, and, for such as need them, the final doses for the night. At nine the bell rings, gas is turned down, and day nurses go to bed. Night nurses go on duty, and sleep and death have the house to themselves.

My work is changed to night watching, or half night and half day, — from twelve to twelve. I like it, as it leaves me time for a morning run, which is what I need to keep well; for bad air, food, and water, work and watching, are getting to be too much for me. I trot up and down the streets in all directions, sometimes to the Heights, then half way to Washington, again to the hill, over which the long trains of army wagons are constantly vanishing and ambulances appearing. That way the fighting lies, and I long to follow.

Ordered to keep my room, being threatened with pneumonia. Sharp pain in the side, cough, fever, and dizziness. A pleasant prospect for a lonely soul five hundred miles from home! Sit and sew on the boys' clothes, write letters, sleep, and read; try to talk and keep merry, but fail decidedly, as day after day goes, and I feel no better. Dream awfully, and wake unrefreshed, think of home, and wonder if I am to die here, as Mrs. R., the matron, is likely to do. Feel too miserable to care much what becomes of me. Dr. S. creaks up twice a day to feel my pulse, give me doses, and ask if I am at all consumptive, or some other cheering question. Dr. O. examines my lungs and looks sober. Dr. J. haunts the room, coming by day and night with wood, cologne, books, and messes, like a motherly little man as he is. Nurses fussy and anxious, matron dying, and everything very gloomy. They want me to go home, but I *won't* yet.

January 16*th.* — Was amazed to see Father enter the room that morning, having been telegraphed to by order of Mrs. R. without asking leave. I was very angry at first, though glad to see him, because I knew I should have to go. Mrs. D. and Miss Dix came, and pretty Miss W., to take me to Willard's to be cared for by them. I would n't go, preferring to keep still, being pretty ill by that time.

On the 21st I suddenly decided to go home, feeling very strangely, and dreading to be worse. Mrs. R. died,

and that frightened the doctors about me; for my trouble
was the same, — typhoid pneumonia. Father, Miss K.,
and Lizzie T. went with me. Miss Dix brought a basket
full of bottles of wine, tea, medicine, and cologne, besides
a little blanket and pillow, a fan, and a testament. She
is a kind old soul, but very queer and arbitrary.

Was very sorry to go, and "my boys" seemed sorry
to have me. Quite a flock came to see me off; but
I was too sick to have but a dim idea of what was
going on.

Had a strange, excited journey of a day and night, —
half asleep, half wandering, just conscious that I was
going home; and, when I got to Boston, of being taken
out of the car, with people looking on as if I was a sight.·
I daresay I was all blowzed, crazy, and weak. Was too
sick to reach Concord that night, though we tried to do
so. Spent it at Mr. Sewall's; had a sort of fit; they
sent for Dr. H., and I had a dreadful time of it.

Next morning felt better, and at four went home.
Just remember seeing May's shocked face at the depot,
Mother's bewildered one at home, and getting to bed in
the firm belief that the house was roofless, and no one
wanted to see me.

As I never shall forget the strange fancies that haunted
me, I shall amuse myself with recording some of them.

The most vivid and enduring was the conviction that I
had married a stout, handsome Spaniard, dressed in black
velvet, with very soft hands, and a voice that was continually saying, "Lie still, my dear!" This was Mother,
I suspect; but with all the comfort I often found in her
presence, there was blended an awful fear of the Spanish
spouse who was always coming after me, appearing out
of closets, in at windows, or threatening me dreadfully
all night long. I appealed to the Pope, and really got

up and made a touching plea in something meant for Latin, they tell me. Once I went to heaven, and found it a twilight place, with people darting through the air in a queer way, — all very busy, and dismal, and ordinary. Miss Dix, W. H. Channing, and other people were there; but I thought it dark and "slow," and wished I had n't come.

A mob at Baltimore breaking down the door to get me, being hung for a witch, burned, stoned, and otherwise maltreated, were some of my fancies. Also being tempted to join Dr. W. and two of the nurses in worshipping the Devil. Also tending millions of rich men who never died or got well.

February. — Recovered my senses after three weeks of delirium, and was told I had had a very bad typhoid fever, had nearly died, and was still very sick. All of which seemed rather curious, for I remembered nothing of it. Found a queer, thin, big-eyed face when I looked in the glass; did n't know myself at all; and when I tried to walk discovered that I could n't, and cried because my legs would n't go.

Never having been sick before, it was all new and very interesting when I got quiet enough to understand matters. Such long, long nights; such feeble, idle days; dozing, fretting about nothing; longing to eat, and no mouth to do it with, — mine being so sore, and full of all manner of queer sensations, it was nothing but a plague. The old fancies still lingered, seeming so real I believed in them, and deluded Mother and May with the most absurd stories, so soberly told that they thought them true.

Dr. B. came every day, and was very kind. Father and Mother were with me night and day, and May sang "Birks of Aberfeldie," or read to me, to wile away the tiresome hours. People sent letters, money, kind inquiries, and goodies for the old "Nuss." I tried to sew, read, and write, and found I had to begin all over again. Received $10 for my labors in Washington. Had all my hair, a yard and a half long, cut off, and went into caps like a grandma. Felt badly about losing my one beauty. Never mind, it might have been my head, and a wig outside is better than a loss of wits inside.

March. — Began to get about a little, sitting up nearly all day, eating more regularly, and falling back into my old ways. My first job was characteristic : I cleared out my piece-bags and dusted my books, feeling as tired as if I had cleaned the whole house. Sat up till nine one night, and took no lunch at three A. M., — two facts which I find carefully recorded in my pocket diary in my own shaky handwriting.

Father had two courses of conversations : one at Mr. Quincy's, very select and fine ; the other at a hall not so good. He was tired out with taking care of me, poor old gentleman ; and typhus was not inspiring.

Read a great deal, being too feeble to do much else. No end of rubbish, with a few good things as ballast. "Titan" was the one I enjoyed the most, though it tired my weak wits to read much at a time. Recalled, and wrote some lines on "Thoreau's Flute," which I composed one night on my watch by little Shaw at the hospital.

On the 28th Father came home from Boston, bringing word that Nan had a fine boy. We all screamed out when he burst in, snowy and beaming ; then Mother began to cry, May to laugh, and I to say, like B. Trotwood, "There, I knew it wouldn't be a girl ! " We were all so glad it was safely over, and a jolly little lad was added to the feminine family.

Mother went straight down to be sure that "mother and child were doing well," and I fell to cleaning house, as good work for an invalid and a vent for a happy *aunt.*

First Birth in the Alcott and Pratt Branch, 1863.

MONDAY EVE.

DEAREST LITTLE MOTHER, — Allow me to ask who was a true prophet.

Also to demand, "Where is my niece, Louisa Caroline?"

No matter, I will forgive you, and propose three cheers for my *nephew.* Hurrah! hurrah! Hurray!

I wish you could have seen the performance on Saturday evening.

We were all sitting deep in a novel, not expecting Father home owing to the snowstorm, when the door burst open, and in he came, all wet and white, waving his bag, and calling out, "Good news! good news! Anna has a fine boy!"

With one accord we opened our mouths and screamed for about two minutes. Then Mother began to cry; I began to laugh; and May to pour out questions; while Papa beamed upon us all, — red, damp, and shiny, the picture of a proud old Grandpa. Such a funny evening as we had! Mother kept breaking down, and each time emerged from her handkerchief saying solemnly, "I must go right down and see that baby!" Father had told every one he met, from Mr. Emerson to the coach driver, and went about the house saying, "Anna's boy! yes, yes, Anna's boy!" in a mild state of satisfaction.

May and I at once taxed our brains for a name, and decided upon "Amos Minot Bridge Bronson May Sewall Alcott Pratt," so that all the families would be suited.

I was so anxious to hear more that I went up to town this A. M. and found John's note.

Grandma and Grandpa Pratt came to hear the great news; but we could only inform them of the one tremendous fact, that Pratt, Jr., had condescended to arrive. Now tell us his weight, inches, color, etc.

I know I shall fall down and adore when I see that mite; yet my soul is rent when I think of the *L. C.* on the pincushion, and all the plans I had made for "my niece."

Now get up quickly, and be a happy mamma. Of course John does *not* consider his son as *the* most amazing product of the nineteenth century.

Bless the baby!

                    Ever your admiring   Lu.

April. — Had some pleasant walks and drives, and felt as if born again, everything seemed so beautiful and new. I hope I was, and that the Washington experience may do me lasting good. To go very near to death teaches one to value life, and this winter will always be a very memorable one to me.

Sewed on little shirts and gowns for my blessed nephew, who increased rapidly in stature and godliness.

Sanborn asked me to do what Conway suggested before he left for Europe; viz., to arrange my letters in a printable shape, and put them in the "Commonwealth." They thought them witty and pathetic. I did n't; but I wanted money; so I made three hospital sketches. Much to my surprise, they made a great hit; and people bought the papers faster than they could be supplied. The second, "A Night" was much liked, and I was glad; for my beautiful "John Sulie" was the hero, and the praise belonged to him. More were wanted; and I added a postscript in the form of a letter, which finished it up, as I then thought.

Received $100 from F. L. for a tale which won the prize last January; paid debts, and was glad that my winter bore visible fruit. Sent L. another tale. Went to Boston, and saw "our baby;" thought him ugly, but promising. Got a set of furniture for my room, — a long-talked-of dream of ours.

May. — Spent the first week or two in putting the house in order. May painted and papered the parlors. I got a new carpet and rug besides the paper, and put things to rights in a thorough manner. Mother was away with Nan, so we had full sweep; and she came home to a clean, fresh house.

Nan and the Royal Infanta came as bright as a whole gross of buttons, and as good as a hairless brown angel. Went to Readville, and saw the 54th Colored Regiment, both there and next day in town as they left for the South. Enjoyed it very much; also the Antislavery meetings.

Had a fresh feather in my cap; for Mrs. Hawthorne showed Fields "Thoreau's Flute," and he desired it for the "Atlantic." Of course I didn't say no. It was printed, copied, praised, and glorified; also *paid for*, and being a mercenary creature, I liked the $10 nearly as well as the honor of being "a new star" and "a literary celebrity."

June. — Began to write again on "Moods," feeling encouraged by the commendation bestowed on "Hospital Sketches," which were noticed, talked of, and inquired about, much to my surprise and delight. Had a fine letter from Henry James, also one from Wasson, and a request from Redpath to be allowed to print the sketches in a book. *Roberts Bros. also asked, but I preferred the*

Redpath, and said yes; so he fell to work with all his might.

Went to Class Day for the first time; had a pleasant day seeing new sights and old friends.

G. H. came to the H.'s. Did n't like her as well as Miss H.; too sharp and full of herself; insisted on talking about religion with Emerson, who glided away from the subject so sweetly, yet resolutely, that the energetic lady gave it up at last.

[1877. — Short-sighted Louisa! Little did you dream that this same Roberts Bros. were to help you to make your fortune a few years later. The "Sketches" never made much money, but showed me "my style," and taking the hint, I went where glory waited me. — L. M. A.]

July. — Sanborn asked for more contributions, and I gave him some of my old Mountain Letters vamped up. They were not good, and though they sold the paper, I was heartily ashamed of them, and stopped in the middle, resolving never again to try to be funny, lest I should be rowdy and nothing more. I 'm glad of the lesson, and hope it will do me good.

Had some pleasant letters from Sergeant Bain, — one of my boys who has not forgotten me, though safely at home far away in Michigan. It gratified me very much, and brought back the hospital days again. He was a merry, brave little fellow, and I liked him very much. His right arm was amputated after Fredericksburg, and he took it very cheerfully, trying at once to train his left hand to do duty for both, and never complained of his loss. "Baby B."

August. — Redpath carried on the publishing of the "Sketches" vigorously, sending letters, proof, and notices dáily, and making all manner of offers, suggestions, and prophecies concerning the success of the book and its author.

Wrote a story, " My Contraband," and sent it to Fields, who accepted and paid $50 for it, with much approbation for it and the " Sketches." L. sent $40 for a story, and wanted another.

Major M. invited me to Gloucester; but I refused, being too busy and too bashful to be made a lion of, even in a very small way. Letters from Dr. Hyde, Wilkie (home with a wound from Wagner), Charles Sumner, Mr. Hale, and others, — all about the little "Sketches," which keep on making friends for me, though I don't get used to the thing at all, and think it must be all a mistake.

On the 25th my first morning-glory bloomed in my room, — a hopeful blue, — and at night up came my book in its new dress. I had added several chapters to it, and it was quite a neat little affair. An edition of one thousand, and I to have five cents on each copy.

September. — Redpath anxious for another book. Send him a volume of stories and part of a book to look at. He likes both; but I decide on waiting a little, as I'm not satisfied with the stories, and the novel needs time. " Sketches " sell well, and a new edition is called for.

Dear old Grandma died at Aunt Betsey's in her eighty-ninth year, — a good woman, and much beloved by her children. I sent money to help lay her away; for Aunt B. is poor, and it was all I could do for the kind little old lady.

Nan and Freddy made us a visit, and we decided that of all splendid babies he was the king. Such a hearty, happy, funny boy, I could only play with and adore him all the while he stayed, and long for him when he went. Nan and John are very fond of " our son," and well they may be. Grandma and Grandpa think him perfect, and even artistic Aunty May condescends to say he is " a very nice thing."

" My Contraband ; or, The Brothers," my story in the "Atlantic," came out, and was liked. Received $40 from Redpath for " Sketches," — first edition ; wanted me to be editor of a paper ; was afraid to try, and let it go.

Poor old " Moods " came out for another touching up.

October. — Thought much about going to Port Royal to teach contrabands. Fields wanted the letters I should write, and asked if I had no book. Father spoke of " Moods," and he desired to see it. So I fell to work, and finished it off, thinking the world must be coming to an end, and all my dreams getting fulfilled in a most amazing way. If there was ever an astonished young woman, it is myself ; for things have gone on so swimmingly of late I don't know who I am. A year ago I had no publisher, and went begging with my wares ; now *three* have asked me for something, several papers are ready to print my contributions, and F. B. S. says " any publisher this side of Baltimore would be glad to get a book." There is a sudden hoist for a meek and lowly scribbler, who was told to " stick to her teaching," and never had a literary friend to lend a helping hand ! Fifteen years of hard grubbing may be coming to something after all ; and I may yet " pay all the debts, fix the house, send May to Italy, and keep the old folks cosey," as I 've said I would so long, yet so hopelessly.

May began to take anatomical drawing lessons of Rimmer. I was very glad to be able to pay her expenses up and down and clothe her neatly. Twenty dollars more from Redpath on account.

December. — Earnings 1863, $380.

The principal event of this otherwise quiet month was the Sanitary Fair in Boston, and our part in it. At G. G. B.'s request, I dramatized six scenes from Dickens, and went to town on the 14th to play. Things did not go well for want of a good manager and more time. Our night was not at all satisfactory to us, owing to the falling through of several scenes for want of actors. People seemed to like what there was of it, and after a wearisome week I very gladly came home again. Our six entertainments made twenty-five hundred dollars for the Fair.

Rewrote the fairy tales, one of which was published; but owing to delays it was late for the holidays, and badly bound in the hurry; so the poor "Rose Family" fared badly.

Had a letter from the publisher of a new magazine, called the "Civil Service Magazine," asking for a long tale. Had no time to write one; but will by and by, if the thing is good.

While in town received $10 of F. B. S. and $20 of Redpath, with which I bought May hat, boots, gloves, ribbons, and other little matters, besides furnishing money for her fares up and down to Rimmer.

January, 1864. — New Year's Day was a very quiet one. Nan and Freddy were here, and in the evening we went to a dance at the hall. A merry time; for all the town was there, as it was for the Soldiers' Aid Society, and every one wanted to help. Nan and I sat in the gallery, and watched the young people dance the old year out, the new year in as the clock struck twelve.

On looking over my accounts, I find I have earned by my *writing* alone nearly *six hundred dollars* since last January, and spent less than a hundred for myself, which

I am glad to know. May has had $70 for herself, and the rest has paid debts or bought necessary things for the family.

Received from the "Commonwealth" $18 for "A Hospital Christmas." Wrote a fairy tale, "Fairy Pinafores." "Picket Duty" and other tales came out, — first of Redpath's series of books for the "Camp Fires." Richardson sent again for a long story for the "Civil Service Magazine." Tried a war story, but could n't make it go.

February. — Nan quite sick again. Mother passed most of the month with her; so I had to be housekeeper, and let my writing go, — as well perhaps, as my wits are tired, and the "divine afflatus" don't descend as readily as it used to do. Must wait and fill up my idea-box before I begin again. There is nothing like work to set fancy a-going.

Redpath came flying up on the 4th to get "Moods," promising to have it out by May. Gave it to him with many fears, and he departed content. The next day received a telegram to come down at once and see the printers. Went, and was told the story was too long for a single volume, and a two-volume novel was bad to begin with. Would I cut the book down about half? No, I would n't, having already shortened it all it would bear. So I took my "opus" and posted home again, promising to try and finish my shorter book in a month.

A dull, heavy month, grubbing in the kitchen, sewing, cleaning house, and trying to like my duty.

Mrs. S. takes a great fancy to May; sends her flowers, offers to pay for her to go to the new Art School, and arranges everything delightfully for her. She is a fortunate girl, and always finds some one to help her as she wants to be helped. Wish I could do the same, but suppose as

I never do that it is best for me to work and wait and do all for myself.

Mr. Storrs, D.D., wrote for a sketch for his little paper, " The Drum Beat," to be printed during the Brooklyn Sanitary Fair. A very cordial, pleasant letter, which I answered by a little sketch called " A Hospital Lamp." He sent me another friendly letter, and all the daily papers as they came out. A very gentlemanly D.D. is Dr. Storrs.

The " Hospital Sketches " were fully entitled to their wide and rapid popularity; and for the first time perhaps Miss Alcott felt sure of her vocation, and knew that it would bring at last the success which would enable her to carry out her plans for the family. And yet the battle was not over. She gained in reputation, was received with great attention in society, and lionized more than she cared for. But she still continued writing stories for the various papers at very low prices. Some of them were refused by the publishers, as she thinks, on account of the Antislavery sentiments expressed in them. Her " blood and thunder " stories continued in demand, and she wrote them rapidly, and was glad of the money they brought. But she had not yet found her true path, and she suffered at times from keen depression of spirits; for the way seemed long and dark, and she did not see the end. In more than one sense she struggled with Moods; for that unhappy book was still tossed from publisher to publisher, who gave her much praise, but no satisfaction.

Journal.

A busy month getting settled. Freddy's birthday on the 28th, one year old. He had a dozen nice little presents laid out in a row when he came down to breakfast, and seemed quite overpowered with his riches. On being told to take what he liked best, he chose the picture of little Samuel which Father gave him, and the good pope was much delighted at that.

Was asked for a poem for the great album at the St. Louis Fair, and sent "Thoreau's Flute" as my best. Also received a letter from the Philadelphia managers asking contributions for the paper to be printed at their Fair.

Wrote nothing this month.

April. — At Father's request I sent "Moods" to T., and got a very friendly note from him, saying they had so many books on hand that they could do nothing about it now. So I put it back on the shelf, and set about my other work. Don't despair, "Moods," we'll try again by and by!

[Alas! we did try again. — L. M. A.]

Wrote the first part of a story for Professor C. called "Love and Loyalty," — flat, patriotic, and done to order. Wrote a new fairy tale, "Nelly's Hospital."

May. — Had a letter from Mrs. Gildersleeve, asking for my photograph and a sketch of my life, for a book called "Heroic Women" which she was getting up. Respectfully refused. Also a letter and flattering notice from "Ruth Hall," and a notice from a Chicago critic with a long extract from "Rose Family." My tale "Enigmas" came out, and was much liked by readers of sensation rubbish. Having got my $50, I was resigned.

June. — To town with Father on the 3d to a Fraternity Festival to which we were invited. Had a fine time, and was amazed to find my "'umble" self made a lion of, set up among the great ones, stared at, waited upon, complimented, and made to hold a "layvee" whether I would or no; for Mr. S. kept bringing up people to be introduced till I was tired of shaking hands and hearing the words "Hospital Sketches" uttered in every tone of interest, admiration, and respect. Mr. Wasson, Whipple, Alger, Clarke, Calthrop, and Chadwick came to speak to me, and many more whose names I forget. It was a very pleasant surprise and a new experience. I liked it, but think a small dose quite as much as is good for me; for after sitting in a corner and grubbing *à la* Cinderella, it rather turns one's head to be taken out and be treated like a princess all of a sudden.

August. — Went to Gloucester for a fortnight with May at the M.'s. Found a family of six pretty daughters, a pleasant mother, and a father who was an image of one of the Cheeryble brothers. Had a jolly time boating, driving, charading, dancing, and picnicking. One mild moonlight night a party of us camped out on Norman's Woe, and had a splendid time, lying on the rocks singing, talking, sleeping, and rioting up and down. Had a fine time, and took coffee at all hours. The moon rose and set beautifully, and the sunrise was a picture I never shall forget.

Wrote another fairy tale, "Jamie's Wonder Book," and sent the "Christmas Stories" to W. & W., with some lovely illustrations by Miss Greene. They liked the book very much, and said they would consult about publishing it, though their hands were full.

September. — Mrs. D. made a visit, and getting hold

of my old book of stories liked them, and insisted on taking " Moods " home to read. As she had had experience with publishers, was a good business woman, and an excellent critic, I let her have it, hoping she might be able to give the poor old book the lift it has been waiting for all these years. She took it, read it, and admired it heartily, saying that "no American author had showed so much promise ; that the plan was admirable ; the execution unequal, but often magnificent ; that I had a great field before me, and my book must be got out."

Mrs. D. sent it to L., who liked it exceedingly, and asked me to shorten it if I could, else it would be too large to sell well. Was much disappointed, said I'd never touch it again, and tossed it into the spidery little cupboard where it had so often returned after fruitless trips.

At last, in the excited hours of a wakeful night, Miss Alcott thought of a way to curtail the objectionable length of the book, and she spent a fortnight in remodelling it, — as she then thought improving it greatly, — although she afterwards returned to her original version as decidedly the best. The book was brought out, and she had the pleasure of presenting the first copy to her mother on her sixty-fourth birthday. She had various projects in her mind, one of which was a novel, with two characters in it like Jean Paul Richter and Goethe. It is needless to say this was never carried out. Miss Alcott had great powers of observation, and a keen insight into character as it fell within her own range of life, but she had not the creative imagination which could paint to the life the subtlest workings of thought and feeling in natures foreign to her own experience. She could not have portrayed such men: but who could?

Journal.

October. — Wrote several chapters of "Work," and was getting on finely, when, as I lay awake one night, a way to shorten and arrange "Moods" came into my head. The whole plan laid itself smoothly out before me, and I slept no more that night, but worked on it as busily as if mind and body had nothing to do with one another. Up early, and began to write it all over again. The fit was on strong, and for a fortnight I hardly ate, slept, or stirred, but wrote, wrote, like a thinking machine in full operation. When it was all rewritten without copying, I found it much improved, though I'd taken out ten chapters, and sacrificed many of my favorite things ; but being resolved to make it simple, strong, and short, I let everything else go, and hoped the book would be better for it.

[It was n't. 1867.]

Sent it to L. ; and a week after, as I sat hammering away at the parlor carpet, — dusty, dismal, and tired, — a letter came from L. praising the story more enthusiastically than ever, thanking me for the improvements, and proposing to bring out the book at once. Of course we all had a rapture, and I finished my work "double quick," regardless of weariness, toothache, or blue devils.

Next day I went to Boston and saw L. A brisk, business-like man who seemed in earnest and said many complimentary things about " Hospital Sketches " and its author. It was agreed to bring out the book immediately, and Mrs. D. offered to read the proof with me.

Was glad to have the old thing under way again, but did n't quite believe it would ever come out after so many delays and disappointments.

Sewed for Nan and Mary, heard Anna Dickinson and liked her. Read " Emily Chester " and thought it an unnatural story, yet just enough like " Moods " in a few things to make me sorry that it came out now.

On Mother's sixty-fourth birthday I gave her " Moods " with this inscription, — " To Mother, my earliest patron, kindest critic, dearest reader, I gratefully and affectionately inscribe my first romance."

A letter from T. asking me to write for the new magazine " Our Young Folks," and saying that " An Hour " was in the hands of the editors.

November. — Proof began to come, and the chapters seemed small, stupid, and no more my own in print. I felt very much afraid that I 'd ventured too much and should be sorry for it. But Emerson says " that what is true for your own private heart is true for others." So I wrote from my own consciousness and observation and hope it may suit some one and at least do no harm.

I sent " An Hour " to the " Commonwealth " and it was considered *excellent.* Also wrote a Christmas Story, " Mrs. Todger's Teapot." T. asked to see the other fairy tales and designs and poems, as he liked " Nelly's Hospital " so much.

On my thirty-second birthday received Richter's Life from Nan and enjoyed it so much that I planned a story of two men something like Jean Paul and Goethe, only more every-day people. Don't know what will come of it, but if " Moods " goes well " Success " shall follow.

Sewed for Wheeler's colored company and sent them comfort-bags, towels, books, and bed-sacks. Mr. W. sent me some relics from Point Look Out and a pleasant letter.

December. — Earnings, 1864, — $476.

On Christmas Eve received ten copies of "Moods" and a friendly note from L. The book was hastily got out, but on the whole suited me, and as the inside was considered good I let the outside go. For a week where-ever I went I saw, heard, and talked "Moods;" found people laughing or crying over it, and was continually told how well it was going, how much it was liked, how fine a thing I'd done. I was glad but not proud, I think, for it has always seemed as if "Moods" grew in spite of me, and that I had little to do with it except to put into words the thoughts that would not let me rest until I had. Don't know why.

By Saturday the first edition was gone and the second ready. Several booksellers ordered a second hundred, the first went so fast, and friends could not get it but had to wait till more were ready.

Spent a fortnight in town at Mary's, shopping, helping Nan, and having plays. Heard Emerson once. Gave C. "Mrs. Todger's Teapot," which was much liked. Sent L. the rest of his story and got $50. S. paid $35 for "An Hour." R. promised $100 for "Love and Loyalty," so my year closes with a novel well-launched and about $300 to pay debts and make the family happy and comfortable till spring. Thank God for the success of the old year, the promise of the new!

The sale of "Moods" was at first very rapid; for "Hospital Sketches" had created an interest in the author, and welcome recognition came to her from many sources. She received a handsome sum from the copyright, and " the year closed with enough to make her feel free of debt and the family comfortable." She ends the year's journal triumphantly.

The following year was spent mostly in Boston. Miss Alcott went into society and enjoyed the friendly attentions of men and women of ability. She continued to write stories for money, but now received fifty, seventy-five, or a hundred dollars for them. She frequently took part in theatrical performances for charities. She was always brilliant and successful and enjoyed them with something of her early zest.

Her long story of " Success," or " Work," as she afterwards named ·it, was still in her mind, but she did not finish it at this time.

Journal.

January, 1865. — The month began with some plays at the town hall to raise funds for the Lyceum. We did very well and some Scenes from Dickens were excellent. Father lectured and preached a good deal, being asked like a regular minister and paid like one. He enjoyed it very much and said good things on the new religion which we ought to and shall have. May had orders from Canada and England for her pretty pen-and-ink work and did well in that line.

Notices of " Moods " came from all directions, and though people did n't understand my ideas owing to my shortening the book so much, the notices were mostly favorable and gave quite as much praise as was good for me. I had letters from Mrs. Parker, Chadwick, Sanborn,

E. B. Greene, the artist, T. W. Higginson and some others. All friendly and flattering.

Saw more notices of "Moods" and received more letters, several from strangers and some very funny. People seemed to think the book finely written, very promising, wise, and interesting ; but some fear it is n't moral, because it speaks freely of marriage.

Wrote a little on poor old "Work" but being tired of novels, I soon dropped it and fell back on rubbishy tales, for they pay best, and I can't afford to starve on praise, when sensation stories are written in half the time and keep the family cosey.

Earned $75 this month.

I went to Boston and heard Father lecture before the Fraternity. Met Henry James, Sr., there, and he asked me to come and dine, also called upon me with Mrs. James. I went, and was treated like the Queen of Sheba. Henry Jr. wrote a notice of "Moods" for the "North American," and was very friendly. Being a literary youth he gave me advice, as if he had been eighty and I a girl. My curly crop made me look young, though thirty-one.

Acted in some public plays for the N. E. Women's Hospital and had a pleasant time.

L. asked me to be a regular contributor to his new paper, and I agreed if he 'd pay beforehand ; he said he would, and bespoke two tales at once, $50 each, longer ones as often as I could, and whatever else I liked to send. So here 's another source of income and Alcott brains seem in demand, whereat I sing "Hallyluyer" and fill up my inkstand.

April. — Richmond taken on the 2d. Hurrah ! Went to Boston and enjoyed the grand jollification. Saw Booth again in Hamlet and thought him finer than ever. Had a pleasant walk and talk with Phillips.

On the 15th in the midst of the rejoicing came the sad news of the President's assassination, and the city went into mourning. I am glad to have seen such a strange and sudden change in a nation's feelings. Saw the great procession, and though few colored men were in it, one was walking arm in arm with a white gentleman, and I exulted thereat.

Nan went to housekeeping in a pleasant house at Jamaica Plain, and I went to help her move. It was beautiful to see how Freddy enjoyed the freedom, after being cooped up all winter, and how every morning, whether it rained or shone, he looked out and said, with a smile of perfect satisfaction, "Oh, pretty day!" — for all days *were* pretty to him, dear little soul!

Had a fine letter from Conway, and a notice in the "Reader," — an English paper. He advised sending copies to several of the best London papers. English people don't understand "transcendental literature," as they call "Moods." My next book shall have no *ideas* in it, only facts, and the people shall be as ordinary as possible; then critics will say it's all right. I seem to have been playing with edge tools without knowing it. The relations between Warwick, Moor, and Sylvia are pronounced impossible; yet a case of the sort exists, and the woman came and asked me how I knew it. I did *not* know or guess, but perhaps felt it, without any other guide, and unconsciously put the thing into my book, for I changed the ending about that time. It was meant to show a life affected by *moods*, not a discussion of marriage, which I knew little about, except observing that very few were happy ones.

June. — Busy writing, keeping house, and sewing. Company often; and strangers begin to come, demanding to see the authoress, who does not like it, and is porcupiny.

Admire the books, but let the woman alone, if you please, dear public!

On the 24th Anna's second boy was born, at half-past three in the morning, — Lizzie's birthday. A fine, stout, little lad, who took to life kindly, and seemed to find the world all right. Freddy could not understand it at first, and told his mother that "the babee" had got his place. But he soon loved the "tunning sing," and would stand watching it with a grave face, till some funny little idea found vent in still funnier words or caresses.

Nan was very happy with her two boys, so was John, though both had wished for a daughter.

July. — While at Nan's Mrs. B. asked me if I would go abroad with her sister. I said "yes;" but as I spoke neither French nor German, she did n't think I'd do. I was sorry; but being used to disappointment, went to work for Nan, and bided my time, which came very soon.

To Anna.

[Date uncertain.]

MY LASS, — This must be a frivolous and dressy letter, because you always want to know about our clothes, and we have been at it lately. May's bonnet is a sight for gods and men. Black and white outside, with a great cockade boiling over the front to meet a red ditto surging from the interior, where a red rainbow darts across the brow, and a surf of white lace foams up on each side. I expect to hear that you and John fell flat in the dust with horror on beholding it.

My bonnet has nearly been the death of me; for, thinking some angel might make it possible for me to go to the mountains, I felt a wish for a tidy hat, after wearing an old one till it fell in tatters from my brow. Mrs. P. promised a bit of gray silk, and I built on that; but

when I went for it I found my hat was founded on sand ;
for she let me down with a crash, saying she wanted the
silk herself, and kindly offering me a flannel petticoat
instead. I was in woe for a spell, having one dollar in
the world, and scorning debt even for that prop of life,
a " bonnet." Then I roused myself, flew to Dodge,
demanded her cheapest bonnet, found one for a dollar,
took it, and went home wondering if the sky would open
and drop me a trimming. I am simple in my tastes, but
a naked straw bonnet is a little too severely chaste even
for me. Sky did not open ; so I went to the " Widow
Cruise's oil bottle " — my ribbon box — which, by the
way, is the eighth wonder of the world, for nothing is
ever put in, yet I always find some old dud when all
other hopes fail. From this salvation bin I extracted the
remains of the old white ribbon (used up, as I thought,
two years ago), and the bits of black lace that have
adorned a long line of departed hats. Of the lace I
made a dish, on which I thriftily served up bows of ribbon, like meat on toast. Inside put the lace bow, which
adorns my form anywhere when needed. A white flower
A. H. gave me sat airily on the brim, — fearfully unbe-
coming, but pretty in itself, and in keeping. Strings are
yet to be evolved from chaos. I feel that they await me
somewhere in the dim future. Green ones *pro tem.* hold
this wonder of the age upon my gifted brow, and I survey
my hat with respectful awe. I trust you will also, and
see in it another great example of the power of mind
over matter, and the convenience of a colossal brain in
the primeval wrestle with the unruly atoms which have
harassed the feminine soul ever since Eve clapped on a
modest fig-leaf and did up her hair with a thorn for a
hairpin.

I feel very moral to-day, having done a big wash alone,

baked, swept the house, picked the hops, got dinner, and written a chapter in "Moods." May gets exhausted with work, though she walks six miles without a murmur.

It is dreadfully dull, and I work so that I may not "brood." Nothing stirring but the wind; nothing to see but dust; no one comes but rose-bugs; so I grub and scold at the "A." because it takes a poor fellow's tales and keeps 'em years without paying for 'em. If I think of my woes I fall into a vortex of debts, dishpans, and despondency awful to see. So I say, "every path has its puddle," and try to play gayly with the tadpoles in *my* puddle, while I wait for the Lord to give me a lift, or some gallant Raleigh to spread his velvet cloak and fetch me over dry shod.

L. W. adds to my woe by writing of the splendors of Gorham, and says, "When tired, run right up here and find rest among these everlasting hills." All very aggravating to a young woman with one dollar, no bonnet, half a gown, and a discontented mind. It's a mercy the mountains are everlasting, for it will be a century before *I* get there. Oh, me, such is life!

Now I've done my Jeremiad, and I will go on twanging my harp in the "willow tree."

You ask what I am writing. Well, two books half done, nine stories simmering, and stacks of fairy stories moulding on the shelf. I can't do much, as I have no time to get into a real good vortex. It unfits me for work, worries Ma to see me look pale, eat nothing, and ply by night. These extinguishers keep genius from burning as I could wish, and I give up ever hoping to do anything unless luck turns for your

Lu.

CHAPTER VIII.

EUROPE AND LITTLE WOMEN.

LITTLE WOMEN.

Four little chests all in a row,
  Dim with dust and worn by time,
All fashioned and filled long ago
  By children now in their prime.
Four little keys hung side by side,
  With faded ribbons, brave and gay
When fastened there with childish pride
  Long ago on a rainy day.
Four little names, one on each lid,
  Carved out by a boyish hand;
And underneath there lieth hid
  Histories of the happy band
Once playing here, and pausing oft
  To hear the sweet refrain
That came and went on the roof aloft
  In the falling summer rain.

  .   .   .   .   .

Four little chests all in a row,
  Dim with dust and worn by time:
Four women, taught by weal and woe
  To love and labor in their prime;
Four sisters parted for an hour, —
  None lost, one only gone before,
Made by love's immortal power
  Nearest and dearest evermore.
Oh! when these hidden stores of ours
  Lie open to the Father's sight,
May they be rich in golden hours, —
  Deeds that show fairer for the light,
Deeds whose brave music long shall ring
  Like a spirit-stirring strain,
Souls that shall gladly soar and sing
  In the long sunshine, after rain.

THE years which followed the war and Miss Alcott's experience as a hospital nurse were rather sad and anxious from many causes. Louisa felt deeply the loss of one sister by death and the separation from another by marriage. The success of "Hospital Sketches" and a few other stories published about the same time had given her confidence in her powers and hopes of a successful future. But for nearly five years she accomplished nothing which met with equal favor. The reception of the novel "Moods," in which she thought she had expressed her best life, was not cheering to her; and she had become wholly dissatisfied with the sensational stories, which formed the most ready resource for earning money. Her health was seriously injured by the fever from which she suffered in the hospital, and she had no longer the physical energy to sustain the unceasing activity of her brain.

Under these difficulties she naturally desired a change of circumstances; and the old longing for a journey to Europe — which she had felt strongly in her youth, and which, like all Americans of culture, she felt more and more as time passed on — became her ruling desire. She was very fond of new scenes and variety of people, and she often expressed a wish to live many years in Europe.

The circumstances of the family were not yet such as to justify Louisa, in her own eyes, in taking her earnings for the desired trip. But in 1865 an opportunity was offered her to go to Europe as companion to an invalid lady. From her experience in nursing — for which she had a

natural gift — she and her friends thought her
suited to the position, and advised her acceptance
of the offer.

Although devotedly kind, unselfish, and generous, Louisa had not the temperament suited to the
needs of a nervous invalid. She was impetuous
and impatient, and her own life was too strong
within her and too earnest in its cravings, for her
to restrain her moods and actions within the narrow
limits of a companion's service. She found even
what she recognized as fair services wearisome and
distasteful, and sometimes chafed severely under
what seemed unnecessary demands on her time,
strength, and patience. Looking back on this experience in later years, she recognized these facts,
and wrote in 1885 : " Now, being a nervous invalid
myself, I understand what seemed whims, selfishness, and folly in others."

Louisa finally decided to leave her companions
and go on alone to Paris and England, where she
would find many of her own and her father's friends.
At Vevay she had made the acquaintance of a
young Polish lad, whom she found very interesting,
and who was the original of the charming Laurie in
" Little Women." He met her again in Paris, and
contributed greatly to the pleasure of her stay there.
He afterwards came to America, and visited her;
but finally returned to his own country.

The journal gives a sufficient account of her life
while on this journey. I have no letters written
at this time, as she wished all her family letters
destroyed. Her few weeks in London passed very
happily. Her wide reading in English history

and in contemporary fiction, especially the works of Dickens and Thackeray, filled London with interesting associations, and she enjoyed thoroughly her free rambles through the old city, as well as the interesting people, who received her with great kindness.

That Louisa might have these few weeks of entire relaxation and enjoyment, her mother had been obliged to borrow means for the support of the family; and Louisa was very anxious to clear off this debt like all others. She was very exact in pecuniary matters. Money to her was not an end, but a most necessary means. She paid every debt that her father had incurred, even though outlawed by time. It is often asked whether she ever sold her beautiful hair, as represented in " Little Women." The deed was never really done; but she and her sisters always held this treasure as a possible resource in case of need; and Louisa once says in her journal, " I will pay my debts, if I have to sell my hair to do it." She even went so far as to inquire of a barber as to its money value.

Journal.

1865. — Mr. W., hearing that I was something of a nurse and wanted to travel, proposed my going with his invalid daughter. I agreed, though I had my doubts. But every one said " Go;" so after a week of worry I did go. On the 19th we sailed in the " China." I could not realize that my long-desired dream was coming true; and fears that I might not see all the dear home faces when I came back made my heart very full as we steamed down the harbor and Boston vanished.

Was not very sick, but uncomfortable all the way, and found the Ladies' Saloon my only refuge till we were nearly across; enjoyed intervals of quiet, and had many fine glimpses of the sea in its various moods, sunsets and sunrises, fogs, icebergs, rain-storms, and summer calms. No very pleasant people on board; so I read, took notes, and *wiled* away the long days as I best could.

We had a very quiet and quick passage of nine days, and on Saturday, the 29th, steamed up the Mersey at dawn, and got to Liverpool at nine. I was heartily glad to set my feet on the solid earth, and thought I'd never go to sea again; rested, and looked about a little.

August. — Went up to London, and there spent four dull, drizzly days. I amused myself in my usual way, looking well about me, and writing down all I saw in my pocket-diary or letters. Went to the parks, Westminster Abbey, and some of the famous streets. I felt as if I'd got into a novel while going about in the places I'd read so much of; saw no one I knew, and thought English weather abominable.

On the 5th to Dover through a lovely green country; took steamer there to Ostende; but was ill all the way, and saw nothing but a basin; spent two days at a queer hotel near the fine promenade, which was a very foreign and brilliant scene. To Brussels on the 7th. Here I enjoyed much, for the quaint old city was full of interesting things. The ancient square, where the statues of Egmont and Horn stand, was my delight; for the old Dutch houses were still standing, and everything was so new and strange I wanted to stay a month.

To Cologne on the 9th, and the country we passed through was like a big picture-book. The city was very hot, dirty, and evil-smelling. We saw the Cathedral, got eau de Cologne, and very gladly left after three days.

On the 12th began a lovely voyage up the Rhine. It was too beautiful to describe, so I shall not try; but I feel richer and better for that memorable day. We reached Coblenz at sunset, and I was up half the night enjoying the splendid view of the fortress opposite the town, the moonlit river with its bridges of boats, and troops crossing at midnight.

A second day, still more charming, took us through the famous parts of the Rhine, and filled my head with pictures that will last all my life.

Before we reached Bieberich we stopped at a queer little Dutch town, and had a queer time; for no one spoke English, and we only a little bad French. Passed the night there, and next day reached Schwalbach after many trials and tribulations.

The place is a narrow valley shut in by high hills, the town being divided into two parts: the lowest is the original town — queer ale-houses, churches, and narrow streets; the upper part, near the springs, is full of fine hotels, pleasure-grounds, and bath-houses.

We took lodgings with Madame Genth, wife of the Forestmeister (forest master), — two rooms, — and began the water under Dr. Genth's care.

We walked a little, talked a little, bathed and rode a little, worried a good deal, and I grubbed away at French, with no master and small success.

September. — Still at Schwalbach, A. doing her best to get well, and I doing mine to help her. Rather dull days, — bathing, walking, and quiddling about.

A letter from home on the 20th. All well and happy, thank God. It touched and pleased me very much to see how they missed me, thought of me, and longed to have me back. Every little thing I ever did for them is now so tenderly and gratefully remembered; and my absence seems to have left so large a gap that I begin to realize how much I am to them in spite of all my faults. The letters made me very happy, and everything brightened immensely. A. got stronger, and when G. came on the 28th was able to start off next day on the way to Vevay, where we are to pass some weeks before we are to go to Nice.

Went to Wiesbaden first, a pleasant, gay place, full of people. Saw the gambling hall and people playing, the fine grounds and drives, and then went on to Frankfort. Here I saw and enjoyed a good deal. The statues of Goethe, Schiller, Faust, Gutenberg, and Schaeffer are in the squares. Goethe's house is a tall, plain building, with each story projecting over the lower, and a Dutch roof; a marble slab over the front door recording the date of Goethe's birth. I took a look at it and wanted to go in, as it was empty, but there was no time. Some Americans said, " Who was Goethe, to fuss about? "

Frankfort is a pleasant old city on the river, and I 'm glad to have been there.

October. — On to Heidelberg, a charming old place surrounded by mountains. We went to the Castle and had a fine time roving about the ruins, looking at the view from the great terrace, admiring the quaint stone images of knights, saints, monsters, and angels, and visiting the big tun in the cellar by torchlight.

The moon rose while we were there and completed the enchantment of the scene.

The drive home was like looking at a picture-book, for the street was narrow, the carriage high, and we looked in at the windows, seeing pretty scenes. Here, men drinking beer in a Dutch-looking room ; there, little children going to bed ; a pair of lovers with a pot of flowers between them ; an old woman brooding over the fire like a witch ; and in one room some one lay dead surrounded by candles.

From H. we went to Baden-Baden, a very fashionable place. The old château was my delight, and we passed a morning going up and down to visit it. Next to Freiburg, where the Cathedral delighted me extremely, being full of old carved images and grotesque designs ; the market-place with the fountains, statues, water running beside the streets, and queer costumes.

Basle came next, and a firemen's fête made the city very gay. The hotel was on the river, and moonlight made a Venetian scene for me with the lighted bridge, covered with gondola-like boats and music from both shores. I walk while A. rests, and enjoy sights from my window when she is asleep, as I cannot leave her at night.

On our way to Berne I caught my first glimpse of the Alps, October 8th, mother's birthday. Tall, white, spectral-looking shapes they were, towering above the green hills and valleys that lay between. Clouds half hid them, and the sun glittered on the everlasting snow that lay upon their tops. Sharp, strange outlines against the sky they became as night came on, and in the morning I had a fine view of the Jungfrau, the Blümlis, the Wetterhorn, and Mönch from the terrace at Berne.

B. was a queer old city, but I saw little of it except the bears and shops. No time.

Freiburg No. 2 was the most romantic place we have been in. The town is built in a wide crevice or valley between two steep hills, so that suspension bridges are hung from height to height over a winding river and the streets of the town. Watch-towers stand all about on the hills, and give a very romantic air to the place. The hotel overhung the valley, and from our rooms we went out along a balcony to a wide, paved platform with a fountain in the middle, an aviary, and flowers all about. The view down the valley was charming, — the airy bridges, green or rocky slopes, busy squares below, cows and goats feeding on the hills, the towers, the old church, and a lovely blue sky overhead. I longed to sketch it.

At Lausanne we stopped at the Hotel Gibbon and saw the garden where the great historian wrote his history. The view of the lake was lovely, with rocky mountains opposite, little towns at their feet, vineyards along the hillsides, and pretty boats on the lake, the water of which was the loveliest blue.

To Vevay at last, — a pleasant hour's sail to a very pleasant place. We took rooms at the Pension Victoria.

Our landlady was an English woman who had married a French courier. Very kind sort of people : rooms comfortable, meals good, and surroundings agreeable. Our fellow-boarders varied from time to time, — an English doctor and wife, a fine old lady with them who looked like Marie Antoinette ; two Scotch ladies named Glennie, very pleasant, well-bred ladies who told me about Beattie who was their grandfather, and Walter Scott whom they knew; Colonel ——— and family, rebels, and very bitter and rude to us. Had queer times with them.

I did not enjoy the life nor the society after the first novelty wore off, for I missed my freedom and grew very tired of the daily worry which I had to go through with.

November. — (Laurie) Took some French lessons with Mademoiselle Germain and learned a little, but found it much harder than I thought, and often got discouraged, I was so stupid. A. got much better, and some new people came. The doctor and his set left, and in their place came a Russian family, an Irish lady and daughter, and a young Pole with whom we struck up a friendship.

Ladislas Wisinewski (Laurie) was very gay and agreeable, and being ill and much younger we petted him. He played beautifully, and was very anxious to learn English, so we taught him that and he taught us French.

On my birthday A. gave me a pretty painting of Chillon. Ladislas promised me the notes of the Polish National Hymn, and played me his sweetest airs as a present after wishing me "All good and happiness on earth, and a high place in Heaven as my reward." It was a mild, windy day, very like me in its fitful changes of sunshine and shade. Usually I am sad on my birthday, but not this time; for though nothing very pleasant happened, I was happy and hopeful and enjoyed everything with unusual relish. I feel rather old with my thirty-three years, but have much to keep me young, and hope I shall not grow older in heart as the time goes on. I thought much of dear father on this his sixty-sixth birthday, and missed the little ceremony that always takes place on these occasions. Hope I shall be safely at home before another November comes.

December. — Laurie very interesting and good. Pleasant walks and talks with him in the château garden and about Vevay. A lovely sail on the lake, and much fun giving English and receiving French lessons. Every one very kind, and the house quite home-like. Much indecision about going to Nice owing to the cholera. At last we decided to go, and started on the 6th to meet G. at Geneva. L. went with us to Lausanne, kissed our hands at parting, and went back to V. disconsolate. Sad times for all, but we journeyed away to Nice and tried to forget our troubles. A flat uninteresting country till we approached the sea.

Nice very pleasant, climate lovely, and sea beautiful. We lived in our own rooms, and saw no one but the doctor and Consul and a few American callers. A pleasant drive every day on the Promenade, — a wide curving wall along the bay with hotels and Pensions on one side and a flowery walk on the other. Gay carriages and people always to be seen ; shops full of fine and curious things ; picturesque castles, towers, and walls on one hill ; a lighthouse on each point of the moon-shaped bay ; boats and our fleet on the water ; gardens, olive and orange-trees, queer cacti, and palms all about on the land ; monks, priests, soldiers, peasants, etc.

A dull Christmas within doors, though a lovely day without. Windows open, roses blooming, air mild, and city gay. With friends, health, and a little money how jolly one might be in this perpetual summer.

January, 1866. — Nice. Rained all New Year's day, and I spent it sewing, writing, and reading an American newspaper which came in the morning, my only present. I hoped for letters but got none, and was much disappointed. A. was ill, so I had to receive in American style. Mr. Perkins, Cooper, and the Consul called. At dinner we drank the healths of all at home, and did not forget Laddie (Laurie).

A quiet, dull time generally, driving sometimes, walking little, and writing letters. Now and then I got a pleasant walk by myself away among the vineyards and olive-trees or down into the queer old city. I soon tired of the fashionable Promenade, for every one was on exhibition. Sometimes before or after the fashionable hour I walked there and enjoyed the sea and sky.

A ball was given at our Pension and we went. A queer set, — Russians, Spaniards, French, English, Americans, Italians, Jews, and Sandwich Islanders. They danced wildly, dressed gayly, and sounded as if the "confusion of tongues" was come again. A few pleasant Americans called on us, but we were very lonely and uncomfortable.

Decided to take an apartment No. 10 Rue Geoffredo, paying six hundred francs for ten weeks, six rooms, all large and handsome. Dr. P. got us a good maid, and on the 17th we went to our new quarters. Madame Rolande was French governess for six years to Victoria's children, and was a funny old party.

Could n't sleep at all for some nights, and felt very poorly, for my life did n't suit me and the air was too exciting.

February. — Got on excellently with our housekeeping, for Julie proved a treasure and we were very comfortable. Had many lovely drives, and saw something of Nice and its beauties. To Cimies, an old Franciscan monastery near the ruins of a Roman amphitheatre. The convent stands where a temple of Diana once stood, and is surrounded by ancient ilex trees. A monk in his cowl, brown robe, sandals, and rope girdle did the honors of the church, which was dark and full of bad pictures. San Andre with its château and grotto, Villa Franca in a lovely little bay, the wood of Var where the daisies grew, Valrosa, a villa in a rose garden, and the Porte were all interesting. Also Castle Hill, which overlooks the town.

I decided to go home in May, though A. wants me to stay. I 'm tired of it, and as she is not going to travel, my time is too valuable to be wasted.

The carnival occurred. Funny, but not so fine a sight as I expected. Also went to the theatre to see "Lady Tartuffe." Had a pleasant time, though I could n't understand much. The acting was so natural and good that I caught the plot, and with a little telling from Hosmer knew what was going on.

Wrote a little on three stories which would come into my head and worry me till I gave them a "vent."

Good letters from home. All well and busy, and longing for me in the spring.

March. — A tedious month, which might have been quite the reverse had I been free to enjoy it in my own way. Read French, walked to my favorite places, and wrote letters when I found time.

Went often to Valrosa, a lovely villa buried in roses. Got a wheeled chair and a man to draw it, then with books, lunch, and work, I tempted A. out into the woods, and we had some pleasant hours.

April. — Went to the Cathedral to see the Easter ceremonies. Fine music, the Gloria was sung, a Franciscan monk preached, the Bishop blessed every one, and was fussed over like a great doll. A very splendid scene.

Saw Ristori twice, once in "Medea" and once in "Elizabeth." Never saw such acting; especially in Queen Bess, it was splendid, as she changes from the young, violent, coquettish woman to the peevish old crone dying with her crown on, vain, ambitious, and remorseful.

May. — On the first day of the month left A. and Nice and started alone for Paris, feeling as happy as a freed bird.

A pleasant journey, Laddie waiting for me in Paris to take me to my room at Madame Dyne's. A very charming fortnight here; the days spent in seeing sights with my Laddie, the evenings in reading, writing, hearing "my boy" play, or resting. Saw all that I wished to see in a very pleasant way, and on the 17th reluctantly went to London.

Passed a fortnight at a lovely old place on Wimbledon Common with the Conways, going to town with them to see the lions, Royal Exhibition, Hampton Court, Kensington and British Museums, Crystal Palace, and many other pleasant places. But none were lovelier to me than the old farm-house with the thatched roof, the common of yellow gorse, larks going up in the morning, nightingales flying at night, hawthorne everywhere, and Richmond Park full of deer close by. Also Robin Hood's barn.

June. — Passed the first ten days of the month at Aubrey House with the Peter Taylors. A lovely English home with kind, pure, and friendly people. Saw many interesting persons, — Miss Cobbe, Jean Ingelow, Dr. Garrett, Madame Bodichon, Matilde Blinde, Mill, Bright, Gladstone, Hughes, and the rest at the House of Commons where Mr. T. took me.

Went to a dinner-party or two, theatres, to hear Dickens read, a concert, *conversazione* and receptions, seeing English society, or rather one class of it, and liking what I saw.

On the 11th went to board with Mrs. Travers in Westbourne Grove Terrace. A pleasant little room, plain living, and for society Mrs. T. and daughter, two sisters from Dublin, and ten young men, — barristers, clerks, ministers, and students. A guinea a week.

Very free and jolly, roaming about London all day, dining late and resting, chatting, music, or fun in the evening.

Saw the Tower, Windsor, Parks, Gardens, and all manner of haunts of famous men and women, — Milton's house, Johnson's in Bolt Court, Lamb's, Sairy Gamp's, Saracen's Head, the Charter House where Thackeray was when a lad, Furnival's Inn where Dickens wrote Pickwick, Bacon's Walk, and endless memorable sights. St. Paul's I liked better than Notre Dame.

July. — At Mrs. Travers's till the 7th. Saw Routledge about "Moods." He took it, would like another book, and was very friendly. Said good-by all round, and at six A. M. on the 7th left for Liverpool with Mr. W., who saw to my luggage and went part way. Reached the "Africa" safely.

A trip of fourteen stormy, dull, long, sick days, but at last at eleven at night we sailed up the harbor in the moonlight, and I saw dear John waiting for me on the wharf. Slept on board, and next day reached home at noon to find Father at the station, Nan and babies at the gate, May flying wildly round the lawn, and Marmee crying at the door. Into her arms I went, and was at home at last.

Happy days, talking and enjoying one another. Many people came to see me, and all said I was much improved ; of which I was glad, as there was, is, and always will be room for it.

Found Mother looking old, sick, and tired ; Father as placid as ever ; Nan poorly, but blest in her babies ; May full of plans, as usual ; Freddy very stout and loving ; and my Jack the dearest, prettiest, merriest baby boy that ever kissed and loved everybody.

August. — Soon fell to work on some stories, for things were, as I expected, behindhand when the money-maker was away. Found plenty to do, as orders from E., L., "Independent," "U. S. C. S. Magazine," and several other offers waited for me. Wrote two long tales for L. and got $200 for them. One for E. for which he paid $75, also a bit of poetry for $5. He wanted a long story in twenty-four chapters, and I wrote it in a fortnight, — one hundred and eighty-five pages, — besides work, sewing, nursing, and company.

Sent S. E. S. the first $100 on my account ; could have sent $300, but it was needed, so I gave it up unwillingly, and must work away for the rest. Mother borrowed the money that I might stay longer and see England, as I had missed much while condemned to "hard work and solitary confinement for nine months," as she expressed it.

September. — Mother sick, did little with my pen. Got a girl, and devoted myself to Mother, writing after she was abed. In this way finished a long tale. But E. would not have it, saying it was too long and too sensational !

November. — Mother slowly mending. A sensible Western woman "rubbed" her, and did her a great deal of good. She left her room and seemed more like herself. I never expect to see the strong, energetic Marmee of old times, but, thank the Lord ! she is still here, though pale and weak, quiet and sad ; all her fine hair gone, and face full of wrinkles, bowed back, and every sign of age. Life has been so hard for her, and she so brave, so glad to spend herself for others. Now we must live for her.

On Miss Alcott's return from Europe in July, 1866, she devoted herself as earnestly as ever to the personal care of her mother and to story-writing for the support of the family. She agreed to write a fifty-dollar tale once a month, and besides this wrote many short stories for other publishers. Her father's return from the West with two hundred dollars, earned on his western trip, gave her some relief; and she was cheered by hearing that "Moods" was selling well in Europe. But she was not well, and she felt anxious and troubled about many things. Her journal of these months is very meagre; and January, 1867, opens with the statement that she is "sick from too hard work." Yet the account of stories furnished to publishers continues till August, when she went to Clark's Island for a few weeks of recreation. Here her spirits returned, and she spent, as she says, "a harem-scarem fortnight," which must have given her great refreshment. She says: "Got to work again after my long vacation, for bills accumulate and worry me. I dread debt more than anything."

In the journal occurs this slight notice of the first step in one of the most important achievements of her life, of which I shall speak more fully hereafter: —

Journal.

September, 1867. — Niles, partner of Roberts, asked me to write a girls' book. Said I'd try.

F. asked me to be the editor of "Merry's Museum." Said I'd try.

Began at once on both new jobs; but did n't like either.

The Radical Club met at Sargent's. Fine time. Bartol inspired; Emerson chairman; Alcott on his legs; strong-minded ladies out in full force; æsthetic tea for refreshment.

October. — Agreed with F. to be editor for $500 a year. Read manuscripts, write one story each month and an editorial. On the strength of this engagement went to Boston, took a room — No. 6 Hayward Place — furnished it, and set up housekeeping for myself. Cannot keep well in C., so must try Boston, and not work too hard.

On the 28th rode to B. on my load of furniture with Fred, feeling as if I was going to camp out in a new country; hoped it would prove a hospitable and healthy land.

This incident appears in "The Old-fashioned

Girl" (p. 153), where the country girl goes into the city in a farmer's cart, with a squash pie in her hand given her at parting by an old friend. Her sister May had a drawing class at her room every day, which gave Louisa the pleasure of companionship.

Miss Alcott was an enthusiastic admirer of Dickens, and she entered into the humor of his homely characters most heartily. She acted " Mrs. Jarley displaying her waxwork " nine times this winter, and was always successful in giving life and variety to the representation. She was constantly called upon to act for charity. She enjoyed the fun, and as she could not give money, it satisfied her generous nature to be able to help in any way.

She wrote an article for Mr. B., called " Happy Women," in which she gratified her love of single life by describing the delightful spinsters of her acquaintance. Her sketches are all taken from life, and are not too highly colored. The Physician, the Artist, the Philanthropist, the Actress, the Lawyer, are easily recognizable. They were a " glorious phalanx of old maids," as Theodore Parker called the single women of his Society, who aided him so much in his work.

To her Mother.

JANUARY, 1868.

Things look promising for the new year. F. $20 for the little tales, and wrote two every month; G. $25 for the " Bells ; " L. $100 for the two " Proverb " stories. L. takes all I 'll send; and F. seems satisfied.

So my plan will work well, and I shall make my $1,000

this year in spite of sickness and worry.   Praise the Lord and keep busy, say I.

I am pretty well, and keep so busy I have n't time to be sick.   Every one is very clever to me ; and I often think as I go larking round, independent, with more work than I can do, and half-a-dozen publishers asking for tales, of the old times when I went meekly from door to door peddling my first poor little stories, and feeling so rich with $10.

It 's clear that Minerva Moody is getting on, in spite of many downfalls, and by the time she is a used up old lady of seventy or so she may finish her job, and see her family well off.   A little late to enjoy much may be ; but I guess I shall turn in for my last long sleep with more content, in spite of the mortal weariness, than if I had folded my hands and been supported in elegant idleness, or gone to the devil in fits of despair because things moved so slowly.

Keep all the money I send ; pay up every bill ; get comforts and enjoy yourselves.   Let 's be merry while we may, and lay up a bit for a rainy day.

With which gem from Aristotle, I am, honored Madam, your dutiful and affectionate   L. M. ALCOTT.

Regards to Plato.   Don't he want new socks?   Are his clothes getting shiny ?

Although, as I have said, little direct European influence is observable in Miss Alcott's writings from her journeys in Europe, yet this first visit had a marked effect upon her life and writings.   She was unfavorably situated to gain the refreshment she sorely needed ; and yet she did get a great deal from the entire change of surroundings, from the larger horizon into which she entered, from her rich enjoyment of scenery, and from the variety

of companions she met. Probably she looked
through new spectacles at her own work, as she describes herself as looking through those of Professor
Bhaer, and she saw all the defects of the pot-boiling
stories which she had been pouring out one after
another, without strong purpose, or regard for artistic excellence. She had also the chance to look
upon her own early life and home from a distance;
and as she thought of the incidents of those years
they grouped into more harmonious lines, and she
saw how much they contained of real life, of true
poetry and humor, as well as moral significance.
So the old idea of "The Pathetic Family" took
shape anew in her mind.

In July, 1863, the enterprising firm of Roberts
Brothers asked her for the publication in book
form of "Hospital Sketches," which were then appearing in the "Commonwealth" newspaper, being
struck by their intense reality and originality. At
the time, as she states in her journal, she preferred
to allow Mr. Redpath to publish them. Later, in
September, 1867, Roberts Brothers asked her to
write a girls' book for them, and in May, 1868,
they repeated the request through her father, who
had brought to them a collection of short stories
for publication.

Miss Alcott's fancy had always been for depict
ing the life of boys rather than girls; but she fortunately took the suggestion of the publisher, and
said, like Col. Miller, "I'll try, sir." The old idea
of "The Pathetic Family" recurred to her mind;
and she set herself to describe the early life of her
home. The book was finished in July, named

" Little Women," and sent to the publishers, who promptly accepted it, making Miss Alcott an outright offer for the copyright, but at the same time advising her not to part with it. It was published in October, and the result is well known. She was quite unconscious of the unusual merit of the book, thinking, as she says, the first chapters dull, and so was quite surprised at her success. " It reads better than I expected," she says; and she truly adds, " We really lived most of it, and if it succeeds, that will be the reason of it."

But that is not the whole secret of its success. Through many trials and many failures Louisa had learned her literary art. By her experience in melodrama she had proved the emptiness of sensational writing, and knew how to present the simple and true, — seemingly without art, but really with the nicest art of discrimination and emphasis. All her previous training and experience were needed to fit her for the production of her masterpiece; for in spite of all the good work she did later, this remains her masterpiece, by which she will be remembered and loved. Already twenty-one years have passed, and another generation has come up since she published this book, yet it still commands a steady sale; and the mothers who read it in their childhood renew their enjoyment as they watch the faces of their little girls brighten with smiles over the theatricals in the barn, or moisten with tears at the death of the beloved sister. One of the greatest charms of the book is its perfect truth to New England life. But it is not merely local; it touches the universal heart deeply.

The excitement of the children was intense; they claimed the author as their own property, and felt as if she were interpreting their very lives and thoughts. The second series was anticipated with the eagerness of a bulletin from the war and the stock market. But unlike Miss Alcott herself, the children took especial interest in the love-story, and when poor Laurie was so obstinately refused by Jo, "they wept aloud, and refused to be comforted," and in some instances were actually made ill by grief and excitement.

Miss Alcott had now secured publishers in whom she placed perfect confidence, and who henceforth relieved her of the worry of business matters, dealing directly and fairly by her, and consulting her interests as well as their own. This is abundantly shown by her private journals and letters.

The success of "Little Women" was so well assured that Miss Alcott at once set about preparing the second part, which was eagerly demanded by the little women outside, who wanted all the girls to marry, and rather troubled her by wishing to settle matters their own way. She finished writing the sequel, which had been rapid work, Jan. 1, 1869.

The success of "Little Women" was not confined to this country. The book was translated into French, German, and Dutch, and has become familiarly known in England and on the Continent. In Holland the first series was published under the title "Under the Mother's Wings," and the second part as "On Their Own Wings;" and these two books with "Work" established her fame among the children, who still continue to read her stories with fresh delight.

It is hardly necessary to analyze or criticise this happy production. It is a realistic transcript of life, but idealized by the tenderness of real feeling. It teaches the lessons of every-day conduct and inculcates the simplest virtues of truth, earnest effort, and loving affection. There is abundant humor, but no caricature, and tender, deep feeling without sentimentality.

Miss Alcott herself did not wish her representative, Jo, to marry; but the demand of the publisher and the public was so imperative that she created her German professor, of whom no prototype existed. While some of her romantic young readers were not satisfied at Jo's preferring him to the charming Laurie, he is certainly a genuine, warm-hearted man, who would probably have held her affections by his strong moral and intellectual traits. That he became a very living personality to the author is evident from his reappearance in "Jo's Boys," where he has the same strong, cheery influence in the school and home that she found from him in her girlhood. The style of the book is thoroughly easy and colloquial; and the girls talk and act like girls, and not like prim little women. The influence of the book has been wide and deep, and has helped to make a whole generation of girls feel a deeper sense of family love and the blessings to be gained from lives of earnest effort, mutual sacrifice, and high aims.

Much interest has been expressed in regard to

the originals of the characters in "Little Women."
This is the author's own statement: —

Facts in the stories that are true, though often changed
as to time and place : —
"Little Women" — The early plays and experiences ;
Beth's death ; Jo's literary and Amy's artistic experiences ;
Meg's happy home ; John Brooke and his death ; Demi's
character. Mr. March did not go to the war, but Jo did.
Mrs. March is all true, only not half good enough.
Laurie is not an American boy, though every lad I ever
knew claims the character. He was a Polish boy, met
abroad in 1865. Mr. Lawrence is my grandfather,
Colonel Joseph May. Aunt March is no one.

Journal.

January, 1868. *Gamp's Garret, Hayward Place,
Boston.* — The year begins well and cheerfully for us
all. Father and Mother comfortable at home ; Anna
and family settled in Chelsea ; May busy with her drawing classes, of which she has five or six, and the prospect
of earning $150 a quarter ; also she is well and in good
spirits.

I am in my little room, spending busy, happy days,
because I have quiet, freedom, work enough, and
strength to do it. F. pays me $500 a year for my name
and some editorial work on Merry's Museum ; "The
Youth's Companion" pays $20 for two short tales each
month ; L. $50 and $100 for all I will send him ; and
others take anything I have. My way seems clear for
the year if I can only keep well. I want to realize
my dream of supporting the family and being perfectly
independent. Heavenly hope !

I have written twenty-five stories the past year, besides the fairy book containing twelve. Have earned $1,000, paid my own way, sent home some, paid up debts, and helped May.

For many years we have not been so comfortable: May and I both earning, Annie with her good John to lean on, and the old people in a cosey home of our own.

After last winter's hard experience, we cannot be too grateful.

To-day my first hyacinth bloomed, white and sweet, — a good omen, — a little flag of truce, perhaps, from the enemies whom we have been fighting all these years. Perhaps we are to win after all, and conquer poverty, neglect, pain, and debt, and march on with flags flying into the new world with the new year.

Thursday, 7th. — A queer day. Up early, and had my bread and milk and baked apples. Fed my doves. Made May a bonnet, and cut out a flannel wrapper for Marmee, who feels the cold in the Concord snowbanks. Did my editorial work in the P. M., and fixed my dresses for the plays. L. sent $50, and F. $40, for tales. A. and boys came.

To Dorchester in evening, and acted Mrs. Pontifex, in "Naval Engagements," to a good house. A gay time, had flowers, etc. Talked half the night with H. A. about the fast ways of young people nowadays, and gave the child much older-sisterly advice, as no one seems to see how much she needs help at this time of her young life.

Dreamed that I was an opera dancer, and waked up prancing.

Wednesday, 15th. — Wrote all day. Did two short tales for F. In the evening with A. M. to hear Fanny Kemble read "The Merchant of Venice." She was a whole stock company in herself. Looked younger and handsomer than ever before, and happy, as she is to be with her daughters now. We went to supper afterwards at Mrs. Parkman's, and saw the lioness feed. It was a study to watch her face, so full of varying expression was it, — always strong, always sweet, then proud and fierce as she sniffed at nobodies who passed about her. Being one, I kept away, and enjoyed the great creature afar off, wondering how a short, stout, red woman *could* look so like a queen in her purple velvet and point lace.

Slipped behind a door, but Dr. Holmes found me out, and affably asked, "How many of you children are there?" As I was looking down on the top of his illustrious head, the question was funny. But I answered the little man with deep respect, "Four, sir." He seemed to catch my naughty thought, and asked, with a twinkle in his eye, looking up as if I were a steeple, "And all as tall as you?" Ha! ha!

18*th.* — Played again at D., and had a jolly time. Home early, and putting off my fine feathers, fell to work on my stories. F. seems to expect me to write the whole magazine, which I did not bargain for.

To Nan's in P. M., to take care of her while the Papa and Freddie went to C. The dear little man, so happy and important with his bit of a bag, six pennies, and a cake for refreshment during the long journey of an hour.

We brooded over Johnny as if he were a heavenly sort of fire to warm and comfort us with his sunny little face and loving ways. She is a happy woman! I sell *my* children; and though they feed me, they don't love me as hers do.

Little Tranquillity played alone all day, and made a pretty picture sitting in "marmar's" lap in his night-gown, talking through the trumpet to her. She never heard his sweet little voice in any other way. Poor Nan!

Wednesday, 22d. — To the Club with Father. A good paper on the "Historical View of Jesus." Father spoke finely. It amuses me to see how people listen and applaud *now* what was hooted at twenty years ago.

The talk lasted until two, and then the hungry philosophers remembered they had bodies and rushed away, still talking.

[Hard to feed. — L. M. A.]

Got a snow-slide on my bonnet, so made another in the P. M., and in the evening to the Antislavery Festival. All the old faces and many new ones. Glad I have lived in the time of this great movement, and known its heroes so well. War times suit me, as I am a fighting *May*.

24th. — My second hyacinth bloomed pale blue, like a timid hope, and I took the omen for a good one, as I *am* getting on, and have more than I can do of the work that I once went begging for. Enjoyed the little spring my little flower made for me, and Buzzy, my pet fly, moved into the sweet mansion from his hanging garden in the ivy pot.

Acted in Cambridge, Lucretia Buzzard and Mrs. Jarley.

Sunday, 31st. — Last day of the month, but I'm not satisfied with my four weeks' work. Acting for charity upsets my work. The change is good for me, and so I do it, and because I have no money to give.

Four tales this month. Received $70; sent $30 home. No debts.

February 1st. — Arranged "Hospital Sketches and War Stories" for a book. By taking out all Biblical allusions, and softening all allusions to rebs., the book may be made "quite perfect," I am told. Anything to suit customers.

Friday, 14*th.* — My third hyacinth bloomed this A. M., a lovely pink. So I found things snug, and had a busy day chasing ———— who dodged. Then I wrote my tales. Made some shirts for my boys, and went out to buy a squash pie for my lonely supper. It snowed; was very cold. No one paid, and I wanted to send some money home. Felt cross and tired as I trudged back at dusk. My pie turned a somersault, a boy laughed, so did I, and felt better. On my doorstep I found a gentleman who asked if Miss A. lived here. I took him up my winding stair and found him a very delightful fly, for he handed me a letter out of which fell a $100 bill. With this bait Mr. B. lured me to write "one column of Advice to Young Women," as Mrs. Shaw and others were doing. If he had asked me for a Greek oration I would have said "yes." So I gave a receipt, and the very elegant agent bowed himself away, leaving my " 'umble " bower full of perfume, and my soul of peace.

Thriftily taking advantage of the enthusiastic moment, I planned my article while I ate my dilapidated pie, and then proceeded to write it with the bill before me. It was about old maids. "Happy Women" was the title, and I put in my list all the busy, useful, independent spinsters I know, for liberty is a better husband than love to many of us. This was a nice little episode in my trials of an authoress, so I record it.

So the pink hyacinth was a true prophet, and I went to bed a happy millionaire, to dream of flannel petticoats for my blessed Mother, paper for Father, a new dress for May, and sleds for my boys.

Monday, 17*th.* — Father came full of plans about his book. Went with him to the Club. P. read a paper, and the Rabbi Nathan talked. A curious jumble of fools and philosophers. The Club should be kept more select, and not be run by one person.

Tuesday, 25th. — Note from Lady Amberly as I sat sewing on my ninepenny dress. She wanted to come and see me, and I told her to do so, and I'd show her how I lived in my sky-parlor, — spinning yarns like a spider. Met her at the Club, and liked her, so simple and natural.

Acted for Mr. Clarke's Church Fair in the evening. Did Mrs. Jarley three times. Very hoarse with a cold, but kept my promise.

"Proverb Stories" suggested, and "Kitty's Class-Day" written.

Friday, 28th. — Packed for home, as I am needed there, and acted Jarley for the third evening. Have done it nine times this week, and my voice is gone.

I am sorry to leave my quiet room, for I've enjoyed it very much.

Written eight long tales, ten short ones, read stacks of manuscripts, and done editorial work. Acted for charity twelve times.

Not a bad two months' work. I can imagine an easier life, but with love, health, and work I can be happy; for these three help one to do, to be, and to endure all things.

March, April, and May. — Had the pleasure of providing Marmee with many comforts, and keeping the hounds of care and debt from worrying her. She sits at rest in her sunny room, and that is better than any amount of fame to me.

May, 1868. — Father saw Mr. Niles about a fairy book. Mr. N. wants a *girls' story*, and I begin "Little Women." Marmee, Anna, and May all approve my plan. So I plod away, though I don't enjoy this sort of thing. Never liked girls or knew many, except my sisters; but our queer plays and experiences may prove interesting, though I doubt it.

[Good joke. — L. M. A.]

June. — Sent twelve chapters of "L. W." to Mr. N. He thought it *dull;* so do I. But work away and mean to try the experiment; for lively, simple books are very much needed for girls, and perhaps I can supply the need.

Wrote two tales for Ford, and one for F. L. clamors for more, but must wait.

July 15*th.* — Have finished "Little Women," and sent it off, — 402 pages. May is designing some pictures for it. Hope it will go, for I shall probably get nothing for " Morning Glories."

Very tired, head full of pain from overwork, and heart heavy about Marmee, who is growing feeble.

[Too much work for one young woman. No wonder she broke down. 1876. — L. M. A.]

August. — Roberts Bros. made an offer for the story, but at the same time advised me to keep the copyright; so I shall.

[An honest publisher and a lucky author, for the copyright made her fortune, and the "dull book" was the first golden egg of the ugly duckling. 1885. — L. M. A.]

August 26*th.* — Proof of whole book came. It reads better than I expected. Not a bit sensational, but simple and true, for we really lived most of it; and if it succeeds that will be the reason of it. Mr. N. likes it better now, and says some girls who have read the manuscripts say it is "splendid!" As it is for them, they are the best critics, so I should be satisfied.

September. — Father's book ["Tablets"] came out. Very simple outside, wise and beautiful within. Hope it will bring him praise and profit, for he has waited long.

No girl, Mother poorly, May busy with pupils, Nan with her boys, and much work to be done. We don't like the kitchen department, and our tastes and gifts lie in other directions, so it is hard to make the various Pegasuses pull the plan steadily.

October 8th. — Marmee's birthday; sixty-eight. After breakfast she found her gifts on a table in the study. Father escorted her to the big red chair, the boys prancing before blowing their trumpets, while we "girls" marched behind, glad to see the dear old Mother better and able to enjoy our little fête. The boys proudly handed her the little parcels, and she laughed and cried over our gifts and verses.

I feel as if the decline had begun for her; and each year will add to the change which is going on, as time alters the energetic, enthusiastic home-mother into a gentle, feeble old woman, to be cherished and helped tenderly down the long hill she has climbed so bravely with her many burdens.

October 26th. — Came to Boston, and took a quiet room in Brookline Street. Heard Emerson in the evening. Sent a report of it to A. P. for the "Standard" at his desire.

Anna is nicely settled in her new house, and Marmee is with her. Helped put down carpets and settle things.

30th. — Saw Mr. N. of Roberts Brothers, and he gave me good news of the book. An order from London for an edition came in. First edition gone and more called for. Expects to sell three or four thousand before the New Year.

Mr. N. wants a second volume for spring. Pleasan'

notices and letters arrive, and much interest in my little women, who seem to find friends by their truth to life, as I hoped.

November 1st. — Began the second part of " Little Women." I can do a chapter a day, and in a month I mean to be done. A little success is so inspiring that I now find my " Marches " sober, nice people, and as I can launch into the future, my fancy has more play. Girls write to ask who the little women marry, as if that was the only end and aim of a woman's life. I *won't* marry Jo to Laurie to please any one.

Monday, 16th. — To the Club for a change, as I have written like a steam engine since the 1st. Weiss read a fine paper on " Woman Suffrage." Good talk afterward. Lunched with Kate Field, Celia Thaxter, and Mr. Linton. Woman's Club in P. M.

17th. — Finished my thirteenth chapter. I am so full of my work, I can't stop to eat or sleep, or for anything but a daily run.

29th. — My birthday; thirty-six. Spent alone, writing hard. No presents but Father's " Tablets."

I never seem to have many presents, as some do, though I give a good many. That is best perhaps, and makes a gift very precious when it does come.

December. — Home to shut up the house, as Father goes West and Mother to Anna's. A cold, hard, dirty time ; but was so glad to be off out of C. that I worked like a beaver, and turned the key on Apple Slump with joy.

May and I went to the new Bellevue Hotel in Beacon Street. She does n't enjoy quiet corners as I do, so we took a sky-parlor, and had a queer time whisking up and down in the elevator, eating in a marble café, and sleeping on a sofa bed, that we might be genteel. It did not suit me at all. A great gale nearly blew the roof off. Steam pipes exploded, and we were hungry. I was very tired with my hard summer, with no rest for the brains that earn the money.

January, 1869. — Left our lofty room at Bellevue and went to Chauncey Street. Sent the sequel of " L. W." to Roberts on New Year's Day. Hope it will do as well as the first, which is selling finely, and receives good notices. F. and F. both want me to continue working for them, and I shall do so if I am able; but my head-aches, cough, and weariness keep me from working as I once could, fourteen hours a day.

In March we went home, as Mother was restless at Nan's, and Father wanted his library. Cold and dull; not able to write; so took care of Marmee and tried to rest.

Paid up all the debts, thank the Lord ! — every penny that money can pay, — and now I feel as if I could die in peace. My dream is beginning to come true; and if my head holds out I 'll do all I once hoped to do.

April. — Very poorly. Feel quite used up. Don't care much for myself, as rest is heavenly even with pain; but the family seem so panic-stricken and helpless when I break down, that I try to keep the mill going. Two short tales for L., $50; two for Ford, $20; and did my editorial work, though two months are unpaid for. Roberts wants a new book, but am afraid to get into a vortex lest I fall ill.

To her Publishers.

BOSTON, Dec. 28, 1869.

Many thanks for the check which made my Christmas an unusually merry one.

After toiling so many years along the uphill road, —

always a hard one to women writers, — it is peculiarly grateful to me to find the way growing easier at last, with pleasant little surprises blossoming on either side, and the rough places made smooth by the courtesy and kindness of those who have proved themselves friends as well as publishers.

With best wishes for the coming year,

I am yours truly,   L. M. ALCOTT.

AUGUST, 1871.

DEAR MR. NILES, — Many thanks for the fortune and the kind note accompanying it. Please hand the money to S. E. S., and he will put it somewhere for me. . . .

You are very kind to find a minute out of your hurried day to attend to this affair. . . . I 'm not sure but I shall try Dr. B. if my present and ninth doctor fails to cure my aching bones. I have n't a bit of faith in any of them; but my friends won't let me gently slip away where bones cease from troubling, so I must keep trying.

Very gratefully your friend,   L. M. A.

Written in 1871, just after the publication of " Little Men " : —

AUGUST 5th.

DEAR MR. NILES, — Thanks for the parcel and notes.

. . . The letters were very gushing from Nellie and Dollie and Sallie Somebody asking for pictures, autographs, family history, and several new books right away.

I must give Dr. R. a fair trial, and if he fails I 'll try Dr. B., just to make up the number of doctors to a round ten.

" Happy Thoughts " is very funny, especially the trip to Antwerp.

Yours truly,   L. M. A.

CHAPTER IX.

EUROPE.

THE LAY OF A GOLDEN GOOSE.

Long ago in a poultry yard
  One dull November morn,
Beneath a motherly soft wing
  A little goose was born.

Who straightway peeped out of the shell
  To view the world beyond,
Longing at once to sally forth
  And paddle in the pond.

"Oh! be not rash," her father said,
  A mild Socratic bird;
Her mother begged her not to stray
  With many a warning word.

But little goosey was perverse,
  And eagerly did cry,
"I've got a lovely pair of wings,
  Of course I ought to fly."

In vain parental cacklings,
  In vain the cold sky's frown,
Ambitious goosey tried to soar,
  But always tumbled down.

The farm-yard jeered at her attempts,
  The peacocks screamed, "Oh fie!
You're only a domestic goose,
  So don't pretend to fly."

Great cock-a-doodle from his perch
  Crowed daily loud and clear,
"Stay in the puddle, foolish bird,
  That is your proper sphere."

The ducks and hens said, one and all,
  In gossip by the pool,
" Our children never play such pranks;
  My dear, that fowl 's a fool."

The owls came out and flew about,
  Hooting above the rest,
" No useful egg was ever hatched
  From transcendental nest."

Good little goslings at their play
  And well-conducted chicks
Were taught to think poor goosey's flights
  Were naughty, ill-bred tricks.

They were content to swim and scratch,
  And not at all inclined
For any wild-goose chase in search
  Of something undefined.

Hard times she had as one may guess,
  That young aspiring bird,
Who still from every fall arose
  Saddened but undeterred.

She knew she was no nightingale,
  Yet spite of much abuse,
She longed to help and cheer the world,
  Although a plain gray goose.

She could not sing, she could not fly,
  Nor even walk with grace,
And all the farm-yard had declared
  A puddle was her place.

But something stronger than herself
  Would cry, " Go on, go on !
Remember, though an humble fowl,
  You 're cousin to a swan."

So up and down poor goosey went,
  A busy, hopeful bird.
Searched many wide unfruitful fields,
  And many waters stirred.

At length she came unto a stream
  Most fertile of all *Niles,*
Where tuneful birds might soar and sing
  Among the leafy isles.

Here did she build a little nest
    Beside the waters still,
Where the parental goose could rest
    Unvexed by any *bill.*

And here she paused to smooth her plumes,
    Ruffled by many plagues ;
When suddenly arose the cry,
    " This goose lays golden eggs."

At once the farm-yard was agog ;
    The ducks began to quack ;
Prim Guinea fowls relenting called,
    " Come back, come back, come back."

Great chanticleer was pleased to give
    A patronizing crow,
And the contemptuous biddies clucked,
    " I wish my chicks did so."

The peacocks spread their shining tails,
    And cried in accents soft,
" We want to know you, gifted one,
    Come up and sit aloft."

Wise owls awoke and gravely said,
    With proudly swelling breasts,
" Rare birds have always been evoked
    From transcendental nests ! "

News-hunting turkeys from afar
    Now ran with all thin legs
To gobble facts and fictions of
    The goose with golden eggs.

But best of all the little fowls
    Still playing on the shore,
Soft downy chicks and goslings gay,
    Chirped out, " Dear Goose, lay more."

But goosey all these weary years
    Had toiled like any ant,
And wearied out she now replied,
    " My little dears, I can't.

" When I was starving, half this corn
    Had been of vital use,
Now I am surfeited with food
    Like any Strasbourg goose."

So to escape too many friends,
  Without uncivil strife,
She ran to the Atlantic pond
  And paddled for her life.

Soon up among the grand old Alps
  She found two blessed things,
The health she had so nearly lost,
  And rest for weary limbs.

But still across the briny deep
  Couched in most friendly words,
Came prayers for letters, tales, or verse,
  From literary birds.

Whereat the renovated fowl
  With grateful thanks profuse,
Took from her wing a quill and wrote
  This lay of a Golden Goose.

BEX, SWITZERLAND, August, 1870.

THE year 1869 was less fruitful in work than the preceding one. Miss Alcott spent the winter in Boston and the summer in Concord. She was ill and very tired, and felt little inclined for mental effort. "Hospital Sketches," which had been first published by Redpath, was now republished by Roberts Brothers, with the addition of six shorter "Camp and Fireside Stories." The interest of the public in either the author or the work had not lessened; for two thousand copies of the book in its new form were sold the first week. In her weary condition she finds her celebrity rather a burden than a pleasure, and says in her journal : —

People begin to come and stare at the Alcotts. Reporters haunt the place to look at the authoress, who dodges into the woods *à la* Hawthorne, and won't be even a very small lion.

Refreshed my soul with Goethe, ever strong and fine and alive. Gave S. E. S. $200 to invest. What richness to have a little not needed !

Miss Alcott had some pleasant refreshment in travelling during the summer.

July. — . . . Spent in Canada with my cousins, the Frothinghams, at their house at Rivière du Loup, — a little village on the St. Lawrence, full of queer people. Drove, read, and walked with the little ones. A pleasant, quiet time.

August. — . . . A month with May at Mt. Desert. A gay time, and a little rest and pleasure before the old pain and worry began again.

Made up $1,000 for S. E. S. to invest. Now I have $1,200 for a rainy day, and no debts. With that thought I can bear neuralgia gayly.

In the autumn the whole family went to Boston, the father and mother staying with Mrs. Pratt; while Louisa and her sister May, "the workers," occupied rooms in Pinckney Street. Not being well enough to do much new work, Louisa began using up her old stories, and found that the little women "helped their rejected sisters to good places where once they went a-begging." In January, 1870, she suffered from loss of voice, for which she tried "heroic treatment" under a distinguished physician. She got well enough to write a little, and in February wrote the conclusion to "The Old-fashioned Girl," which was published in March. She says : —

I wrote it with left hand in a sling, one foot up, head aching, and no voice. Yet, as the book is funny, people will say, " Did n't you enjoy doing it ? " I often think of poor Tom Hood as I scribble, rather than lie and groan. I certainly earn my living by the sweat of my brow.

The book does not reveal this condition ; for nothing could be fresher, brighter, and more wholesome than the heroine Polly, many of whose adventures are drawn from the author's own experience. She steps out of her usual surroundings into the fashionable life of the city, but betrays her own want of sympathy with it. The book has always been very popular.

In 1870, the success of " Hospital Sketches " and the continued receipts from " Little Women " put their author in a pecuniary position which enabled her to go abroad for the rest and refreshment which she sorely needed. The younger sister was invited to go by her friend A. B. on condition that Louisa would accompany them. This journey was very free and independent. She has given an account — somewhat travestied certainly, but very true to the general facts — in " Shawl Straps," although the reader would hardly suppose the old lady described in that book had not yet reached her fortieth year. These sketches were arranged after her return, at the request of Mrs. Stowe, for the " Christian Union," and were published in a book forming one volume of " Aunt Jo's Scrap-Bag " in 1872.

Fortunately we have many of Louisa's original letters preserved in her father's copies, which have

14

escaped the destruction of her correspondence.
With some extracts from her journals, they give
a sufficient account of this journey.   In many re-
spects the contrast to her former visit to Europe is
most pleasant.   She has now become pecuniarily independent by her own exertions, and has a popular
reputation which brings her welcome and recognition wherever she goes.   But she has paid a heavy
price for these gains.   Her health has become seriously shattered.   The long application to writing,
sometimes even for fourteen hours a day, — a pressure of excitement which kept her from eating and
sleeping, — added to sorrow and anxiety, have told
upon her nerves and strength, and she is often un-
fitted to enjoy the pleasures which are open to her.
Yet her journal and letters are as full of wit and
humor as ever; and she laid up stores of pleasant
memories which lasted her through life.   Readers
of " Shawl Straps " will recognize the originals of
those bright sketches in the series of letters from
Dinan.

Second Trip to Europe.

April. — . . . On the first day of the month (fit day
for *my* undertaking I thought) May and I went to N. Y.
to meet A. B., with John for escort.   Every one very kind.
Thirty gifts, a parting ball among our house-mates, and
a great cake.   Half-a-dozen devoted beings at the station
to see us off.   But I remember only Father and Mother
as they went away the day before, leaving the two am•
bitious daughters to sail away, perhaps forever.

Marmee kept up bravely, and nodded and smiled ; but
at the corner I saw the white handkerchief go up to the

eyes, after being gayly waved to us. May and I broke down, and said, " We won't go ; " but next day we set forth, as young birds will, and left the nest empty for a year.

Sailed on the 2d in a gale of wind in the French steamer " Lafayette " for Brest. Our adventures are told in " Shawl Straps."

" O. F. G." came out in March, and sold well. Train-boy going to N. Y. put it into my lap ; and when I said I did n't care for it, exclaimed with surprise, —

" Bully book, ma'am ! Sell a lot ; better have it."

John told him I wrote it ; and his chuckle, stare, and astonished " No ! " was great fun. On the steamer little girls had it, and came in a party to call on me, very sea-sick in my berth, done up like a mummy.

Spent some charming weeks in Brittany.

June and July. — " O. F. G." was published in London by Sampson Low & Co. We left Dinan on the 15th, and had a lovely trip through France to Vevay and Bex.

Talk of war between France and Prussia.

Much excitement at. Vevay. Refugees from Lyons come in. Isabella and Don Carlos were there, with queer followers.

September. — . . . On the 3d came news of the Emperor's surrender. Great wailing among the French here. All well at home. Books going finely ; no debts.

We decide to go to Rome for the winter, as May pines for the artist's Paradise ; and war will not trouble us I hope.

SHIP " LAFAYETTE," April 9, 1870.

DEAREST MARMEE, — To-morrow we come to our long journey's end [Brest, France], thank the Lord. It has been a good one on the whole, and I have got along as well as I expected. But it is tiresome to be day after day doing nothing; for my head will not let me read. May has done well, and has been very kind to me and good, and is the life of the table, I guess. I never go up to meals, for Marie takes such good care of me; I lie and peck all sorts of funny messes, and receive calls in my den. People seem to think we are " guns," and want to know us; but as they are not interesting, we are on the reserve, and it has a fine effect. About three thousand miles away does not seem possible in so little while. How do you all get along, — Marmee, Father, the laddies, my lass, and dear old John? He was so good and kind all the way I had no care or worry, but just lopped round and let him do all the work. Bless the dear!

I shall despatch a good long letter as soon as we arrive and have something to tell. We send this to ease your mind. Letters here are not prepaid, so pay for mine out of my money. Don't forget to tell the postmaster in Boston about my letters.

Bless you all, says your   LU.

                                    · MORLAIX, April 14, 1870.

DEAREST MARMEE, — Having got our " poise " a bit by a day and night on land, I begin at once to scribble to you, as I mean to keep a letter on hand all the time, and send them off as fast as they are done. We had a twelve days' passage, owing to a double screw which they were trying and which delayed us, though it is safer than one. The weather was cold and rainy, and the sea rough, so I only went up once or twice, and kept warm in my den most of the time. After the first two days I did n't feel sick, except my head as usual. I slept, ate, ruminated, and counted the hours. May poked about more, and was liked by all.

We got to Brest about noon Wednesday. A. and I got our trunks through the custom-house, and after some squabbling with the men, got all aboard for Morlaix, which is a curious old place worth seeing. It was a lovely day, warm as our June, and we had a charming trip of three hours through a country already green and flowery. We reached our hotel all right, and after a nice dinner had baths and went to bed. May's room being some way from mine, she came and bunked in with me in my little bed, and we slept.

To-day is lovely, warm, and I am sitting at an open window looking at the square, enjoying the queer sights and sounds; for the air resounds with the rattle of wooden shoes on the stones.

Market-women sit all about selling queer things, among which are snails; they buy them by the pint, pick them out with a pin like nuts, and seem to relish them mightily. We went out this A. M. after breakfast, and took a stroll about the queer old town. May was in heaven, and kept having raptures over the gables, the turrets with storks on them, the fountains, people, and churches. She is now sketching the tower of St. Melanie, with a crowd of small boys round her enjoying the sight and criticising the work. It don't seem very new to me, but I enjoy it, and feel pretty well. We are to study French every day when we settle, and I am to do the mending, etc., for A., who is to talk for us, and make our bargains. So far we go well together.

To-morrow we go on to Lamballe, where we take the diligence to Dinan, fourteen miles farther, and there settle for some weeks. I wish the boys could see the funny children here in little wooden shoes like boats, the girls in blue cloth caps, aprons, and shawls, just like the women, and the boys in funny hats and sheepskin jackets. Now

I must go and get May, who can't speak a word of French, and has a panic if any one speaks to her. The beggars afflict her, and she wants to give them money on all occasions. This P. M. we go for a drive to see all there is, as neither A. nor I are good walkers; "adoo" till by and by. I wish I could send you this balmy day.

DINAN, Sunday, April 17, 1870.

Here we are, all settled at our first neat stopping-place, and are in clover, as you will see when I tell you how plummy and lovely it is. We left Morlaix Friday at 8 A. M., and were so amazed at the small bill presented us that we could n't praise the town enough. You can judge of the cheapness of things, when I say that my share of the expenses from Brest here, including two days at a hotel, car, 'bus, and diligence fare, fees, and everything, was $8. The day was divine, and we had a fine little journey to Lamballe, where the fun began; for instead of a big diligence, we found only a queer ramshackle thing like an insane carryall, with a wooden boot and queer porch for the driver.

Our four trunks were piled up behind and tied on with old ropes, our bags stowed in a wooden box on top, and ourselves inside with a fat Frenchman. The humpbacked driver "ya hooped" to the horses, and away we clattered at a wild pace, all feeling dead sure that something would happen, for the old thing bounded and swayed awfully, the trunks were in danger of tumbling off, and to our dismay we soon discovered that the big Frenchman was tipsy. He gabbled to A. as only a tipsy person could, quoted poetry; said he was Victor Hugo's best friend, and a child of Nature; that English ladies were all divine, but too cold, — for when he pressed A.'s hand she told him it was not allowed in England, and he was overwhelmed with remorse; bowed, sighed, rolled his eyes, and told her that he drank much ale, because it flew to his head and gave him "commercial ideas."

I never saw anything so perfectly absurd as it was, and after we got used to it we laughed ourselves sick over the lark. You ought to have seen us and our turnout, tearing over the road at a breakneck pace, pitching, creaking, and rattling, the funny driver hooting at the horses, who had their tails done up in chignons, blue harness, and strings of bells, the drunken man warbling, exhorting, and languishing at us all by turns, while A. headed him off with great skill. I sat, a mass of English dignity and coolness, suffering alternate agonies of anxiety and amusement, and May, who tied her head up in a bundle, looked like a wooden image.

It was rich; and when we took up first a peasant woman in wooden shoes and fly-away cap, and then a red-nosed priest smoking a long pipe, we were a superb spectacle. In this style we banged into Dinan, stopped at the gate, and were dumped bag and baggage in the square. Finding Madame Coste's man was not here for us, we hired a man to bring our trunks up. To our great amazement, an oldish woman, who was greasing the wheels of a diligence, came, and catching up our big trunks, whipped them into two broad carts, and taking one trotted down the street at a fine pace, followed by the man with the other. That was the finishing touch; and we went laughing after them through the great arched gate into the quaintest, prettiest, most romantic town I ever saw. Narrow streets with overhanging gables, distracting roofs, windows, and porches, carved beams, and every sort of richness. The strong old lady beat the man, and finally landed us close by another old gate at a charming house fronting the south, overlooking a lovely green valley, full of gardens, blooming plum and peach trees, windmills, and a ruined castle, at sight of which we all skipped. Madame Coste received us with rapture, for A. brought a letter from Mrs. L., who stayed here and was the joy of the old lady's soul. We were in great luck, for being early in the season she had three rooms left, and we nabbed them at once, — a salon with old oak walls and wardrobes, blue damask furniture, a fireplace, funny windows, and quaint furniture. A little room out of it for A., and upstairs a larger room for May and me, with two beds draped in green chintz, and carved big wardrobe, etc., and best of all, a sunny window toward the valley. For these rooms and our board we each pay $1 a day, and I call that cheap. It would be worth that to get the fun and air alone, for it is like June, and we sit about with open windows, flowers in the fields, birds singing, and everything spring-like.

We took possession at once, and dressed for a dinner at six. We were then presented to our fellow-boarders, — Madame Forney, a buxom widow, her son Gaston, a handsome Frenchy youth of twenty-three, and her daughter, a homely girl of twenty, who is to be married here on the 3d of May. After a great bowing and scraping we had a funny fish dinner, it being Good Friday. When they found we did n't speak French they were "desolated," and begged us to learn at once, which we solemnly vowed to do. Gaston "knew English," so May at once began to teach him more, and the ice being broken we got gay and friendly at once. I could understand them pretty well, but can't talk, and A. told them that I was forbidden to say much on account of my throat. This will give me a chance to get a fair start. May pegs away at her grammar, and with that and the elegant Gaston, she will soon begin to " parlez-vous."

After dinner we were borne to the great salon, where a fire, lights, and a piano appeared. Every one sat round and gabbled except the Alcotts, who looked and laughed. Mademoiselle Forney played, and then May convulsed them by singing some *Chants Amériques*, which they thought very lively and droll. They were all attention and devotion to Madame Coste, — a tall old lady with whiskers, who kept embracing A. and beaming at us in her great content at being friends of *chère* Madame L. A. told them that I was a celebrated authoress, and May a very fine artist, and we were beamed at more than ever. Being tired, we turned in early, after a jolly time in our own little salon, eating chocolate and laying plans.

DINAN, April 20, 1870.

. . . A. and I went shopping. A. got a little bird to enliven our parlor, a sort of sparrow, gray with a red head and a lively song. We named him Bernard du Guesclin (the hero of the town), and call him Bernie. I got some nice gloves for three francs (sixty cents), and a white sun-umbrella for May (forty cents). She needs it when she sketches, and there is always a crowd of children round her to watch and admire ; she gives one of them a sou to hold the umbrella, and so gets on nicely.

In the P. M. A. and I went to the little village of Lahou, in the valley where the ruined castle is, to a fair. It was a very picturesque sight, for the white-capped women, sitting about on the green hillside, looked like flowers, and the blue blouses of the men and wide-brimmed hats added to the effect. The little street was lined with booths, where they sold nuts, queer cakes, hot sausages, and pancakes, toys, etc. I got a funny cake, just the size and shape of a deep pie-dish, and a jack-knife, for a sou. We also indulged in nuts, and sat on our campstools in a shady place and ate them boldly in the public mart, while enjoying the lively scene. French and English people went by in droll parties, and we coolly sat and stared at them. May is going to sketch the castle, so I won't waste paper describing the pretty place with the ruined church full of rooks, the old mill with the water-wheel housed in vines, or the winding river, and meadows full of blue hyacinths and rosy daisies.

Yesterday, A. and I had to return the call of Mademoiselle M., and as she speaks English I got on very well. The stairs to her apartment were so steep that we held on by a velvet-covered rope as we climbed up. In the P. M. we had fun, for we took two donkey carriages and rode to the mineral spring. Gaston was sick and could n't go, as we had planned, so May drove herself in one, and A. and I in the other. I wish the boys could have seen us, it was so funny. The carriages were bath-chairs with a wee donkey harnessed to each, so small, so neat, and looking so venerable with thin long ears and bits of feet that I felt as if I was driving my grandmother. May was a very imposing sight, alone in her chair under her new umbrella, in her gray suit, with bright gloves and a big whip, driving a gray rat who would n't trot unless pounded and banged and howled at in the maddest way. Our steed was bigger, but the most pig-headed old scamp you ever saw, for it took two big women to make him go. I drove, and A. thrashed away with all her might, — our joint efforts only producing occasional short trots which enraged us dreadfully.

We laughed till we were sick, it was so very absurd; while May trundled serenely along, enjoying the fine views regardless of her rat, who paced along at his ease, wagging his ears and meditating.

We had a nice trip, but did n't drink the water, as iron

don't suit us. Coming home, we passed the home of the donkeys, and they at once turned in, and were with much difficulty persuaded to go on by two short girls in caps and short gowns, who ran and shouted "E ! E ! va oui ! " and punched sticks into the poor asses, rattling us over the stones till our eyes danced in our heads. We found it rather hard work, and A. means to buy a horse and straw pony-chaise, so we can drive ourselves in peace where we like. . . .

A. is bargaining for a horse which an Englishman wishes to sell for $50, including harness and cart. We can't hire horses for less than $2 a drive, and donkeys are vile, so it is cheaper to buy, and sell when we go away, and so drive as much as we like. A. knows about such things, and takes all the responsibility. . . . To-morrow we go on a little excursion in the steamboat down the river, and return *à la* donkey with the English ladies, who have returned our call and are very friendly.

Please forward this little note in an envelope to its address. The child wrote me a pretty letter, which N. sent, and the pa said I would n't answer. The child said, " I know she will, she is so nice." So I do. Best love to every one. Don't go home too soon. I shall write to Fred and Jack next time. Good-by.

Lu.

To M. S.

. . . They call each other pet names that convulse us, — " my little pig," " my sweet hen," " my cabbage," and " my tom-cat." A French lady with her son and daughter board here, and their ways amuse us mightily. The girl is to be married next week to a man whom she has seen twice, and never talked to but an hour in her life. She writes to him what her mother dictates, and says she should be ashamed to love him before they were married.

Her wedding clothes absorb her entire mind, and her Jules will get a pretty doll when he takes Mademoiselle A. F. to wife. Gaston, the son, puts on *blasé* airs, though only twenty-two, and languishes at May, for they can't talk, as he does not know English nor she French.

April 27.

I left my letter to drive to a ruined château, which we went all over, as a part is inhabited by a farmer who keeps his hog in the great banqueting hall, his grain in the chapel, and his hens in the lady's chamber. It was very picturesque; the old rooms, with ivy coming in at the windows, choking up the well, and climbing up the broken towers. The lady of the château was starved to death by her cruel brothers, and buried in the moat, where her bones were found long afterward, and her ghost still haunts the place they say. Here we had cider, tell Pa.

Coming home we saw a Dolmen, one of the Druidical remains. It stood in a grove of old pines, — a great post of gray stone, some twenty-five feet high, and very big round. It leaned as if falling, and had queer holes in it. Brittany is full of these relics, which no one can explain, and I was glad to see the mysterious things.

Yesterday we took a little trip down the river in a tiny steamer, going through a lock and skimming along between the green banks of the narrow river to Miss M.'s country-house, where we had new milk, and lay on the grass for an hour or so. Then May and Miss M. walked home, and A. and I went in a donkey cart.

To-day the girls have gone to La Garaye with Gaston on donkeys. The weather has been cold for a day or two with easterly winds. So I feel it at once and keep warm. It is very unusual at this time, but comes, I suppose, because I 've travelled hundreds of miles to get rid of them. It won't last long, and then we shall be hot enough.

We lead such quiet, lazy lives I really have nothing to tell.

Oh, yes, the *fiancé* of Mademoiselle has arrived, and amuses us very much. He is a tiny man in uniform, with a red face, big moustache, and blue eyes. He thinks he talks English, and makes such very funny mistakes. He asked us if we had been to "promenade on monkeys" meaning donkeys, and called the Casino "the establishment of dance." He addresses all his attentions to the ma, and only bows to his future wife, who admires her diamonds and is contented. We are going away on the day of the wedding, as it is private.

The girls have just returned in great spirits, for A.'s donkey kept lying down, and it took all three to get him up again. They sat in a sort of chair, and looked very funny with the four little legs under them and long ears flopping before. I shall go to Garaye some fine day, and will tell you about it.

Adieu, love to all. Yours, Lu.

DINAN, May 6, 1870.

DEAR PEOPLE,—I have just got a fat letter full of notices from N.,—all good, and news generally pleasant.

The great event of the season is over, and Miss F. is Mrs. C. It was a funny scene, for they had a breakfast the day before, then on Tuesday the wedding. We did not go, as the church is like a tomb, but we saw the bride, in white satin, pearls, orange flowers, and lace, very pretty, and like other brides. Her ma, in purple moire and black lace, was fine to see; and the little groom, in full regimentals, with a sabre as large as himself, was very funny. A lot of people came in carriages

to escort them to church; and our little square was full
of queer turnouts, smartly dressed people, and a great
bustle. There was some mistake about the bride's carriage, and it did not drive up in time, so she stood on
the steps till it came as near as it could, and then she
trotted out to it on Gaston's arm, with her maid holding
up her satin train. Uncle, ma, bride, and brother drove
off, but the groom's carriage was delayed by the breaking
of a trace, and there he sat, with his fat pa and ma, after
every one had gone, fuming, and poking his little cocked
hat out of the window, while the man mended the harness, and every one looked on with breathless interest.

We went to D—— with Coste in the P. M., and had a
fine view of the sea and San Malo. We didn't like
D——, and won't go there. When we got home about
eight o'clock the wedding dinner was in full blast, and I
caught a glimpse of a happy pair at the head of the
table, surrounded by a lot of rigged-up ladies and fine
men, all gabbing and gabbling as only French folk can.
The couple are still here, resting and getting acquainted
before they go to Lamballe for a week of festivity. A
church wedding is a very funny thing, and I wish you
could have seen it.

The dry season continues, and the people have pro-
cessions and masses to pray for rain. One short flurry
of hail is all we have had, and the cold winds still blow.
When our month is out we shall go somewhere near the
sea if it is at all warm. Nothing could be kinder than
dear old Coste, and I couldn't be in a better place to be
poorly in than this; she coddles me like a mother, and
is so grieved that I don't get better.

Send Ma a bit of the gorse flower with which the fields
are now yellow.

Yours,

Lu.

DINAN, May 13, 1870.

DEAREST FOLKS, — We drove to Guildo yesterday to
see if we should like it for July. It is a queer little town
on the seashore, with ruins near by, bright houses, and
lots of boats. Rooms a franc a day, and food very
cheap. The man of the house — a big, brown, Peggotty
sailor — has a sloop, and promised the girls as much
sailing as they liked. We may go, but our plans are
very vague, and one day we say we will go to one place
and the next to another, and shall probably end by staying where we are.

Yours,   LU.

DINAN, May 17, 1870.

DEAREST PEOPLE, — We run out and do errands in the
cool before breakfast at ten, then we write, sew, and
read, and look round, till four, when we go to drive.
May and I in the cherry bounce with M. Harmon to
drive us, and A. on horseback; for, after endless fuss, she
has at last evoked a horse out of chaos, and comes gal-
loping gayly after us as we drive about the lovely roads
with the gallant hotel-keeper, Adolph Harmon. We are
getting satiated with ruins and châteaux, and plan a trip
by water to Nantes; for the way they do it is to hire a
big boat and be towed by a horse in the most luxurious
manner.

To Anna.

DINAN, May 25, 1870.

DEAR BETSEY,[1] — All well. We have also had fun
about the queer food, as we don't like brains, liver, etc.
A. does; and when we eat some mess, not knowing what

[1] Betsey Prig was a pet name for her sister, as she herself was
Sairey Gamp.

it is, and find it is sheep's tails or eels, she exults over us, and writes poems.

I wander dreadfully, but the girls are racketing, birdie singing like mad, and nine horses neighing to one another in the place, so my ideas do not flow as clearly as they should. Besides, I expect Gaston to come in every minute to show us his rig ; for he is going to a picnic in Breton costume, — a very French affair, for the party are to march two and two, with fiddlers in front, and donkeys bearing the feast in the rear. Such larks !

Yesterday we had a funny time. We went to drive in a basket chair, very fine, with a perch behind and a smart harness ; but most of the horses here are stallions, and act like time. Ours went very well at first, but in the town took to cutting up, and suddenly pounced on to a pile of brush, and stuck his head into a bake-shop. We tried to get him out, but he only danced and neighed, and all the horses in town seemed to reply. A man came and led him on a bit, but he did n't mean to go, and whisked over to the other side, where he tangled us and himself up with a long string of team horses. I flew out and May soon followed. A. was driving, and kept in while the man led the "critter" back to the stable. I declined my drive with the insane beast, and so we left him and bundled home in the most ignominious manner. All the animals are very queer here, and, unlike ours, excessively big.

We went to a ruin one day, and were about to explore the castle, when a sow, with her family of twelve, charged through the gateway at us so fiercely that we fled in dismay ; for pigs are not nice when they attack, as we don't know where to bone 'em, and I saw a woman one day whose nose had been bitten off by an angry pig. I

flew over a hedge; May tried to follow. I pulled her
over head first, and we tumbled into the tower like a
routed garrison. It wasn't a nice ruin, but we were
bound to see it, having suffered so much. And we did
see it, in spite of the pigs, who waylaid us on all sides,
and squealed in triumph when we left, — dirty, torn, and
tired. The ugly things wander at their own sweet will,
and are tall, round-backed, thin wretches, who run like
race horses, and are no respecters of persons.

Sunday was a great day here, for the children were
confirmed. It was a pretty sight to see the long procession of little girls, in white gowns and veils, winding
through the flowery garden and the antique square, into
the old church, with their happy mothers following, and
the boys in their church robes singing as they went. The
old priest was too ill to perform the service, but the
young one who did announced afterward that if the children would pass the house the old man would bless
them from his bed. So all marched away down the
street, with crosses and candles, and it was very touching
to see the feeble old man stretch out his hands above
them as the little white birds passed by with bended
heads, while the fresh, boyish voices chanted the re-
sponses. This old priest is a very interesting man, for
he is a regular saint, helping every one, keeping his
house as a refuge for poor and old priests, settling quarrels
among the people, and watching over the young people
as if they were his own. I shall put him in a story.

Voilà! Gaston has just come in, rigged in a white
embroidered jacket, with the Dinan coat-of-arms worked
in scarlet and yellow silk on it fore and aft; a funny hat,
with streamers, and a belt, with a knife, horn, etc. He
is handsome, and as fond of finery as a girl. I'll send
you his picture next time, and one of Dinan.

You will see that Marmee has all she needs, and a girl, and as much money as she wants for being cosey and comfortable. S. E. S. will let her have all she wants, and make her take it. I'm sorry the chapel $100 did n't come, for she likes to feel that she has some of her very own.

I have written to Conway and Mrs. Taylor, so that if we decide to take a run to England before we go to Italy, the way will be open. . . .

But Dinan is so healthy and cosey, that we shall linger till the heat makes us long for the sea. Roses, cherries, strawberries, and early vegetables are come, and we are in clover. Dear old Coste broods over us like a motherly hen, and just now desired me to give her affectionate and respectful compliments to my *bonne mère.*

Now I'm spun out; so adieu, my darling Nan. Write often, and I will keep sending, — trusting that you will get them in time.

Kisses all round.

Yours,   Lu.

DINAN, May 30, 1870.

DEAR FOLKS, — May has made up such a big letter that I will only add a line to give you the last news of the health of her Highness Princess Louisa. She is such a public character nowadays that even her bones are not her own, and her wails of woe cannot be kept from the long ears of the world, — old donkey as it is !

Dr. Kane, who was army surgeon in India, and doctor in England for forty years, says my leg trouble and many of my other woes come from the calomel they gave me in Washington. He has been through the same thing with an Indian jungle fever, and has never got the calomel out of him. . . . I don't know anything about it, only my leg is the curse of my life. But I think

Dr. K.'s iodine of potash will cure it in the end, as it did his arms, after taking it for three months. It is simple, pleasant, and seems to do something to the bones that gives them ease ; so I shall sip away and give it a good trial.

We are now revelling in big strawberries, green peas, early potatoes, and other nice things, on which we shall grow fat as pigs.

We are beginning to think of a trip into Normandy, where the H.'s are.

Love to all. By-by !   Your loving   Lu.

No news except through N., who yesterday sent me a nice letter with July account of $6,212, — a neat little sum for " the Alcotts, who can't make money ! " With $10,000 well invested, and more coming in all the time, I think we may venture to enjoy ourselves, after the hard times we have all had.

The cream of the joke is, that we made our own money ourselves, and no one gave us a blessed penny. That does soothe my rumpled soul so much that the glory is not worth thinking of.

To Anna.

DINAN, June 4, 1870.

. . . .

The present excitement is the wood which Coste is having put in. Loads keep coming in queer, heavy carts drawn by four horses each, and two men to work the machine. Two men chop the great oak stumps, and a woman puts it in down cellar by the armful. The men get two francs a day, — forty cents ! (Would n't our $3 a day workmen howl at that sort of wages !) When several carts arrive at once the place is a lively scene. Just now there were three carts and twelve horses, and eight were all up in a snarl, while half-a-dozen ladies stood at their doors and gave advice. One had a half-dressed baby in her arms; one a lettuce she was washing; another her distaff; and a fourth her little bowl of soup, which she ate at on the sidewalk, in the intervals gesticulating so frantically that her sabots rattled on the stones. The horses had a free fight, and the man couldn't seem to manage one big one, who romped about like a wild elephant, till the lady with the baby suddenly set the half-naked cherub on the doorsteps, charged in among the rampant beasts, and, by some magic howl or jerk, brought the bad horse to order, when she quietly returned to her baby, who had sat placidly eating dirt, and with a calm *Voilà, messieurs,* she skipped little Jean into his shirt, and the men sat down to smoke.

We are now in great excitement over Gaston, who has lately become so very amiable that we don't know him. We began by letting the spoiled child severely alone. This treatment worked well, and now he offers us things at table, bows when we enter, and to-day presented us with green tulips, violet shrubs, and queer medals all round. We have let little bits of news leak out about us, and they think we are dukes and duchesses in *Amérique,* and pronounce us *très spirituelles; très charmantes; très seductives femmes.* We laugh in private, and are used to having the entire company rise when we enter, and embrace us with ardor, listen with uplifted hands and shrieks of *mon Dieu! grand ciel!* etc., to all remarks, and point us out in public as *les dames Américaines.* Such is fame!

An English lady arrived to-day—a Miss B.—dressed, with English taste, in a little green skirt, pink calico waist, a large crumpled frill, her hair in a tight knot, one front tooth sticking straight out, and a golden oriole in a large

cage. She is about forty, very meek and pursy, and the
old ladies have been sitting in a heap since breakfast,
talking like mad.

May has "sack" on the brain just now, and A. has
"hose" on the brain; and at this moment they are both
gabbling wildly, one saying, "I shall trim it with blue
and have it pinked!" the other shrieking, "My hose
must be red, with little dragons in black all over it, like
small-pox!" and the bird flies to her upper perch in dismay at the riot, while I sit and laugh, with an occasional
duennaish, "Young ladies, less noise if you please!"

It rained last eve, and we are waiting for it to dry
before going out in the donkey chaise to buy a warm
bun and some strawberries for lunch, to be eaten as we
parade the town and drink ale at intervals.

. . . .

Do tell me how things are about my pictures. I see
they are advertised, and if they sell I want my share
of the profits. Send me one of those that are in the
market, after taking off the heavy card.

Love to all, and the best of luck.

Ever your   Lu.

HOTEL D'UNIVERSE, TOURS, June 17, 1870.

DEAREST PEOPLE, — Our wanderings have begun again,
and here we are in this fine old city in a cosey hotel, as
independent and happy as three old girls can be. We
left Dinan Wednesday at 7 A.M. Gaston got up to see us
off, — a most unusual and unexpected honor; also Mrs. B.
and all the old ladies, whom we left dissolved in tears.

We had a lovely sail down the river to St. Malo,
where we breakfasted at Hotel Franklin, a quaint old
house in a flowery corner. At twelve we went by rail to
Le Mans, — a long trip, — and arrived at 6 P.M. so tired

that we went to bed in the moonlight while a band played in the square before the hotel, and the sidewalks before the café were full of people taking ices and coffee round little tables.

Next morning we went to see the famous cathedral and had raptures, for it is like a dream in stone. Pure Gothic of the twelfth century, with the tomb of Berengaria, wife of Cœur de Leon, stained glass of the richest kind, dim old chapels with lamps burning, a gorgeous high altar all crimson and gold and carmine, and several organs. Anything more lovely and divine I never saw, for the arches, so light and graceful, seemed to soar up one above the other like the natural curves of trees or the spray of a great fountain. We spent a long time here and I sat above in the quaint old chapel with my eyes and heart full, and prayed a little prayer for my family. Old women and men knelt about in corners telling their beads, and the priest was quietly saying his prayers at the altar. Outside it was a pile of gray stone, with towers and airy pinnacles full of carved saints and busy rooks. I don't think we shall see anything finer anywhere. It was very hot for there had been no rain for four months, so we desired to start for town at 5 and get in about 8 as it is light then.

We had a pleasant trip in the cool of the day, and found Tours a great city, like Paris on a small scale. Our hotel is on the boulevard, and the trees, fountains, and fine carriages make our windows very tempting. We popped into bed early; and my bones are so much better that I slept without any opium or anything, — a feat I have not performed for some time.

This morning we had coffee and rolls in bed, then as it was a fine cool day we dressed up clean and nice and went out for a walk. At the post-office we found your

letters of May 31, one from Nan and Ma, and one from
L. We were exalted, and went into the garden and
read them in bliss, with the grand cathedral right before
us. Cathedral St. Martin, twelfth century, with tomb of
Charles XIII.'s children, the armor of Saint Louis, fine
pictures of Saint Martin, his cloak, etc. May will tell you
about it and I shall put in a photograph, if I can find
one. We are now — 12 o'clock — in our pleasant room
all round the table writing letters and resting for another
trip by and by.

The *Fête Dieu* is on Monday, — very splendid, — and
we shall then see the cathedral in its glory. To-day a few
hundred children were having their first communion
there, girls all in white, with scarlet boys, crosses, candles,
music, priests, etc. Get a Murray, and on the map of
France follow us to Geneva, *via* St. Malo, Le Mans,
Tours, Amboise and Blois, Orleans, Nevers, Autun.
We may go to the Vosges instead of the Jura if Mrs. H.
can go, as A. wants to see her again. But we head for
the Alps of some sort and will report progress as we go.

My money holds out well so far, as we go second class.

To her Father.

TOURS, June 20, 1870.

DEAR PAPA, — Before we go on to fresh "châteaux
and churches new," I must tell you about the sights here
in this pleasant, clean, handsome old city. May has
done the church for you, and I send a photograph to
give some idea of it. The inside is very beautiful; and
we go at sunset to see the red light make the gray walls
lovely outside and the shadows steal from chapel to
chapel inside, filling the great church with what is really
"a dim religious gloom." We wandered about it the

other evening till moonrise, and it was very interesting to see the people scattered here and there at their prayers ; some kneeling before Saint Martin's shrine, some in a flowery little nook dedicated to the infant Christ, and one, a dark corner with a single candle lighting up a fine picture of the Mater Dolorosa, where a widow all in her weeds sat alone, crying and praying. In another a sick old man sat, while his old wife knelt by him praying with all her might to Saint Gratien (the patron saint of the church) for her dear old invalid. Nuns and priests glided about, and it was all very poetical and fine, till I came to an imposing priest in a first class chapel who was taking snuff and gaping, instead of piously praying.

The *Fête Dieu* was yesterday, and I went out to see the procession. The streets were hung with old tapestry, and sheets covered with flowers. Crosses, crowns, and bouquets were suspended from house to house, and as the procession approached, women ran out and scattered green boughs and rose-leaves before the train. A fine band and a lot of red soldiers came first, then the different saints on banners, carried by girls, and followed by long trains of girls bearing the different emblems. Saint Agnes and her lamb was followed by a flock of pretty young children all in white, carrying tall white lilies that filled the air with their fragrance.

"Mary our Mother" was followed by orphans with black ribbons crossed on their breasts. Saint Martin led the charity boys in their gray suits, etc. The Host under a golden canopy was borne by priests in gorgeous rig, and every one knelt as it passed with censors swinging, candles burning, boys chanting, and flowers dropping from the windows. A pretty young lady ran out and set her baby in a pile of green leaves in the middle of the street before the Host, and it passed over the little thing who sat placidly staring at the show and admiring its blue shoes. I suppose it is a saved and sacred baby henceforth.

It was a fine pageant and quite touching, some of it; but as usual, I saw something funny to spoil the solemnity. A very fat and fine priest, who walked with his eyes upon his book and sung like a pious bumblebee, suddenly destroyed the effect by rapping a boy over the head with his gold prayer-book, as the black sheep strayed a little from the flock. I thought the old saint swore also.

The procession went from the cathedral to Charlemagne's Tower, an old, old relic, all that is left of the famous church which once covered a great square. We went to see it, and the stones looked as if they were able to tell wonderful tales of the scenes they had witnessed all these hundreds of years. I think the " Reminiscences of a Rook " would be a good story, for these old towers are full of them, and they are long-lived birds.

AMBOISE, THE GOLDEN LION,
Tuesday, June 21, 1870.

Here we go again! now in an utterly different scene from Tours. We left at 5 P. M., and in half an hour were here on the banks of the Loire in a queer little inn where we are considered duchesses at least, owing to our big trunks and A.'s good French. I am the Madame, May Mam'selle, and A. the companion.

Last evening being lovely, we went after dinner up to the castle where Charles VIII. was born in 1470. The Arab chief, Abd-el-Kader, and family were kept prisoners here, and in the old garden is a tomb with the crescent over it where some of them were buried. May was told about the terrace where the Huguenots hung thick and

the court enjoyed the sight till the Loire, choked up with
dead bodies, forced them to leave.   We saw the little
low door where Anne of Brittany's first husband Charles
VIII. " bumped his head " and killed himself, as he was
running through to play bowls with his wife.

It has been modernized and is now being restored as
in old times, so the interior was all in a toss.   But we
went down the winding road inside the tower, up which
the knights and ladies used to ride.   Father would
have enjoyed the *pleached* walks, for they are cut so
that looking down on them, it is like a green floor, and
looking up it is a thick green wall.   There also Margaret
of Anjou and her son were reconciled to Warwick.   Read
Murray, I beg, and see all about it.   We sat in the twilight on the terrace and saw what Fred would have liked,
a little naked boy ride into the river on one horse after
another, and swim them round in the deep water till
they were all clean and cool.

This morning at 7 o'clock we drove to Chenonceaux,
the chateau given by Henry II. to Diane de Poictiers.
It was a lovely day, and we went rolling along through the
most fruitful country I ever saw.   Acre on acre of yellow
grain, vineyards miles long, gardens and orchards full of
roses and cherries.   The Cher is a fine river winding
through the meadows, where haymakers were at work
and fat cattle feeding.   It was a very happy hour, and
the best thing I saw was May's rapturous face opposite, as
she sat silently enjoying everything, too happy to talk.

The château built over the water is very interesting;
Catherine de Medicis took it away from Diane when the
king died, and her room is still seen as she left it; also
a picture of Diane, a tall simpering woman in a tunic,
with hounds, stag, cupids, and other rubbish round her.
The gallery of pictures was fine; for here were old, old

portraits and bas-reliefs, Agnes Sorel, Montaigne, Rabelais, many kings and queens, and among them Lafayette and dear old Ben Franklin.

There is a little theatre where Rousseau's plays were acted. This place at the time of the Revolution belonged to the grandmother of George Sand, and she was so much respected that no harm was done to it. So three cheers for Madame Dupin ! Among the pictures were Ninon D'Enclos, and Madame Sevigné holding a picture of her beloved daughter. The Guidos, etc. I don't care for so much as they were all grimy and convulsive, and I prefer pictures of people who really lived, to these impossible Venuses and repulsive saints, — bad taste, but I can't help it. The walls were hung with stamped leather and tapestry, carved chairs in which queens had sat, tables at which kings had eaten, books they had read, and glasses that had reflected their faces were all about, and I just revelled. The old kitchen had a fireplace quaint enough to suit Pa, with immense turn-spits, cranes, andirons, etc. The chapel, balcony, avenue, draw-bridge, and all the other pleasing bits were enjoyed, and I stole a sprig of jasmine from the terrace which I shall press for Mamma. Pray take extra care of the photographs, for if lost, we cannot replace them, and I want to make a fine album of pictures with flowers and descriptions after I get home. . . . But all goes well and we enjoy much every day. Love to all, LU.

To her Mother.

BLOIS, June 24, 1870.

DEAR MARMEE, — On this, Lizzie's and Johnny's birthday, I 'll begin a letter to you. We found at the Poste Restante here two " Moods " and a paper for me, one book from L., and one from N. I think the pictures horrid, and sent them floating down the Loire as soon as possible, and put one book at the bottom of my trunk and left the other where no one will find it. I could n't read the story, and try to forget that I ever wrote it.

Blois is a noisy, dusty, soldierly city with nothing to admire but the river, nearly dry now with this four months' drought, and the old castle where Francis I., Louis XII., Catherine de Medicis, and other great folks lived. It has been very splendidly restored by the Government, and the ceilings are made with beams blazoned with coats-of-arms, the walls hung with cameos, painted with the same design as the stamped leather in old times, and the floors inlaid with colored tiles. Brown and gold, scarlet, blue, and silver, quaint dragons and flowers, porcupines and salamanders, crowns and letters, glittered everywhere. We saw the guard-room and the very chimney where the Duc de Guise was leaning when the king Henry III. sent for him; the little door where the king's gentlemen fell upon and stabbed him with forty wounds; the cabinet where the king and his mother plotted the deed; the chapel where the monks prayed for success; and the great hall where the body lay covered with a cloak till the king came and looked at it and kicked his dead enemy, saying, " I did not think he was so tall.". We also saw the cell where the brother of the duke was murdered the next day, and the attic entire where their bodies were burnt, after which the ashes were thrown into the Loire by order of the king; the window out of which Marie de Medicis lowered herself when her son Louis XIII. imprisoned her there; the recess where Catherine de Medicis died; and many other interesting places. What a set of rascals these old kings and queens were !

The *Salle des États* was very gorgeous, and here in a week or so are to be tried the men who lately fired at the Emperor. It will be a grand, a fine sight when the great arched hall is full. I got a picture of the castle, and one of a fireplace for Pa. It is a mass of gold and color, with the porcupine of Louis XIII. and the ermine of his wife Anne of Brittany, their arms, in medallion over it.

At 5 P. M. we go on to Orleans for a day, where I shall get some relics of Joan of Arc for Nan. We shall pass Sunday at Bourges where the great church is, and then either to Geneva or the Jura, for a few weeks of rest.

GENEVA, June 29, 1870.

It seems almost like getting home again to be here where I never thought to come again when I went away five years ago. We are at the Metropole Hotel right on the lake with a glimpse of Mount Blanc from our windows. It is rather fine after the grimy little inns of Brittany, and we enjoy a sip of luxury and put on our best gowns with feminine satisfaction after living in old travelling suits for a fortnight.

I began my letter at Blois, where we spent a day or two. At Orleans we only passed a night, but we had time to see the famous statue of the Maid, put up in gratitude by the people of the city she saved. It is a fine statue of Joan in her armor on horseback, with her sword drawn. Round the base of the statue are bronzed bas-reliefs of her life from the girl with her sheep, to the martyr at the stake. They were very fine, but don't show much in the photograph which I got for Nan, remembering the time when she translated Schiller's play for me.

At Bourges we saw the great cathedral, but did n't like it as well as that in Tours. We only spent a night there, and A. bought an antique ring of the time of

Francis I., — an emerald set in diamonds. It cost $9, and is very quaint and handsome.

Moulins we reached Sunday noon, and at 3 o'clock went to vespers in the old church, where we saw a good deal of mumbo-jumbo by red, purple, and yellow priests, and heard a boy with a lovely voice sing in the hidden choir like a little angel among the clouds. A. had a fancy to stay a week, if we could find rooms out of town in some farm-house ; for the handsome white cattle have captivated her, and we were rather tired. So the old lady at the hotel said she had a little farm-house out in the fields, and we should go see it with her in basket *chay*. After dinner we all piled in and went along a dusty road to a little dirty garden-house with two rooms and a few cabbages and rose-bushes round it. She said we could sleep and eat at the hotel and come down here for the day. That did n't suit at all, so we declined ; and on Monday morning we set out for Lyons. It was a very interesting trip under, over, and through the mountains with two engines and much tunnelling and up-and-down grading. May was greatly excited at the queer things we did, and never knew that cars could turn such sharp corners. We wound about so that we could see the engine whisking out of sight round one corner while we were turning another, and the long train looked like a snake winding through the hills. The tunnels were so long that lamps were lighted, and so cold we put on our sacks while passing in the darkness. The scenery was very fine ; and after we left Lyons, where we merely slept, the Alps began to appear, and May and I stared in blissful silence ; for we had two tall old men opposite, and a little priest, so young that we called him the Rev. boy. He slept and said his prayers most of the time, stealing sly looks at May's hair, A.'s pretty hands, and my buckled shoes, which were like his own and seemed to strike him as a liberty on my part. The old boys were very jolly, especially the one with three chins, who smiled paternally upon us and tried to talk. But we were very English and mum, and he thought we did n't understand French, and confided to his friend that he did n't see "how the English could travel and know not the French tongue." They sang, gabbled, slept, and slapped one another at intervals, and were very amusing till they left, and another very handsome Booth-like priest took their places.

To her Father.

BEX, July 14, 1870.

DEAR PA, — As I have not written to you yet, I will send you a picture-letter and tell you about the very interesting old Count Sz— who is here. This morning he asked us to go to the hills and see some curious trees which he says were planted from acorns and nuts brought from Mexico by Atala. We found some very ancient oaks and chestnuts, and the enthusiastic old man told us the story about the Druids who once had a church, amphitheatre, and sacrifical altar up there. No one knows much about it, and he imagines a good deal to suit his own pet theory. You would have liked to hear him hold forth about the races and Zoroaster, Plato, etc. He is a Hungarian of a very old family, descended from Semiramide and Zenobia. He believes that the body can be cured often by influencing the soul, and that doctors should be priests, and priests doctors, as the two affect the body and soul which depend on one another. He is doing a great deal for Miss W., who has tried many doctors and got no help. I never saw such a kindly, simple, enthusiastic, old soul, for at sixty-seven he is as full of hope and faith and good-will as a young man. I told him I should like my father to see a little book he has written, and he is going to give me one.

We like this quiet little place among the mountains, and pass lazy days ; for it is very warm, and we sit about on our balconies enjoying the soft air, the moonlight, and the changing aspect of the hills.

May had a fine exciting time going up St. Bernard, and is now ready for another. . . .

The Polish Countess and her daughter have been reading my books and are charmed with them. Madame says she is not obliged to turn down any pages so that the girls may not read them, as she does in many books, " All is so true, so sweet, so pious, she may read every word."

I send by this mail the count's little pamphlet. I don't know as it amounts to much, but I thought you might like to see it.

Love to every one, and write often to your

Affectionate daughter   L. M. A.

BEX, July 18, 1870.

DEAR PEOPLE, — The breaking out of this silly little war between France and Prussia will play the deuce with our letters. I have had none from you for a long time ; and Alexandre, the English waiter here, says that the mails will be left to come as they can, for the railroads are all devoted to carrying troops to the seat of war. The French have already crossed the Rhine, and rumors of a battle came last eve ; but the papers have not arrived, and no letters for any one, so all are fuming for news, public and private, and I am howling for my home letter, which is more important than all the papers on the continent. . . .

Don't be worried if you don't hear regularly, or think us in danger. Switzerland is out of the mess, and if she gets in, we can skip over into Italy, and be as cosey as possible. It will make some difference in money, perhaps, as Munroe in Paris˚ is our banker, and we shall be plagued about our letters, otherwise the war won't effect us a bit; I dare say you know as much about it as we do, and Marmee is predicting "a civil war" all over the world. We hear accounts of the frightful heat with you. Don't wilt away before we come. . . .

Lady Amberley is a trump, and I am glad she says a word for her poor sex though she *is* a peeress. . . .

I should like to have said of me what Hedge says of Dickens; and when I die, I should prefer such a memory rather than a tomb in Westminster Abbey.

. . . .

I hope to have a good letter from Nan soon. May does the descriptions so well that I don't try it, being lazy.   Lu.

To Anna.

Sunday, July 24, 1870.

. . . The war along the Rhine is sending troops of travellers to Switzerland for refuge; and all the large towns are brimful of people flying from Germany. It won't trouble us, for we have done France and don't mean to do Germany. So when August is over, we shall trot forward to Italy, and find a warm place for our winter-quarters. At any time twenty-four hours carries us over the Simplon, so we sit at ease and don't care a straw for old France and Prussia. Russia, it is reported, has joined in the fight, but Italy and England are not going to meddle, so we can fly to either "in case of fire." [1]

---

[1] This was a family joke as Mrs. Alcott always ended her in-structions to her children " in case of fire."

BEX, July 27, 1870.

We heard of Dickens's death some weeks ago and have been reading notices, etc., in all the papers since. One by G. Greenwood in the Tribune was very nice. I shall miss my old Charlie, but he is not the old idol he once was. . . .

Did you know that Higginson and a little girl friend had written out the Operatic Tragedy in " Little Women " and set the songs to music and it was all to be put in " Our Young Folks." What are we coming to in our old age? Also I hope to see the next designs N. has got for " Little Women." I know nothing about them.

To her Mother.

3 P.M., BEX, July 31, 1870.

Papers are suppressed by the Government so we know nothing about the war, except the rumors that float about. But people seem to think that Europe is in for a general fight, and there is no guessing when it will end.

The trouble about getting into Italy is, that civil war always breaks out there and things are so mixed up that strangers get into scrapes among the different squabblers. When the P.'s were abroad during the last Italian fuss, they got shut up in some little city and would have been killed by Austrians, who were rampaging round the place drunk and mad, if a woman had not hid them in a closet for a day and night, and smuggled them out at last, when they ran for their lives. I don't mean to get into any mess, and between Switzerland and England we can manage for a winter. London is so near home and so home-like that we shall be quite handy and can run up to Boston at any time. Perhaps Pa will step across to see us.

All these plans may be knocked in the head to-morrow and my next letter may be dated from the Pope's

best parlor or Windsor Castle ; but I like to spin about on
ups and downs so you can have something to talk about
at Apple Slump. Uncertainty gives a relish to things, so
we chase about and have a dozen plans a day. It is an
Alcott failing you know. . . .

Love to all and bless you,

Ever yours, Lu.

BEX, Aug. 7, 1870.

DEAR MR. NILES, — I keep receiving requests from
editors to write for their papers and magazines. I am
truly grateful, but having come abroad for rest I am not
inclined to try the treadmill till my year's vacation is
over. So to appease these worthy gentlemen and excuse
my seeming idleness I send you a trifle in rhyme,[1] which
you can (if you think it worth the trouble) set going as
a general answer to everybody; for I can't pay postage
in replies to each separately, — "it's very costly." Mr.
F. said he would pay me $10, $15, $20 for any little
things I would send him; so perhaps you will let him
have it first.

The war makes the bankers take double toll on our
money, so we feel very poor and as if we ought to be
earning, not spending; only we are *so* lazy we can't bear
to think of it in earnest. . . .

We shall probably go to London next month if the
war forbid Italy for the winter; and if we can't get one
dollar without paying five for it, we shall come home
disgusted.

Perhaps if I can do nothing else this year I could have
a book of short stories, old and new, for Christmas. F.
and F. have some good ones, and I have the right to
use them. We could call them "Jo March's Necessity

---

[1] This is the poem prefixed to the chapter.

Stories." Would it go with new ones added and good illustrations?

I am rising from my ashes in a most phœnix-like manner.   L. M. A.

To her Mother.

VEVAY, PENSION PARADIS, Aug. 11, 1870.

DEAR MARMEE, — . . . This house is very cosey, and the food excellent. I thought it would be when I heard gentlemen liked it, — they always want good fodder. There are only three now, — an old Spaniard and his son, and a young Frenchman. We see them at meals, and the girls play croquet with them. . . .

This is the gay season here, and in spite of the war Vevay is full. The ex-Queen of Spain and her family are here at the Grand Hotel; also Don Carlos, the rightful heir to the Spanish throne. Our landlady says that her house used to be full of Spaniards, who every day went in crowds to call on the two kings, Alphonse and Carlos. We see brown men and women with black eyes driving round in fine coaches, with servants in livery, who I suppose are the Court people.

The papers tell us that the French have lost two big battles; the Prussians are in Strasbourg, and Paris in a state of siege. The papers are also full of theatrical messages from the French to the people, asking them to come up and be slaughtered for *la patrie*, and sober, cool reports from the Prussians. I side with the Prussians, for they sympathized with us in our war. Hooray for old Pruss! . . .

France is having a bad time. Princess Clotilde passed through Geneva the other day with loads of baggage, flying to Italy; and last week a closed car with the imperial arms on it went by here in the night, — supposed to be Matilde and other royal folks flying away from Paris. The Prince Imperial has been sent home from the seat of war; and poor Eugénie is doing her best to keep things quiet in Paris. The French here say that a republic is already talked of; and the Emperor is on his last legs in every way. He is sick, and his doctor won't let him ride, and so nervous he can't command the army as he wanted to. Poor old man! one can't help pitying him when all his plans fail.

We still dawdle along, getting fat and hearty. The food is excellent. A breakfast of coffee and tip-top bread, fresh butter, with eggs or fried potatoes, at 8; a real French dinner at 1.30, of soup, fish, meat, game, salad, sweet messes, and fruit, with wine; and at 7 cold meat, salad, sauce, tea, and bread and butter. It is grape time now, and for a few cents we get pounds, on which we feast all day at intervals. We walk and play as well as any one, and feel so well I ought to do something. . . .

Fred and Jack would like to look out of my window now and see the little boys playing in the lake. They are there all day long like little pigs, and lie around on the warm stones to dry, splashing one another for exercise. One boy, having washed himself, is now washing his clothes, and all lying out to dry together. . . .

Ever yours, Lu.

To Anna.

VEVAY, Aug. 21, 1870.

I had such a droll dream last night I must tell you. I thought I was returning to Concord after my trip, and was alone. As I walked from the station I missed Mr. Moore's house, and turning the corner, found the scene so changed that I did not know where I was. Our house was gone, and in its place stood a great gray stone castle, with towers and arches and lawns and bridges, very fine and antique. Somehow I got into it without meeting any one of you, and wandered about trying to find my family. At last I came across Mr. Moore, papering a room, and asked him where his house was. He did n't know me, and said, —

"Oh! I sold it to Mr. Alcott for his school, and we live in Acton now."

"Where did Mr. Alcott get the means to build this great concern?" I asked.

"Well, he *gave* his own land, and took the great pasture his daughter left him, — the one that died some ten years ago."

"So I am dead, am I?" says I to myself, feeling so queerly.

"Government helped build this place, and Mr. A. has a fine college here," said Mr. Moore, papering away again.

I went on, wondering at the news, and looked into a glass to see how I looked dead. I found myself a fat old lady, with gray hair and specs, — very like E. P. P. I laughed, and coming to a Gothic window, looked out and saw hundreds of young men and boys in a queer flowing dress, roaming about the parks and lawns; and among them was Pa, looking as he looked thirty years ago, with brown hair and a big white neckcloth, as in the old times. He looked so plump and placid and young and happy I was charmed to see him, and nodded; but he did n't know me; and I was so grieved and troubled at being a Rip Van Winkle, I cried, and said I had better go away and not disturb any one, — and in the midst of my woe, I woke up. It was all so clear and funny, I can't help thinking that it may be a foreshadowing of something real. I used to dream of being famous, and it has partly become true; so why not Pa's college blossom, and he get young and happy with his disciples? I only hope he won't quite forget me when I come back, fat and gray and old. Perhaps his dream is to come in another world, where everything is fresh and calm, and the reason why he did n't recognize me was because I was still in this work-a-day world, and so felt old and strange in this lovely castle in the air. Well, he is welcome to my fortune ; but the daughter who did die ten years ago is more likely to be the one who helped him build his School of Concord up aloft.

I can see how the dream came ; for I had been looking at Silling's boys in their fine garden, and wishing I could go in and know the dear little lads walking about there, in the forenoon. I had got a topknot at the barber's, and talked about my gray hairs, and looking in the glass thought how fat and old I was getting, and had shown the B.'s Pa's picture, which they thought saintly, etc. I believe in dreams, though I am free to confess that "cowcumbers" for tea may have been the basis of this "ally-gorry-cal wision." . . .

As we know the Consul at Spezzia, — that is, we have letters to him, as well as to many folks in Rome, etc., — I guess we shall go ; for the danger of Europe getting into the fight is over now, and we can sail to England or home any time from Italy. . . . Love to every one.

Kiss my *cousin* for me.

Ever your LU.

To Mr. Niles.

AUGUST 23, 1870.

Your note of August 2 has just come, with a fine budget of magazines and a paper, for all of which many thanks.

.   .   .   .

Don't give my address to any one. I don't want the young ladies' notes. They can send them to Concord, and I shall get them next year.

. . . .

The boys at Silling's school are a perpetual source of delight to me ; and I stand at the gate, like the Peri, longing to go in and play with the lads. The young ladies who want to find live Lauries can be supplied here, for Silling has a large assortment always on hand.

My B. says she is constantly trying to incite me to literary effort, but I hang fire. So I do, — but only that I may go off with a bang by and by, *à la mitrailleuse.*

L. M. A.

To her Family.

VEVAY, Aug. 29, 1870.

DEAR PEOPLE, — . . . M. Nicaud, the owner of this house, — a funny old man, with a face so like a parrot that we call him M. Perrot, — asked us to come and visit him at his *châlet* up among the hills. He is building a barn there, and stays to see that all goes well; so we only see him on Sundays, when he convulses us by his funny ways. Last week seven of us went up in a big landau, and the old dear entertained us like a prince. We left the carriage at the foot of a little steep path, and climbed up to the dearest old *châlet* we ever saw. Here Pa Nicaud met us, took us up the outside steps into his queer little salon, and regaled us with his sixty-year old wine and nice little cakes. We then set forth, in spite of clouds and wind, to view the farm and wood. It showered at intervals, but no one seemed to care ; so we trotted about under umbrellas, getting mushrooms, flowers, and colds, viewing the Tarpeian Rock, and sitting on rustic seats to enjoy the *belle vue*, which consisted of fog. It was such a droll lark that we laughed and ran, and enjoyed the damp picnic very much. Then we had a tip-top Swiss dinner, followed by coffee, three sorts of wine, and cigars. Every one smoked, and as it poured guns, the old Perrot had a blazing fire made, round which we sat, talking many languages, singing, and revelling. We had hardly got through dinner and seen another foggy view when tea was announced, and we stuffed again, having pitchers of cream, fruit, and a queer but very nice dish of slices of light bread dipped in egg and fried, and eaten with sugar. The buxom Swiss maid flew and grinned, and kept serving up some new mess from her tiny dark kitchen. It cleared off, and we walked home in spite of our immense exploits in the eating line. Old Perrot escorted us part way down, and we gave three cheers for him as we parted. Then we showed Madame and the French governess and Don Juan (the Spanish boy) some tall walking, though the roads were very steep and rough and muddy. We tramped some five miles; and our party (May, A., the governess, and I) got home long before Madame and Don Juan, who took a short cut, and would n't believe that we did n't get a lift somehow. I felt quite proud of my old pins; for they were not tired, and none the worse for the long walk. I think they are really all right now, for the late cold weather has not troubled them in the least; and I sleep — O ye gods, how I do sleep ! — ten or twelve hours sound, and get up so drunk with dizziness it is lovely to see. Aint I grateful? Oh, yes ! oh, yes !

We began French lessons to-day, May and I, of the French governess, — a kind old girl who only asks two francs a lesson. We *must* speak the language, for it is disgraceful to be so stupid ; so we have got to work, and mean to be able to *parlez-vous* or die. The war is still a nuisance, and we may be here some time, and really need some work; for we are so lazy we shall be spoilt, if we don't fall to. . . .

I gave Count C. Pa's message, and he was pleased. He reads no English, and is going to Hungary soon; so Pa had better not send the book. . . .   Lu.

VEVAY, Sept. 10, 1870.

DEAR PEOPLE, — As all Europe seems to be going to destruction, I hasten to drop a line before the grand smash arrives. We mean to skip over the Alps next week, if weather and war permit; for we are bound to see Milan and the lakes, even if we have to turn and come back without a glimpse of Rome. The Pope is beginning to perk up; and Italy and England and Russia seem ready to join in the war, now that France is down. Think of Paris being bombarded and smashed up like Strasbourg. We never shall see the grand old cathedral at Strasbourg now, it is so spoilt.

Vevay is crammed with refugees from Paris and Strasbourg. Ten families applied here yesterday. . . .

Our house is brimful, and we have funny times. The sick Russian lady and her old Ma make a great fuss if a breath of air comes in at meal times, and expect twenty people to sit shut tight in a smallish room for an hour on a hot day. We protested, and Madame put them in the parlor, where they glower as we pass, and lock the door when they can. The German Professor is learning English, and is a quiet, pleasant man. The Polish General, a little cracked, is very droll, and bursts out in the middle of the general chat with stories about transparent apples and golden horses. . . . Benda, the crack book-and-picture man, has asked May if she was the Miss Alcott who wrote the popular books; for he said he had many calls for them, and wished to know where they could be found. We told him "at London," and felt puffed up. . . .

May and I delve away at French; but it makes my head ache, and I don't learn enough to pay for the trouble. I never could *study*, you know, and suffer such agony when I try that it is piteous to behold. The little brains I have left I want to keep for future works, and not exhaust them on grammar, — vile invention of Satan! May gets on slowly, and don't have fits after it; so she had better go on (the lessons only cost two francs). . . . L. M. A.

To her Mother.

LAGO DI COMO, Oct. 8, 1870.

DEAREST MARMEE, — A happy birthday, and many of em! Here we actually are in the long-desired Italy, and find it as lovely as we hoped. Our journey was a perfect success, — sunlight, moonlight, magnificent scenery, pleasant company, no mishaps, and one long series of beautiful pictures all the way.

Crossing the Simplon is an experience worth having; for without any real danger, fatigue, or hardship, one sees some of the finest as well as most awful parts of these wonderful Alps.

The road, — a miracle in itself! for all Nature seems to protest against it, and the elements never tire of trying to destroy it. Only a Napoleon would have dreamed of making a path through such a place; and he only cared for it as a way to get his men and cannon into an enemy's country by this truly royal road.

May has told you about our trip; so I will only add a few bits that she forgot.

Our start in the dawn from Brieg, with two diligences, a carriage, and a cart, was something between a funeral

and a caravan: first an immense diligence with seven
horses, then a smaller one with four, then oui *calèche*
with two, and finally the carrier's cart with one.   It was
very exciting, — the general gathering of sleepy travellers
in the dark square, the tramping of horses, the packing
in, the grand stir of getting off; then the slow winding
up, up, up out of the valley toward the sun, which came
slowly over the great hills, rising as we never saw it rise
before.   The still, damp pine-forests kept us in shadow
a long time after the white mountain-tops began to shine.
Little by little we wound through a great gorge, and then
the sun came dazzling between these grand hills, showing
us a new world.   Peak after peak of the Bernese Ober-
land rose behind us, and great white glaciers lay before
us; while the road crept like a narrow line, in and out
over chasms that made us dizzy to look at, under tunnels,
and through stone galleries with windows over which
dashed waterfalls from the glaciers above.   Here and
there were refuges, a hospice, and a few *châlets*, where
shepherds live their wild, lonely lives.   In the P. M.
we drove rapidly down toward Italy through the great
Valley of Gondo, — a deep rift in rock thousands of feet
deep, and just wide enough for the road and a wild stream
that was our guide; a never-to-be-forgotten place, and a
fit gateway to Italy, which soon lay smiling below us.
The change is very striking; and when we came to Lago
Maggiore lying in the moonlight we could only sigh for
happiness, and love and look and look.   After a good
night's rest at Stresa, we went in a charming gondola-sort
of boat to see Isola Bella, — the island you see in the
chromo over the fireplace at home, — a lovely island,
with famous castle, garden, and town on it.   The day was
as balmy as summer, and we felt like butterflies after a
frost, and fluttered about, enjoying the sunshine all day.

A sail by steamer brought us to Luino, where we went on the diligence to Lugano. Moonlight all the way, and a gay driver, who wound his horn as we clattered into market-places and over bridges in the most gallant style. The girls were on top, and in a state of rapture all the way. After supper in a vaulted, frescoed hall, with marble floors, pillars, and galleries, we went to a room which had green doors, red carpet, blue walls, and yellow bed-covers, — all so gay! It was like sleeping i.ı rainbow.

As if a heavenly lake under our windows with moonlight *ad libitum* was n't enough, we had music next door; and on leaning out of a little back window, we made the splendid discovery that we could look on to the stage of the opera-house across a little alley. My Nan can imagine with what rapture I stared at the scenes going on below me, and how I longed for her as I stood there wrapped in my yellow bed-quilt, and saw gallant knights in armor warble sweetly to plump ladies in masks, or pretty peasants fly wildly from ardent lovers in red tights; also a dishevelled maid who tore her hair in a forest, while a man aloft made thunder and lightning, — and *I saw him do it!*

It was the climax to a splendid day; for few travellers can go to the opera luxuriously in their night-gowns, and take naps between the acts as I did.

A lovely sail next morning down the lake; then a carriage to Menaggio; and then a droll boat, like a big covered market-wagon with a table and red-cushioned seats, took us and our trunks to Cadenabbia, for there is only a donkey road to the little town. At the hotel on the edge of the lake we found Nelly L., a sweet girl as lovely as Minnie, and so glad to see us; for since her mother died in Venice last year she has lived alone with her maid. She had waited for us, and next day went to

Milan, where we join her on Monday. She paints; and May and she made plans at once to study together, and enjoy some of the free art-schools at Milan and Naples or Florence, if we can all be together. It is a great chance for May, and I mean she shall have a good time, and not wait for tools and teachers; for all is in the way of her profession, and of use to her.

Cadenabbia is only two hotels and a few villas opposite Bellagio, which is a town, and fashionable. We were rowed over to see it by our boatman, who spends his time at the front of the stone steps before the hotel, and whenever we go out he tells us, "The lake is tranquil; the hour is come for a walk on the water," and is as coaxing as only an Italian can be. He is amiably tipsy most of the time.

To-day it rains so we cannot go out, and I rest and write to my Marmee in a funny room with a stone floor inlaid till it looks like castile soap, a ceiling in fat cupids and trumpeting fairies, a window on the lake, with balcony, etc. Hand-organs with jolly singing boys jingle all day, and two big bears go by led by a man with a drum. The boys would laugh to see them dance on their hind legs, and shoulder sticks like soldiers.

. . . All looks well, and if the winter goes on rapidly and pleasantly as the summer we shall soon be thinking of home, unless one of us decides to stay. I shall post this at Milan to-morrow, and hope to find letters there from you. By-by till then.

Journal.

October, 1870. — A memorable month. . . . Off for Italy on the 2d. A splendid journey over the Alps and Maggiore by moonlight.

Heavenly days at the lakes, and so to Milan, Parma,
Pisa, Bologna, and Florence. Disappointed in some
things, but found Nature always lovely and wonderful;
so did n't mind faded pictures, damp rooms, and the
cold winds of "sunny Italy." Bought furs at Florence,
and arrived in Rome one rainy night.

November 10*th.* — In Rome, and felt as if I had been
there before and knew all about it. Always oppressed
with a sense of sin, dirt, and general decay of all things.
Not well; so saw things through blue glasses. May in
bliss with lessons, sketching, and her dreams. A. had
society, her house, and old friends. The artists were
the best company; counts and princes very dull, what
we saw of them. May and I went off on the Cam-
pagna, and criticised all the world like two audacious
Yankees.

Our apartment in Piazza Barbarini was warm and
cosey; and I thanked Heaven for it, as it rained for
two months, and my first view most of the time was the
poor Triton with an icicle on his nose.

We pay $60 a month for six good rooms, and $6 a
month for a girl, who cooks and takes care of us.

29*th.* — My thirty-eighth birthday. May gave me a
pretty sketch, and A. a fine nosegay.

In Rome Miss Alcott was shocked and grieved by
the news of the death of her well-beloved brother-
in-law, Mr. Pratt. She has drawn so beautiful a
picture of him in "Little Women" and in "Little
Men," that it is hardly needful to dwell upon his
character or the grief which his death caused her.
With her usual care for others, her thoughts at
once turned to the support of the surviving family,
and she found comfort in writing "Little Men"

with the thought of the dear sister and nephews constantly in her heart.

In spite of this great sorrow and anxiety for the dear ones at home, the year of travel was very refreshing to her. Her companions were congenial, she took great delight in her sister's work, and she was independent in her plans, and could go whither and when she would.

The voyage home was a hard one; there was small-pox on board, but Miss Alcott fortunately escaped the infection. "Little Men" was out the day she arrived, as a bright red placard in the carriage announced, and besides all the loving welcomes from family and friends, she received the pleasing news that fifty thousand of the books were already sold.

But the old pains and weariness came home with her also. She could not stay in Concord, and went again to Boston, hoping to rest and work. Her young sister came home to brighten up the family with her hopeful, helpful spirit.

At forty years of age Louisa had accomplished the task she set for herself in youth. By unceasing toil she had made herself and her family independent; debts were all paid, and enough was invested to preserve them from want. And yet wants seemed to increase with their satisfaction, and she felt impelled to work enough to give to all the enjoyments and luxuries which were fitted to them after the necessaries were provided for. It may be that her own exhausted nervous condition made it impossible for her to rest, and the demand which she fancied came from without was the projection of her own thought.

Journal.

1871. — *Rome.* — Great inundation. Streets flooded, churches with four feet of water in them, and queer times for those who were in the overflowed quarters. Meals hoisted up at the window; people carried across the river-like streets to make calls; and all manner of funny doings. We were high and dry at Piazza Barbarini, and enjoyed the flurry.

To the Capitol often, to spend the A. M. with the Roman emperors and other great men. M. Aurelius as a boy was fine; Cicero looked very like W. Phillips; Agrippina in her chair was charming; but the other ladies, with hair *à la sponge*, were ugly; Nero & Co. a set of brutes and bad men. But a better sight to me was the crowd of poor people going to get the bread and money sent by the king; and the splendid snow-covered hills were finer than the marble beauty inside. Art tires; Nature never.

Professor Pierce and his party just from Sicily, where they had been to see the eclipse, — all beaming with delight, and well repaid for the long journey by a *two minutes'* squint at the sun when darkest.

Began to write a new book, "Little Men," that John's death may not leave A. and the dear little boys in want. John took care that they should have enough while the boys are young, and worked very hard to have a little sum to leave, without a debt anywhere.

In writing and thinking of the little lads, to whom I must be a father now, I found comfort for my sorrow. May went on with her lessons, "learning," as she wisely said, how little she knew and how to go on.

February. — A gay month in Rome, with the carnival, artists' fancy ball, many parties, and much calling.

Decided to leave May for another year, as L. sends $700 on "Moods," and the new book will provide $1,000 for the dear girl; so she may be happy and free to follow her talent.

March. — Spent at Albano. A lovely place. Walk, write, and rest. A troop of handsome officers from Turin, who clatter by, casting soft glances at my two blonde signorinas, who enjoy it very much.[1] Baron and Baroness Rothschild were there, and the W.'s from Philadelphia, Dr. O. W. and wife, and S. B. Mrs. W. and A. B. talk *all day*, May sketches, I write, and so we go on. Went to look at rooms at the Bonapartes.

April. — Venice. Floated about for two weeks seeing sights. A lovely city for a short visit. Not enough going on to suit brisk Americans. May painted, A. hunted up old jewelry and friends, and I dawdled after them.

A very interesting trip to London, — over the Brenner Pass to Munich, Cologne, Antwerp, and by boat to London.

May. — A busy month. Settled in lodgings, Brompton Road, and went sight-seeing. Mrs. P. Taylor, Conway, and others very kind. Enjoyed showing May my favorite places and people.

A. B. went home on the 11th, after a pleasant year with us. I am glad to know her, for she is true and very interesting. May took lessons of Rowbotham and was happy. "Little Men" came out in London.

I decided to go home on the 25th. as I am needed. A very pleasant year in spite of constant pain, John's death, and home anxieties. Very glad I came, for May's sake. It has been a very useful year for her.

June. — After an anxious passage of twelve days, got safely home. Small-pox on board, and my room-mate,

[1] See Shawl Straps, p. 179.

Miss D., very ill. I escaped, but had a sober time lying next door to her, waiting to see if my turn was to come. She was left at the island, and I went up the harbor with Judge Russell, who took some of us off in his tug.

Father and T. N. came to meet me with a great red placard of "Little Men" pinned up in the carriage. After due precautions, hurried home and found all well. My room refurnished and much adorned by Father's earnings.

Nan well and calm, but under her sweet serenity is a very sad soul, and she mourns for her mate like a tender turtle-dove.

The boys were tall, bright lads, devoted to Marmee, and the life of the house.

Mother feeble and much aged by this year of trouble. I shall never go far away from her again. Much company, and loads of letters, all full of good wishes and welcome.

"Little Men" was out the day I arrived. Fifty thousand sold before it was out.

A happy month, for I felt well for the first time in two years. I knew it would n't last, but enjoyed it heartily while it did, and was grateful for rest from pain and a touch of the old cheerfulness. It was much needed at home.

July, August, September. — Sick. Holiday soon over. Too much company and care and change of climate upset the poor nerves again. Dear Uncle S. J. May died; our best friend for years. Peace to his ashes. He leaves a sweeter memory behind him than any man I know. Poor Marmee is the last of her family now.

October. — Decided to go to B.; Concord is so hard for me, with its dampness and worry. Get two girls to do the work, and leave plenty of money and go to Beacon Street to rest and try to get well that I may work. A lazy life, but it seemed to suit; and anything is better than the invalidism I hate worse than death.

Bones ached less, and I gave up morphine, as sunshine, air, and quiet made sleep possible without it. Saw people, pictures, plays, and read all I could, but did not enjoy much, for the dreadful weariness of nerves makes even pleasure hard.

November. — May sent pleasant letters and some fine copies of Turner. She decides to come home, as she feels she is needed as I give out. Marmee is feeble, Nan has her boys and her sorrow, and one strong head and hand is wanted at home. A year and a half of holiday is a good deal, and duty comes first always. Sorry to call her back, but her eyes are troublesome, and housework will rest them and set her up. Then she can go again when I am better, for I don't want her to be thwarted in her work more than just enough to make her want it very much.

On the 19th she came. Well, happy, and full of sensible plans. A lively time enjoying the cheerful element she always brings into the house. Piles of pictures, merry adventures, and interesting tales of the fine London lovers.

Kept my thirty-ninth and Father's seventy-second birthday in the old way.

Thanksgiving dinner at Pratt Farm. All well and all together. Much to give thanks for.

December. — Enjoyed my quiet, sunny room very much; and this lazy life seems to suit me, for I am better, mind and body. All goes well at home, with May to run the machine in her cheery, energetic style, and amuse Marmee and Nan with gay histories. Had a

furnace put in, and all enjoyed the new climate. No
more rheumatic fevers and colds, with picturesque open
fires. Mother is to be cosey if money can do it. She
seems to be now, and my long-cherished dream has come
true; for she sits in a pleasant room, with no work, no
care, no poverty to worry, but peace and comfort all
about her, and children glad and able to stand between
trouble and her. Thank the Lord! I like to stop and
"remember my mercies." Working and waiting for them
makes them very welcome.

Went to the ball for the Grand Duke Alexis. A fine
sight, and the big blonde boy the best of all. Would
dance with the pretty girls, and leave the Boston dowa-
gers and their diamonds in the lurch.

To the Radical Club, where the philosophers mount
their hobbies and prance away into time and space, while
we gaze after them and try to look wise.

A merry Christmas at home. Tree for the boys,
family dinner, and frolic in the evening.

A varied, but on the whole a good year, in spite of
pain. Last Christmas we were in Rome, mourning for
John. What will next Christmas bring forth? I have no
ambition now but to keep the family comfortable and not
ache any more. Pain has taught me patience, I hope, if
nothing more.

January, 1872. — Roberts Brothers paid $4,400 as six
months' receipts for the books. A fine New Year's gift.
S. E. S. invested $3,000, and the rest I put in the bank
for family needs. Paid for the furnace and all the bills.
What bliss it is to be able to do that and ask no help!

. . . .

Mysterious bouquets came from some unknown admirer or friend. Enjoyed them very much, and felt
quite grateful and romantic as day after day the lovely

great nosegays were handed in by the servant of the unknown.

February and March. — At Mrs. Stowe's desire, wrote for the "Christian Union" an account of our journey through France, and called it "Shawl Straps." . . . Many calls and letters and invitations, but I kept quiet, health being too precious to risk, and sleep still hard to get for the brain that would work instead of rest.

Heard lectures, — Higginson, Bartol, Frothingham, and Rabbi Lilienthal. Much talk about religion. I'd like to see a little more really *lived.*

April and May. — Wrote another sketch for the "Independent," — "A French Wedding;" and the events of my travels paid my winter's expenses. All is fish that comes to the literary net. Goethe puts his joys and sorrows into poems; I turn my adventures into bread and butter.

.   .   .   .

June, 1872. — Home, and begin a new task. Twenty years ago I resolved to make the family independent if I could. At forty that is done. Debts all paid, even the outlawed ones, and we have enough to be comfortable. It has cost me my health, perhaps; but as I still live, there is more for me to do, I suppose.

From a photograph of Miss Alcott taken about 1862.

LOUISA M. ALCOTT'S FAMOUS BOOKS

"'I'm not hurt, all right in a minute,' he said, sitting up, a little pale and dizzy, as the boys gathered round him, full of admiration and alarm." — PAGE 2

LITTLE MEN; OR, LIFE AT PLUMFIELD WITH JO'S BOYS. Price, $1.50.

ROBERTS BROTHERS, *Publishers, Boston*

LOUISA M. ALCOTT'S FAMOUS BOOKS.

"Sing, Tessa, Sing!" cried Tommo, twanging away with all his might.—PAGE 47.

AUNT JO'S SCRAP-BAG: Containing "My Boys," "Shawl-Straps," "Cupid and Chow-Chow," "My Girls," "Jimmy's Cruise in the Pinafore," "An Old-Fashioned Thanksgiving." 6 vols. Price of each, $1.00.

ROBERTS BROTHERS, Publishers. *Boston.*

CHAPTER X.

FAMILY CHANGES.

TRANSFIGURATION.[1]

IN MEMORIAM.

Lines written by Louisa M. Alcott on the death of her mother.

> MYSTERIOUS death! who in a single hour
> Life's gold can so refine,
> And by thy art divine
> Change mortal weakness to immortal power!

> Bending beneath the weight of eighty years,
> Spent with the noble strife
> Of a victorious life,
> We watched her fading heavenward, through our tears.

> But ere the sense of loss our hearts had wrung,
> A miracle was wrought;
> And swift as happy thought
> She lived again,—brave, beautiful, and young.

> Age, pain, and sorrow dropped the veils they wore
> And showed the tender eyes
> Of angels in disguise,
> Whose discipline so patiently she bore.

> The past years brought their harvest rich and fair;
> While memory and love,
> Together, fondly wove
> A golden garland for the silver hair.

[1] This poem was first published anonymously in " The Masque of Poets," in 1878.

How could we mourn like those who are bereft,
    When every pang of grief
    Found balm for its relief
In counting up the treasures she had left ? —

Faith that withstood the shocks of toil and time;
    Hope that defied despair ;
    Patience that conquered care ;
And loyalty, whose courage was sublime ;

The great deep heart that was a home for all, —
    Just, eloquent, and strong
    In protest against wrong;
Wide charity, that knew no sin, no fall ;

The spartan spirit that made life so grand,
    Mating poor daily needs
    With high, heroic deeds,
That wrested happiness from Fate's hard hand.

We thought to weep, but sing for joy instead,
    Full of the grateful peace
    That follows her release ;
For nothing but the weary dust lies dead.

Oh, noble woman ! never more a queen
    Than in the laying down
    Of sceptre and of crown
To win a greater kingdom, yet unseen :

Teaching us how to seek the highest goal,
    To earn the true success, —
    To live, to love. to bless, —
And make death proud to take a royal soul.

THE history of the next six years offers little variety of incident in Miss Alcott's busy life. She could not work at home in Concord as well as in some quiet lodging in Boston, where she was more free from interruption from visitors; but she spent her summers with her mother, often taking charge of the housekeeping. In 1872 she wrote "Work," one of her most successful books. She had begun it some time before, and originally called it "Success." It represents her own personal experience more than any other book. She says to a friend: "Christie's adventures are many of them my own; Mr. Power is Mr. Parker; Mrs. Wilkins is imaginary, and all the rest. This was begun at eighteen, and never finished till H. W. Beecher wrote to me for a serial for the 'Christian Union' in 1872, and paid $3,000 for it."

Miss Alcott again sent May to Europe in 1873 to finish her studies, and herself continued writing stories to pay the expenses of the family. The mother's serious illness weighed heavily on Louisa's heart, and through the summer of 1873 she was devoted to the invalid, rejoicing in her partial recovery, though sadly feeling that she would never be her bright energetic self again. Mrs. Alcott was able, however, to keep her birthday (October 8) pleasantly, and out of this experience came a story called "A Happy Birthday." This little tale paid for carriages for the invalid. It is included in "Aunt Jo's Scrap-Bag."

Louisa and her mother decided to spend the winter in Boston, while Mr. Alcott was at the West. Her thoughts dwell much upon her father's life, and she is not content that he has not all the recognition and enjoyment that she would gladly give him. She helps her mother to perform the sacred duty of placing a tablet on Colonel May's grave, and the dear old lady recognizes that her life has gone down into the past, and says, "This is n't my Boston, and I never want to see it any more."

Louisa was at this time engaged in writing for "St. Nicholas" and "The Independent."

The return of the young artist, happy in her success, brings brightness to the home-circle. In the winter of 1875 Miss Alcott takes her old place at the Bellevue, where May can have her drawing-classes. She was herself ill, and the words, "No sleep without morphine!" tell the story of nervous suffering.

Journal.

July, 1872. — May makes a lovely hostess, and I fly round behind the scenes, or skip out of the back window when ordered out for inspection by the inquisitive public. Hard work to keep things running smoothly, for this sight-seeing fiend is a new torment to us.

August. — May goes to Clark's Island for rest, having kept hotel long enough. I say "No," and shut the door. People *must* learn that authors have some rights; I can't entertain a dozen a day, and write the tales they demand also. I'm but a human worm, and when walked on must turn in self-defence.

Reporters sit on the wall and take notes; artists sketch me as I pick pears in the garden; and strange women interview Johnny as he plays in the orchard.

It looks like impertinent curiosity to me; but it is called "fame," and considered a blessing to be grateful for, I find. Let 'em try it.

September. — To Wolcott, with Father and Fred. A quaint, lovely old place is the little house on Spindle Hill, where the boy Amos dreamed the dreams that have come true at last.

Got hints for my novel, "The Cost of an Idea," if I ever find time to write it.

Don't wonder the boy longed to climb those hills, and see what lay beyond.

October. — Went to a room in Allston Street, in a quiet, old-fashioned house. I can't work at home, and need to be alone to spin, like a spider.

Rested; walked; to the theatre now and then. Home once a week with books, etc., for Marmee and Nan. Prepared "Shawl Straps" for Roberts.

November. — Forty on the 29th. Got Father off for the West, all neat and comfortable. I enjoyed every penny spent, and had a happy time packing his new trunk with warm flannels, neat shirts, gloves, etc., and seeing the dear man go off in a new suit, overcoat, hat, and all, like a gentleman. We both laughed over the pathetic old times with tears in our eyes, and I reminded him of the "poor as poverty, but serene as heaven" saying.

Something to do came just as I was trying to see what to take up, for work is my salvation. H. W. Beecher sent one of the editors of the "Christian Union" to ask for a serial story. They have asked before, and offered $2,000, which I refused; now they offered $3,000, and I accepted.

Got out the old manuscript of "Success," and called it "Work." Fired up the engine, and plunged into a vortex, with many doubts about getting out. Can't work slowly; the thing possesses me, and I must obey till it 's done. One thousand dollars was sent as a seal on the bargain, so I was bound, and sat at the oar like a galley-slave.

F. wanted eight little tales, and offered $35 apiece; used to pay $10. Such is fame! At odd minutes I wrote the short ones, and so paid my own expenses. "Shawl Straps," Scrap-Bag, No. 2, came out, and went well.

Great Boston fire; up all night. Very splendid and terrible sight.

December. — Busy with "Work." Write three pages at once on impression paper, as Beecher, Roberts, and Low of London all want copy at once.

[This was the cause of the paralysis of my thumb, which disabled me for the rest of my life. — L. M. A.]

Nan and the boys came to visit me, and break up the winter. Rested a little, and played with them.

Father very busy and happy. On his birthday had a gold-headed cane given him. He is appreciated out there.

During these western trips, Mr. Alcott found that his daughter's fame added much to the warmth of his reception. On his return he loved to tell how he was welcomed as the " grandfather of ' Little Women.' " When he visited schools, he delighted the young audiences by satisfying their curiosity as to the author of their favorite book, and the truth of the characters and circumstances described in it.

BOSTON, 1872.

DEAR MARMEE, — Had a very transcendental day yesterday, and at night my head was " swelling wisibly " with the ideas cast into it.

The club was a funny mixture of rabbis and weedy old ladies, the " oversoul " and oysters. Papa and B. flew clean out of sight like a pair of Platonic balloons, and we tried to follow, but could n't.

In the P.M. went to R. W. E.'s reading. All the literary birds were out in full feather. This " 'umble " worm was treated with distinguished condescension. Dr. B. gave me his noble hand to press, and murmured compliments with the air of a bishop bestowing a benediction. Dear B. beamed upon me from the depths of his funny little cloak and said, "We are getting on well, ain't we?" W. bowed his Jewish head, and rolled his fine eye at me. Several dreadful women purred about me, and I fled.

M. said what I liked, — that he 'd sent my works to his mother, and the good old lady told him to tell me that she could n't do a stroke of work, but just sat and read 'em right through; she wished she was young so as to have a long life in which to keep on enjoying such books. The peacock liked that.

I have paid all my own expenses out of the money earned by my little tales; so I have not touched the family income.

Did n't mean to write; but it has been an expensive winter, and my five hundred has made me all right. The $500 I lent K. makes a difference in the income; but I could not refuse her, she was so kind in the old hard times

At the reading a man in front of me sat listening and knitting his brows for a time, but had to give it up and go to sleep. After it was over some one said to him, "Well, what do you think of it?" "It 's all very fine I have no doubt; but I 'm blessed if I can understand a word of it," was the reply. . . .

The believers glow when the oracle is stuck, rustle and beam when he is audible, and nod and smile as if they understood perfectly when he murmurs under the desk! We are a foolish set!

Journal.

January, 1873. — Getting on well with "Work;" have to go slowly now for fear of a break-down. All well at home.

A week at Newport with Miss Jane Stewart. Dinners, balls, calls, etc. Saw Higginson and " H. H." Soon tired of gayety, and glad to get home to my quiet den and pen.

Roberts Brothers paid me $2,022 for books. S. E. S. invested most of it, with the $1,000 F. sent. Gave C. M. $100, — a thank-offering for my success. I like to help the class of "silent poor" to which we belonged for so many years, — needy, but respectable, and forgotten because too proud to beg. Work difficult to find for such people, and life made very hard for want of a little money to ease the necessary needs.

February and March. — Anna very ill with pneumonia; home to nurse her. Father telegraphed to come home. as we thought her dying. She gave me her boys; but the dear saint got well, and kept the lads for herself. Thank God!

Back to my work with what wits nursing left me.

Had Johnny for a week, to keep all quiet at home. Enjoyed the sweet little soul very much, and sent him back much better.

Finished " Work," — twenty chapters. Not what it should be, — too many interruptions. Should like to do one book in peace, and see if it would n't be good.

April. — The job being done I went home to take May's place. Gave her $1,000, and sent her to London for a year of study. She sailed on the 26th, brave and happy and hopeful. I felt that she needed it, and was glad to be able to help her.

I spent seven months in Boston; wrote a book and ten tales; earned $3,250 by my pen, and am satisfied with my winter's work.

May. — D. F. wanted a dozen little tales, and agreed to pay $50 apiece, if I give up other things for this.

Said I would, as I can do two a day, and keep house between times. Cleaned and grubbed, and did n't mind
the change. Let head rest, and heels and feet do the
work.

Cold and dull; but the thought of May free and happy
was my comfort as I messed about.

June and July. — Settled the servant question by getting a neat American woman to cook and help me with
the housework.

Peace fell upon our troubled souls, and all went well.
Good meals, tidy house, cheerful service, and in the P. M.
an intelligent young person to read and sew with us.

It was curious how she came to us. She had taught
and sewed, and was tired, and wanted something else;
decided to try for a housekeeper's place, but happened
to read "Work," and thought she 'd do as Christie did,
— take anything that came.

I was the first who answered her advertisement, and
when she found I wrote the book, she said, "I 'll go and
see if Miss A. practises as she preaches."

She found I did, and we had a good time together.
My new helper did so well I took pale Johnny to the
seaside for a week; but was sent for in haste, as poor
Marmee was very ill. Mental bewilderment came after
one of her heart troubles (the dropsy affected the brain),
and for three weeks we had a sad time. Father and I
took care of her, and my good A. S. kept house nicely
and faithfully for me.

Marmee slowly came back to herself, but sadly feeble,
— never to be our brave, energetic leader any more.
She felt it, and it was hard to convince her that there was
no need of her doing anything but rest.

August, September, October. — Mother improved steadily. Father went to the Alcott festival in Walcott, A

and boys to Conway for a month; and it did them all much good.

I had quiet days with Marmee; drove with her, and had the great pleasure of supplying all her needs and fancies.

May busy and happy in London. A merry time on Mother's birthday, October 8. All so glad to have her still here; for it seemed as if we were to lose her.

Made a little story of it for F., — "A Happy Birthday," — and spent the $50 in carriages for her.

November and December. — Decided that it was best not to try a cold, lonely winter in C., but go to B. with Mother, Nan, and boys, and leave Father free for the West.

Took sunny rooms at the South End, near the Park, so the lads could play out and Marmee walk. She enjoyed the change, and sat at her window watching people, horse-cars, and sparrows with great interest. Old friends came to see her, and she was happy. Found a nice school for the boys; and Nan enjoyed her quiet days.

January, 1874. — Mother quite ill this month. Dr. Wesselhoeft does his best for the poor old body, now such a burden to her. The slow decline has begun, and she knows it, having nursed her mother to the same end.

Father disappointed and rather sad, to be left out of so much that he would enjoy and should be asked to help and adorn. A little more money, a pleasant house and time to attend to it, and I 'd bring all the best people to see and entertain *him*. When I see so much twaddle going on I wonder those who can don't get up something better, and have really good things.

When I had the youth I had no money; now I have the money I have no time; and when I get the time, if

I ever do, I shall have no health to enjoy life. I suppose it's the discipline I need; but it's rather hard to love the things I do and see them go by because duty chains me to my galley. If I come into port at last with all sail set that will be reward perhaps.

Life always was a puzzle to me, and gets more mysterious as I go on. I shall find it out by and by and see that it's all right, if I can only keep brave and patient to the end.

May still in London painting Turners, and doing pretty panels as "pot-boilers." They sell well, and she is a thrifty child. Good luck to our mid-summer girl.

February. — Father has several conversations at the Clubs and Societies and Divinity School. No one pays anything; but they seem glad to listen. There ought to be a place for him.

Nan busy with her boys, and they doing well at school, — good, gay, and intelligent; a happy mother and most loving little sons.

I wrote two tales, and got $200. Saw Charles Kingsley, — a pleasant man. His wife has Alcott relations, and likes my books. Asked us to come and see him in England; is to bring his daughters to Concord by and by.

March. — May came home with a portfolio full of fine work. Must have worked like a busy bee to have done so much.

Very happy in her success; for she has proved her talent, having copied Turner so well that Ruskin (meeting her in the National Gallery at work) told her that she had "caught Turner's spirit wonderfully." She has begun to copy Nature, and done well. Lovely sketches of the cloisters in Westminster Abbey, and other charming things.

I write a story for all my men, and make up the $1,000 I planned to earn by my "pot-boilers" before we go back to C.

A tablet to Grandfather May is put in Stone Chapel, and one Sunday A. M. we take Mother to see it. A pathetic sight to see Father walk up the broad aisle with the feeble old wife on his arm as they went to be married nearly fifty years ago. Mother sat alone in the old pew a little while and sung softly the old hymns; for it was early, and only the sexton there. He asked who she was, and said his father was sexton in Grandfather's time.

Several old ladies came in and knew Mother. She broke down thinking of the time when she and her mother and sisters and father and brothers all went to church together, and we took her home saying, "This is n't my Boston; all my friends are gone; I never want to see it any more."

[She never did. — L. M. A.]

April and May. — Back to Concord, after ·May and I had put all in fine order and made the old house lovely with her pictures. When all were settled, with May to· keep house, I went to B. for rest, and took a room in Joy Street.

The Elgin Watch Company offered me a gold watch or $100 for a tale. Chose the money, and wrote the story "My Rococo Watch"[1] for them.

October. — Took two nice rooms at the Hotel Bellevue for the winter; May to use one for her classes. Tried to work on my book, but was in such pain could not do much. Got no sleep without morphine. Tried old Dr. Hewett, who was sure he could cure the woe. . . .

November. — Funny time with the publishers about the

---

[1] In Spinning-Wheel Stories.

tale; for all wanted it at once, and each tried to outbid the other for an unwritten story. I rather enjoyed it, and felt important with Roberts, Low, and Scribner all clamoring for my "'umble" works. No peddling poor little manuscripts now, and feeling rich with $10. The golden goose can sell her eggs for a good price, if she is n't killed by too much driving.

December. — Better and busier than last month.

All well at home, and Father happy among his kind Westerners. Finish "Eight Cousins," and get ready to do the temperance tale, for F. offers $700 for six chapters, — "Silver Pitchers."

January, 1875. — . . . Father flourishing about the Western cities, "riding in Louisa's chariot, and adored as the grandfather of 'Little Women,'" he says.

February. — Finish my tale and go to Vassar College on a visit. See M. M., talk with four hundred girls, write in stacks of albums and school-books, and kiss every one who asks me. Go to New York; am rather lionized, and run away; but things look rather jolly, and I may try a winter there some time, as I need a change and new ideas.

March. — Home again, getting ready for the centennial fuss.

April. — On the 19th a grand celebration. General *break-down,* owing to an unwise desire to outdo all the other towns; too many people. . . .

Miss Alcott was very much interested in the question of Woman Suffrage, and exerted herself to get up a meeting in Concord. The subject was then very unpopular, and there was an ill-bred effort to destroy the meeting by noise and riot. Although not fond of speaking in public, she always put herself bravely on the side of the unpopular cause, and lent to it all the argument of her heroic life. When Mrs. Livermore lectured at Concord, Miss Alcott sat up all night talking with her on the great question. She had an opportunity of trying which was most exhausting, abuse or admiration, when she went to a meeting of the Women's Congress at Syracuse, in October. She was introduced to the audience by Mrs. Livermore, and the young people crowded about her like bees about a honeycomb. She was waylaid in the streets, petitioned for autographs, kissed by gushing young maidens, and made emphatically the lion of the hour. It was all so genial and spontaneous, that she enjoyed the fun. No amount of adulation ever affected the natural simplicity of her manners. She neither despised nor overrated her fame; but was glad of it as a proof of success in what she was ever aiming to do. She spent a few weeks in New York enjoying the gay and literary society which was freely opened to her; but finding most satisfaction in visiting the Tombs, Newsboys' Home, and Randall's Island, for she liked these things better than parties and dinners.

Journal.

June, July, August, 1875. — Kept house at home, with two Irish incapables to trot after, and ninety-two guests in one month to entertain. Fame is an expensive luxury. I can do without it. This is my worst scrape, I think. I asked for bread, and got a stone, — in the shape of a pedestal.

September and October, 1875. — I go to Woman's Congress in Syracuse, and see Niagara. Funny time with the girls.

Write loads of autographs, dodge at the theatre, and am kissed to death by gushing damsels. One energetic lady grasped my hand in the crowd, exclaiming, "If you ever come to Oshkosh, your feet will not be allowed to touch the ground : you will be borne in the arms of the people ! Will you come?" "Never," responded Miss A., trying to look affable, and dying to laugh as the good soul worked my arm like a pump-handle, and from the gallery generations of girls were looking on. "This, this, is fame !"

November, December. — Take a room at Bath Hotel, New York, and look about me. Miss Sally Holly is here, and we go about together. She tells me much of her life among the freedmen, and Mother is soon deep in barrels of clothes, food, books, etc., for Miss A. to take back with her.

See many people, and am very gay for a country-mouse. Society unlike either London or Boston.

Go to Sorosis, and to Mrs. Botta's, O. B. Frothingham's, Miss Booth's, and Mrs. Croly's receptions.

Visit the Tombs, Newsboys' Home, and Randall's Island on Christmas Day with Mrs. Gibbons. A memorable day. Make a story of it. Enjoy these things more than the parties and dinners.

To Mrs. Dodge.

NEW YORK, Oct. 5, 1875

DEAR MRS. DODGE, — So far, New York seems inviting, though I have not seen or done much but "gawk round" as the country folks do. I have seen Niagara, and enjoyed my vacation very much, especially the Woman's Congress in Syracuse. I was made a member, so have the honor to sign myself,

Yours truly,   L. M. ALCOTT, M. C.

To her Father.

NEW YORK, Nov. 26, 1875.

DEAR SEVENTY-SIX, — As I have nothing else to send you on our joint birthday, I 'll despatch a letter about some of the people I have lately seen in whom you take an interest.

Tuesday we heard Gough on " Blunders," and it was very good, — both witty and wise, earnest and sensible. Wednesday eve to Mr. Frothingham's for his Fraternity Club meeting. Pleasant people. Ellen F.; Abby Sage Richardson, a very lovely woman; young Putnam and wife; Mrs. Stedman; Mattie G. and her spouse, Dr. B., who read a lively story of Mormon life; Mrs. Dodge; O. Johnson and wife, and many more whose names I forget.

After the story the given subject for discussion was brought up, — " Conformity and Noncomformity." Mr. B., a promising young lawyer, led one side, Miss B. the other, and Mr. F. was in the chair. It was very lively; and being called upon, I piped up, and went in for non-conformity when principle was concerned. Got patted on the head for my remarks, and did n't disgrace myself except by getting very red and talking fast.

Ellen F. was very pleasant, and asked much about May. Proudly I told of our girl's achievements, and E. hoped she would come to New York. Mrs. Richardson was presented, and we had some agreeable chat. She is a great friend of O. B. F., and is lecturing here on

"Literature." Shall go and hear her, as she is coming to see me.

O. B. F. was as polished and clear and cool and witty as usual; most gracious to the "'umble" Concord worm; and Mrs. F. asked me to come and see them.

Yesterday took a drive with Sally H. in Central Park as it was fine, and she had no fun on her Thanksgiving. I dined at Mrs. Botta's, for she kindly came and asked me. Had a delightful time, and felt as if I'd been to Washington; for Professor Byng, a German ex-consul, was there, full of Capitol gossip about Sumner and all the great beings that there do congregate. Mr. Botta you know, — a handsome, long-haired Italian, very culti-vated and affable.

Also about Lord H., whom B. thought "an amiable old woman," glad to say pretty things, and fond of being lionized. Byng knew Rose and Una, and asked about them; also told funny tales of Victor Emmanuel and his Court, and queer adventures in Greece, where he, B., was a consul, or something official. It was a glimpse into a new sort of world; and as the man was very accomplished, elegant, and witty, I enjoyed it much.

We had music later, and saw some fine pictures. Durant knew Miss Thackeray, J. Ingelow, and other English people whom I did, so we had a good dish of gossip with Mrs. Botta, while the others talked three or four languages at once.

It is a delightful house, and I shall go as often as I may, for it is the sort of thing I like much better than B. H. and champagne.

To-night we go to hear Bradlaugh; to-morrow, a new play; Sunday, Frothingham and Bellows; and Monday, Mrs. Richardson and Shakespeare.

But it is n't all play, I assure you. I'm a thrifty but

terfly, and have written three stories. The "G." has paid for the little Christmas tale ; the " I." has " Letty's Tramp ; " and my " girl paper " for " St. Nick " is about ready. Several other papers are waiting for tales, so I have a ballast of work to keep me steady in spite of much fun.

Mr. Powell has been twice to see me, and we go to visit the charities of New York next week. I like to see both sides, and generally find the busy people most interesting.

So far I like New York very much, and feel so well I shall stay on till I'm tired of it. People begin to tell me how much better I look than when I came, and I have not an ache to fret over. This, after such a long lesson in bodily ails, is a blessing for which I am duly grateful.

Hope all goes well with you, and that I shall get a line now and then. I'll keep them for you to *bind* up by and by instead of mine. . . .

We can buy a carriage some other time, and a barn likewise, and a few other necessities of life. Rosa has proved such a good speculation we shall dare to let May venture another when the ship comes in. I am glad the dear " rack-a-bones " is a comfort to her mistress, only don't let her break my boy's bones by any antics when she feels her oats.

I suppose you are thinking of Wilson just now, and his quiet slipping away to the heavenly council chambers where the good senators go. Rather like Sumner's end, was n't it? No wife or children, only men and servants. Wilson was such a genial, friendly soul I should have thought he would have felt the loneliness very much. Hope if he left any last wishes his mates will carry them out faithfully. . . .

Now, dear Plato, the Lord bless you, and keep you serene and happy for as many years as He sees fit, and me likewise, to be a comfort as well as a pride to you.

Ever your loving   FORTY-THREE

To her Nephews.

NEW YORK, Dec. 4, 1875.

DEAR FRED AND DONNY, — We went to see the news-boys, and I wish you 'd been with us, it was so interesting. A nice big house has been built for them, with dining-room and kitchen on the first floor, bath-rooms and school-room next, two big sleeping-places, — third and fourth stories, — and at the top a laundry and gymnasium. We saw all the tables set for breakfast, — a plate and bowl for each, — and in the kitchen great kettles, four times as big as our copper boiler, for tea and coffee, soup, and meat. They have bread and meat and coffee for breakfast, and bread and cheese and tea for supper, and get their own dinners out. School was just over when we got there, and one hundred and eighty boys were in the immense room with desks down the middle, and all around the walls were little cupboards numbered. Each boy on coming in gives his name, pays six cents, gets a key, and puts away his hat, books, and jacket (if he has 'em) in his own cubby for the night. They pay five cents for supper, and schooling, baths, etc., are free. They were a smart-looking set, larking round in shirts and trousers, barefooted, but the faces were clean, and the heads smooth, and clothes pretty decent; yet they support themselves, for not one of them has any parents or home but this. One little chap, only six, was trotting round as busy as a bee, locking up his small shoes and ragged jacket as if they were great treasures. I asked about little Pete, and the man told us his brother, only nine, supported him and took care of him entirely; and would n't let Pete be sent away to any home, because *he* wished to have "his family" with him.

Think of that, Fred! How would it seem to be all alone in a big city, with no mamma to cuddle you; no two grandpa's houses to take you in; not a penny but what you earned, and Donny to take care of? Could you do it? Nine-year-old Patsey does it capitally; buys Pete's clothes, pays for his bed and supper, and puts pennies in the savings-bank. There's a brave little man for you! I wanted to see him; but he is a newsboy, and sells late papers, because, though harder work, it pays better, and the coast is clear for those who do it.

The savings-bank was a great table all full of slits, each one leading to a little place below and numbered outside, so each boy knew his own. Once a month the bank is opened, and the lads take out what they like, or have it invested in a big bank for them to have when they find homes out West, as many do, and make good farmers. One boy was putting in some pennies as we looked, and I asked how much he had saved this month. "Fourteen dollars, ma'am," says the thirteen-year-older, proudly slipping in the last cent. A prize of $3 is offered to the lad who saves the most in a month.

The beds upstairs were in two immense rooms, ever so much larger than our town hall, — one hundred in one, and one hundred and eighty in another, — all narrow beds with a blue quilt, neat pillow, and clean sheet. They are built in long rows, one over another, and the upper boy has to climb up as on board ship. I'd have liked to see one hundred and eighty all in their "by-lows" at once, and I asked the man if they did n't train when all were in. "Lord, ma'am, they're up at five, poor little chaps, and are so tired at night that they drop off right away. Now and then some boy kicks up a little row, but we have a watchman, and he soon settles 'em."

He also told me how that very day a neat, smart young man came in, and said he was one of their boys who went West with a farmer only a little while ago; and now he owned eighty acres of land, had a good house, and was doing well, and had come to New York to find his sister, and to take her away to live with him. Was n't that nice? Lots of boys do as well. Instead of loafing round the streets and getting into mischief, they are taught to be tidy, industrious, and honest, and then sent away into the wholesome country to support themselves.

It was funny to see 'em scrub in the bath-room, — feet and faces, — comb their hair, fold up their old clothes in the dear cubbies, which make them so happy because they feel that they *own* something.

The man said every boy wanted one, even though he had neither shoes nor jacket to put in it; but would lay away an old rag of a cap or a dirty tippet with an air of satisfaction fine to see. Some lads sat reading, and the man said they loved it so they 'd read all night, if allowed. At nine he gave the word, " Bed ! " and away went the lads, trooping up to sleep in shirts and trousers, as nightgowns are not provided. How would a boy I know like that, — a boy who likes to have " trommin " on his nighties? Of course, I don't mean dandy Don ! Oh, dear no !

After nine [if late in coming in] they are fined five cents; after ten, ten cents; and after eleven they can't come in at all. This makes them steady, keeps them out of harm, and gives them time for study. Some go to the theatre, and sleep anywhere; some sleep at the Home, but go out for a better breakfast than they get there, as the swell ones are fond of goodies, and live well in their funny way. Coffee and cakes at Fulton Market is "the tip-top grub," and they often spend all their day's earnings in a play and a supper, and sleep in boxes or cellars after it.

Lots of pussies were round the kitchen; and one black one I called a bootblack, and a gray kit that yowled loud was a newsboy. That made some chaps laugh, and they nodded at me as I went out. Nice boys! but I know some nicer ones. Write and tell me something about my poor Squabby.

By-by, your

WEEDY.

To her Family.

SATURDAY EVENING, Dec. 25, 1875.

DEAR FAMILY, — . . . I had only time for a word this A. M., as the fourth letter was from Mrs. P. to say they could not go; so I trotted off in the fog at ten to the boat, and there found Mr. and Mrs. G. and piles of goodies for the poor children. She is a dear little old lady in a close, Quakerish bonnet and plain suit, but wide-awake and full of energy. It was grand to see her tackle the big mayor and a still bigger commissioner, and tell then. what *ought* to be done for the poor things on the Island, as they are to be routed; for the city wants the land for some dodge or other. Both men fled soon, for the brave little woman was down on 'em in a way that would have made Marmee cry "Ankore!" and clap her dress-gloves to rags.

When the rotundities had retired, she fell upon a demure priest, and read him a sermon; and then won the heart of a boyish reporter so entirely that he stuck to us all day, and helped serve out dolls and candy like a man and a brother. Long life to him!

Mr. G. and I discussed pauperism and crime like two old wiseacres; and it was sweet to hear the gray-headed couple say "thee" and "thou," "Abby" and "James," to one another, he following with the bundles wherever the little poke-bonnet led the way. I've had a pretty good variety of Christmases in my day, but never one like this before. First we drove in an old ramshackle hack to the chapel, whither a boy had raced before us, crying joyfully to all he met, "She's come! Miss G.—she's come!" And all faces beamed, as well they might, since for thirty years she has gone to make set after set of little forlornities happy on this day.

The chapel was full. On one side, in front, girls in blue gowns and white pinafores; on the other, small chaps in pinafores likewise; and behind them, bigger boys in gray suits with cropped heads, and larger girls with ribbons in their hair and pink calico gowns. They sang alternately; the girls gave "Juanita" very well, the little chaps a pretty song about poor children asking a "little white angel" to leave the gates of heaven ajar, so they could peep in, if no more. Quite pathetic, coming from poor babies who had no home but this.

The big boys spoke pieces, and I was amused when one bright lad in gray, with a red band on his arm, spoke the lines I gave G.,—"Merry Christmas." No one knew me, so I had the joke to myself; and I found afterward that I was taken for the mayoress, who was expected. Then we drove to the hospital, and there the heart-ache began, for me at least, so sad it was to see these poor babies, born of want and sin, suffering every sort of deformity, disease, and pain. Cripples half blind, scarred with scrofula, burns, and abuse,—it was simply awful and indescribable!

As we went in, I with a great box of dolls and the

young reporter with a bigger box of candy, a general cry of delight greeted us. Some children tried to run, half-blind ones stretched out their groping hands, little ones crawled, and big ones grinned, while several poor babies sat up in their bed, beckoning us to "come quick."

One poor mite, so eaten up with sores that its whole face was painted with some white salve, — its head covered with an oilskin cap; one eye gone, and the other half filmed over; hands bandaged, and ears bleeding, — could only moan and move its feet till I put a gay red dolly in one hand and a pink candy in the other; then the dim eye brightened, the hoarse voice said feebly, "Tanky, lady!" and I left it contentedly sucking the sweetie, and *trying* to *see* its dear new toy. It can't see another Christmas, and I like to think I helped make this one happy, even for a minute.

It was pleasant to watch the young reporter trot round with the candy-box, and come up to me all interest to say, "One girl has n't got a doll, ma'am, and looks *so* disappointed."

After the hospital, we went to the idiot house; and there I had a chance to see faces and figures that will haunt me a long time. A hundred or so of half-grown boys and girls ranged down a long hall, a table of toys in the middle, and an empty one for Mrs. G.'s gifts. A cheer broke out as the little lady hurried in waving her handkerchief and a handful of gay bead necklaces, and "Oh! Ohs!" followed the appearance of the doll-lady and the candy man.

A pile of gay pictures was a new idea, and Mrs. G. told me to hold up some bright ones and see if the poor innocents would understand and enjoy them. I held up one of two kittens lapping spilt milk, and the girls began to mew and say "Cat! ah, pretty." Then a fine horse, and the boys bounced on their benches with pleasure; while a ship in full sail produced a cheer of rapture from them all.

Some were given out to the good ones, and the rest are to be pinned round the room; so the pictures were a great success. All wanted dolls, even boys of nineteen; for all were children in mind. But the girls had them, and young women of eighteen cuddled their babies and were happy. The boys chose from the toy-table, and it was pathetic to see great fellows pick out a squeaking dog without even the wit to pinch it when it was theirs. One dwarf of thirty-five chose a little Noah's ark, and brooded over it in silent bliss.

Some with beards sucked their candy, and stared at a toy cow or box of blocks as if their cup was full. One French girl sang the Marseillaise in a feeble voice, and was so overcome by her new doll that she had an epileptic fit on the spot, which made two others go off likewise; and a slight pause took place while they were kindly removed to sleep it off.

A little tot of four, who had n't sense to put candy in its mouth, was so fond of music that when the girls sang the poor vacant face woke up, and a pair of lovely soft hazel eyes stopped staring dully at nothing, and went wandering to and fro with light in them, as if to find the only sound that can reach its poor mind.

I guess I gave away two hundred dolls, and a soap-box of candy was empty when we left. But rows of sticky faces beamed at us, and an array of gay toys wildly waved after us, as if we were angels who had showered goodies on the poor souls.

Pauper women are nurses; and Mrs. G. says the babies die like sheep, many being deserted so young nothing

can be hoped or done for them. One of the teachers in
the idiot home was a Miss C., who remembered Nan at
Dr. Wilbur's. Very lady-like, and all devotion to me.
But such a life! Oh, me! Who *can* lead it, and not
go mad?

At four, we left and came home, Mrs. G. giving a box
of toys and sweeties on board the boat for the children
of the men who run it. So leaving a stream of blessings
and pleasures behind her, the dear old lady drove away,
simply saying, "There now, I shall feel better for the
next year!" Well she may; bless her!

She made a speech to the chapel children after the
Commissioner had prosed in the usual way, and she told
'em that *she* should come as long as she could, and when
she was gone her children would still keep it up in memory of her; so for thirty years more she hoped this, their
one holiday, would be made happy for them. I could
have hugged her on the spot, the motherly old dear!

Next Wednesday we go to the Tombs, and some day
I am to visit the hospital with her, for I like this better
than parties, etc.

I got home at five, and then remembered that I'd had
no lunch; so I took an apple till six, when I discovered
that all had dined at one so the helpers could go early
this evening. Thus my Christmas day was without dinner or presents, for the first time since I can remember.
Yet it has been a very memorable day, and I feel as if
I'd had a splendid feast seeing the poor babies wallow
in turkey soup, and that every gift I put into their hands
had come back to me in the dumb delight of their
unchild-like faces trying to smile.

After the pleasant visit in New York, Miss Alcott
returned to Boston, where she went into society

more than usual, often attending clubs, theatres, and receptions. She was more lionized than ever, and had a natural pleasure in the attention she received.

The summer of 1876 she spent at Concord, nursing her mother, who was very ill. She here wrote "Rose in Bloom," the sequel to "Eight Cousins," in three weeks. It was published in November.

Louisa was anxious that her sister should have a home for her young family. Mrs. Pratt invested what she could of her husband's money in the purchase, and Louisa contributed the rest. This was the so-called Thoreau House on the main street in Concord, which became Mrs. Pratt's home, and finally that of her father.

Louisa spent the summer of 1877 in Concord. Her mother's illness increased, and she was herself very ill in August. Yet she wrote this summer one of her brightest and sweetest stories, "Under the Lilacs." Her love of animals is specially apparent in this book, and she records going to the circus to make studies for the performing dog Sanch.

During the winter of 1877, Miss Alcott went to the Bellevue for some weeks, and having secured the necessary quiet, devoted herself to the writing of a novel for the famous No Name Series published by Roberts Brothers. This book had been in her mind for some time, as is seen by the journal. As it was to appear anonymously, and was not intended for children, she was able to depart from her usual manner, and indulge the weird and lurid fancies which took possession of her in

her dramatic days, and when writing sensational
stories. She was much interested, and must have
written it very rapidly, as it was published in April.
She enjoyed the excitement of her *incognito*, and
was much amused at the guesses of critics and
friends, who attributed the book to others, and
were sure Louisa Alcott did not write it, because
its style was so unlike hers.

It certainly is very unlike the books Miss Alcott
had lately written. It has nothing of the home-
like simplicity and charm of " Little Women,"
" Old-Fashioned Girl," and the other stories with
which she was delighting the children, and, with
" Moods," must always be named as exceptional
when speaking of her works. Still, a closer study
of her life and nature will reveal much of her own
tastes and habits of thought in the book; and it is
evident that she wrote *con amore*, and was fascinated by the familiars she evoked, however little
charm they may seem to possess to others. She
was fond of Hawthorne's books. The influence of
his subtle and weird romances is undoubtedly per-
ceptible in the book, and it is not strange that it
was attributed to his son. She says it had been
simmering in her brain ever since she read " Faust "
the year before; and she clearly wished to work
according to Goethe's thought, — that the Prince
of Darkness was a gentleman, and must be represented as belonging to the best society.

The plot is powerful and original. A young poet,
with more ambition than genius or self-knowledge,
finds himself, at nineteen, friendless, penniless, and
hopeless, and is on the point of committing suicide.

He is saved by Helwyze, a middle-aged man,
who has been severely crippled by a terrible fall,
and his heart seared by the desertion of the woman
he loved. A man of intellect, power, imagination,
and wealth, but incapable of conscientious feeling
or true love, he is a dangerous savior for the impulsive poet; but he takes him to his home, warms,
feeds, and shelters him, and promises to bring out
his book. The brilliant, passionate woman who
gave up her lover when his health and beauty were
gone, returned to him when youth had passed,
and would gladly have devoted herself to soothing his pain and enriching his life. Her feeling
is painted with delicacy and tenderness.

But Helwyze's heart knew nothing of the divine
quality of forgiveness; for his love there was no res-
urrection; and he only valued the power he could
exercise over a brilliant woman, and the intellectual
entertainment she could bring him. A sweet young
girl, Olivia's protegee, completes the very limited
dramatis personæ.

The young poet, Felix Canaris, under the guidance of his new friend, wins fame, success, and the
young girl's heart; but his wayward fancy turns
rather to the magnificent Olivia. The demoniac
Helwyze works upon this feeling, and claims of
Olivia her fair young friend Gladys as a wife for
Felix, who is forced to accept her at the hands of
his master. She is entirely responsive to the love
which she fancies she has won, and is grateful for
her fortunate lot, and devotes herself to the comfort and happiness of the poor invalid who delights in her beauty and grace. For a time Felix

enjoys a society success, to which his charming
wife, as well as his book, contribute. But at last
this excitement flags. He writes another book,
which he threatens to burn because he is dissatisfied with it. Gladys entreats him to spare it, and
Helwyze offers to read it to her. She is overcome
and melted with emotion at the passion and pathos
of the story; and when Helwyze asks, "Shall I
burn it?" Felix answers, "No!" Again the book
brings success and admiration, but the tender wife
sees that it does not insure happiness, and that
her husband is plunging into the excitement of
gambling.

The demon Helwyze has complete control over
the poet, which he exercises with such subtle tyranny that the young man is driven to the dreadful
thought of murder to escape from him; but he is
saved from the deed by the gentle influence of his
wife, who has won his heart at last, unconscious
that it had not always been hers.

Helwyze finds his own punishment. One being
resists his power, — Gladys breathes his poisoned
atmosphere unharmed. He sends for Olivia as his
ally to separate the wife from her husband's love.
A passion of curiosity possesses him to read her
very heart; and at last he resorts to a strange
means to accomplish his purpose. He gives her
an exciting drug without her knowledge, and under its influence she speaks and acts with a rare
genius which calls forth the admiration of all the
group. Left alone with her, Helwyze exercises his
magnetic power to draw forth the secrets of her
heart; but he reads there only a pure and true

love for her husband, and fear of the unhallowed passion which he is cherishing. The secret of his power over the husband is at last revealed. Canaris has published as his own the work of Helwyze, and all the fame and glory he has received has been won by deceit, and is a miserable mockery.

The tragic result is inevitable. Gladys dies under the pressure of a burden too heavy for her, — the knowledge of deceit in him she had loved and trusted; while the stricken Helwyze is paralyzed, and lives henceforth only a death in life.

With all the elements of power and beauty in this singular book, it fails to charm and win the heart of the reader. The circumstances are in a romantic setting, but still they are prosaic; and tragedy is only endurable when taken up into the region of the ideal, where the thought of the universal rounds out all traits of the individual. In Goethe's Faust, Margaret is the sweetest and simplest of maidens; but in her is the life of all wronged and suffering womanhood.

The realism which is delightful in the pictures of little women and merry boys is painful when connected with passions so morbid and lives so far removed from joy and sanity. As in her early dramas and sensational stories, we do not find Louisa Alcott's own broad, generous, healthy life, or that which lay around her, in this book, but the reminiscences of her reading, which she had striven to make her own by invention and fancy.

This note refers to "A Modern Mephistoph eles": —

[1877.]

DEAR MR. NILES, — I had to keep the proof longer than I meant because a funeral came in the way.

The book as last sent is lovely, and much bigger than I expected.

Poor "Marmee," ill in bed, hugged it, and said, "It is perfect! only I do wish your name could be on it." She is very proud of it; and tender-hearted Anna weeps and broods over it, calling Gladys the best and sweetest character I ever did. So much for home opinion; now let's see what the public will say.

May clamors for it; but I don't want to send this till she has had one or two of the others. Have you sent her "Is That All?" If not, please do; then it won't look suspicious to send only "M. M."

I am so glad the job is done, and hope it won't disgrace the series. Is not another to come before this? I hope so; for many people suspect what is up, and I could tell my fibs about No. 6 better if it was *not* mine.

Thanks for the trouble you have taken to keep the secret. Now the fun will begin.

Yours truly,   L. M. A.

P. S. — Bean's expressman grins when he hands in the daily parcel. He is a Concord man.

By Louisa's help the younger sister again went abroad in 1876; and her bright affectionate letters cheered the little household, much saddened by the mother's illness.

Journal.

January, 1876. — Helped Mrs. Croly receive two hundred gentlemen.

A letter from Baron Tauchnitz asking leave to put my

book in his foreign library, and sending 600 marks to pay for it. Said, " Yes, thank you, Baron."

Went to Philadelphia to see Cousin J. May installed in Dr. Furness's pulpit. Dull place is Philadelphia. Heard Beecher preach; did not like him. . . .

Went home on the 21st, finding I could not work here. Soon tire of being a fine lady.

February and March. — Took a room in B., and fell to work on short tales for F. T. N. wanted a centennial story; but my frivolous New York life left me no ideas. Went to Centennial Ball at Music Hall, and got an idea.

Wrote a tale of "'76," which with others will make a catchpenny book. Mother poorly, so I go home to nurse her.

April, May, and June. — Mother better. Nan and boys go to P. farm. May and I clean the old house. It seems as if the dust of two centuries haunted the ancient mansion, and came out spring and fall in a ghostly way for us to clear up.

Great freshets and trouble.

Exposition in Philadelphia; don't care to go. America ought to pay her debts before she gives parties. " Silver Pitchers," etc., comes out, and goes well. Poor stuff; but the mill must keep on grinding even chaff.

June. — Lovely month! Keep hotel and wait on Marmee.

Try to get up steam for a new serial, as Mrs. Dodge wants one, and Scribner offers $3,000 for it. Roberts Brothers want a novel; and the various newspapers and magazines clamor for tales. My brain is squeezed dry, and I can only wait for help.

July, August. — Get an idea and start "Rose in Bloom," though I hate sequels.

September. — On the 9th my dear girl sails in the

"China" for a year in London or Paris. God be with her! She has done her distasteful duty faithfully, and deserved a reward. She cannot find the help she needs here, and is happy and busy in her own world over there.

[She never came home. — L. M. A.]

Finish "Rose."

.   .   .   .

November. — "Rose" comes out; sells well.

. . . Forty-four years old. My new task gets on slowly; but I keep at it, and can be a prop, if not an angel, in the house, as Nan is.

December. — Miss P. sends us a pretty oil sketch of May, — so like the dear soul in her violet wrapper, with yellow curls piled up, and the long hand at work. Mother delights in it.

She (M.) is doing finely, and says, "I am getting on, and I feel as if it was not all a mistake; for I have some talent, and will prove it." Modesty is a sign of genius, and I think our girl has both. The money I invest in her pays the sort of interest I like. I am proud to have her show what she can do, and have her depend upon no one but me. Success to little Raphael! My dull winter is much cheered by her happiness and success.

January, February, 1877. — The year begins well. Nan keeps house; boys fine, tall lads, good and gay; Father busy with his new book; Mother cosey with her sewing, letters, Johnson, and success of her "girls."

Went for some weeks to the Bellevue, and wrote "A Modern Mephistopheles" for the No Name Series. It has been simmering ever since I read Faust last year. Enjoyed doing it, being tired of providing moral pap for the young. Long to write a novel, but cannot get time enough.

May's letters our delight. She is so in earnest she will not stop for pleasure, rest, or society, but works away like a Trojan. Her work admired by masters and mates for its vigor and character.

March. — Begin to think of buying the Thoreau place for Nan. The $4,000 received from the Vt. and Eastern R. Rs. must be invested, and she wants a home of her own, now the lads are growing up.

Mother can be with her in the winter for a change, and leave me free to write in B. Concord has no inspiration for me.

April. — May, at the request of her teacher, M. Muller, sends a study of still life to the Salon. The little picture is accepted, well hung, and praised by the judges. No friend at court, and the modest work stood on its own merits. She is very proud to see her six months' hard work bear fruit. A happy girl, and all say she deserves the honor.

"M. M." appears and causes much guessing. It is praised and criticised, and I enjoy the fun, especially when friends say, "I know *you* did n't write it, for you can't hide your peculiar style."

Help to buy the house for Nan, — $4,500. So she has *her* wish, and is happy. When shall I have mine? Ought to be contented with knowing I help both sisters by my brains. But I 'm selfish, and want to go away and rest in Europe. Never shall.

May, June. — Quiet days keeping house and attending to Marmee, who grows more and more feeble. Helped Nan get ready for her new home.

Felt very well, and began to hope I had outlived the neuralgic worries and nervous woes born of the hospital fever and the hard years following.

May living alone in Paris, while her mates go jaunting,

— a solitary life; but she is so busy she is happy and safe. A good angel watches over her. Take pleasant drives early in the A. M. with Marmee. She takes her comfort in a basket wagon, and we drive to the woods, picking flowers and stopping where we like. It keeps her young, and rests her weary nerves.

July. — Got too tired, and was laid up for some weeks. A curious time, lying quite happily at rest, wondering what was to come next.

August. — As soon as able began "Under the Lilacs," but could not do much.

Mrs. Alcott grew rapidly worse, and her devoted daughter recognized that the final parting was near. As Louisa watched by the bedside she wrote "My Girls," and finished "Under the Lilacs."

The journal tells the story of the last days of watching, and of the peaceful close of the mother's self-sacrificing yet blessed life. Louisa was very brave in the presence of death. She had no dark thoughts connected with it; and in her mother's case, after her long, hard life, she recognized how "growing age longed for its peaceful sleep."

The tie between this mother and daughter was exceptionally strong and tender. The mother saw all her own fine powers reproduced and developed in her daughter; and if she also recognized the passionate energy which had been the strength and the bane of her own life, it gave her only a more constant watchfulness to save her child from the struggles and regrets from which she had suffered herself.

Journal.

September, 1877. — On the 7th Marmee had a very ill turn, and the doctor told me it was the beginning of the end. [Water on the chest.] She was so ill we sent for Father from Walcott; and I forgot myself in taking care of poor Marmee, who suffered much and longed to go.

As I watched with her I wrote "My Girls," to go with other tales in a new "Scrap Bag," and finished "Under the Lilacs." I foresaw a busy or a sick winter, and wanted to finish while I could, so keeping my promise and earning my $3,000.

Brain very lively and pen flew. It always takes an exigency to spur me up and wring out a book. Never have time to go slowly and do my best.

October. — Fearing I might give out, got a nurse and rested a little, so that when the last hard days come I might not fail Marmee, who says, "Stay by, Louy, and help me if I suffer too much." I promised, and watched her sit panting life away day after day. We thought she would not outlive her seventy-seventh birthday, but, thanks to Dr. W. and homœopathy, she got relief, and we had a sad little celebration, well knowing it would be the last. Aunt B. and L. W. came up, and with fruit, flowers, smiling faces, and full hearts, we sat round the brave soul who faced death so calmly and was ready to go.

I overdid and was very ill, — in danger of my life for a week, — and feared to go before Marmee. But pulled through, and got up slowly to help her die. A strange month.

November. — Still feeble, and Mother failing fast. On the 14th we were both moved to Anna's at Mother's earnest wish.

A week in the new home, and then she ceased to care

for anything. Kept her bed for three days, lying down after weeks in a chair, and on the 25th, at dusk, that rainy Sunday, fell quietly asleep in my arms.

She was very happy all day, thinking herself a girl again, with parents and sisters round her. Said her Sunday hymn to me, whom she called "Mother," and smiled at us, saying, "A smile is as good as a prayer." Looked often at the little picture of May, and waved her hand to it, "Good-by, little May, good-by!"

Her last words to Father were, "You are laying a very soft pillow for me to go to sleep cn."

We feared great suffering, but she was spared that, and slipped peacefully away. I was so glad when the last weary breath was drawn, and silence came, with its rest and peace.

On the 27th it was necessary to bury her, and we took her quietly away to Sleepy Hollow. A hard day, but the last duty we could do for her; and there we left her at sunset beside dear Lizzie's dust, — alone so long.

On the 28th a memorial service, and all the friends at Anna's, — Dr. Bartol and Mr. Foote of Stone Chapel. A simple, cheerful service, as she would have liked it.

Quiet days afterward resting in her rest.

My duty is done, and now I shall be glad to follow her.

December. — Many kind letters from all who best knew and loved the noble woman.

I never wish her back, but a great warmth seems gone out of life, and there is no motive to go on now.

My only comfort is that I *could* make her last years comfortable, and lift off the burden she had carried so bravely all these years. She was so loyal, tender, and true ; life was hard for her, and no one understood all she had to bear but we, her children. I think I shall soon follow her, and am quite ready to go now she no longer needs me.

January, 1878. — An idle month at Nan's, for I can only suffer.

Father goes about, being restless with his anchor gone. Dear Nan is house-mother now, — so patient, so thoughtful and tender; I need nothing but that cherishing which only mothers can give.

May busy in London. Very sad about Marmee; but it was best not to send for her, and Marmee forbade it, and she has some very *tender friends* near her.

February. — . . . Wrote some lines on Marmee.

To Mrs. Dodge.

CONCORD, June 3 [1877].

DEAR MRS. DODGE, — The tale [1] goes slowly owing to interruptions, for summer is a busy time, and I get few quiet days. Twelve chapters are done, but are short ones, and so will make about six or seven numbers in "St. Nicholas."

I will leave them divided in this way that you may put in as many as you please each month; for trying to suit the magazine hurts the story in its book form, though this way does no harm to the monthly parts, I think.

I will send you the first few chapters during the week for Mrs. Foote, and with them the schedule you suggest, so that my infants may not be drawn with whiskers, and my big boys and girls in pinafores, as in "Eight Cousins."

I hope the new baby won't be set aside too soon for my illustrations; but I do feel a natural wish to have one story prettily adorned with good pictures, as hitherto artists have much afflicted me.

[1] Under the Lilacs.

I am daily waiting with anxiety for an illumination of some sort, as my plot is very vague so far; and though I don't approve of "sensations" in children's books, one must have a certain thread on which to string the small events which make up the true sort of child-life.

I intend to go and simmer an afternoon at Van Amburg's great show, that I may get hints for the further embellishment of Ben and his dog. I have also put in a poem by F. B. S.'s small son,[1] and that hit will give Mrs. Foote a good scene with the six-year-old poet reciting his verses under the lilacs.

I shall expect the small tots to be unusually good, since the artist has a live model to study from. Please present my congratulations to the happy mamma and Mr. Foote, Jr.

Yours *warmly,*

L. M. A.

AUGUST 21, 1879.

DEAR MRS. DODGE, — I have not been able to do anything on the serial. . . . But after a week at the seaside, to get braced up for work, I intend to begin. The Revolutionary tale does not seem to possess me. I have casually asked many of my young folks, when they demand a new story, which they would like, one of that sort or the old "Eight Cousin" style, and they all say the latter. It would be much the easier to do, as I have a beginning and a plan all ready, — a village, and the affairs of a party of children. We have many little romances going on among the Concord boys and girls, and all sorts of queer things, which will work into "Jack and Jill" nicely. Mrs. Croly has been anxious for a story, and I am trying to do a short one, as I told her

---

[1] Under the Lilacs, page 78.

you had the refusal of my next serial. I hope you will not be very much disappointed about the old-time tale. It would take study to do it well, and leisure is just what I have not got, and I shall never have, I fear, when writing is to be done. I will send you a few chapters of "Jack and Jill" when in order, if you like, and you can decide if they will suit. I shall try to have it unlike the others if possible, but the dears *will* cling to the "Little Women" style.

I have had a very busy summer, but have been pretty well, and able to do my part in entertaining the four hundred philosophers.

Yours truly,
L. M. A.

SEPTEMBER 17 [1879].

DEAR MRS. DODGE, —. . Don't let me *prose*. If I seem to be declining and falling into it, pull me up, and I 'll try to prance as of old. Years tame down one's spirit and fancy, though they only deepen one's love for the little people, and strengthen the desire to serve them wisely as well as cheerfully. Fathers and mothers tell me they use my books as helps for themselves; so now and then I like to slip in a page for them, fresh from the experience of some other parent, for education seems to me to be *the* problem in our times.

Jack and Jill are right out of our own little circle, and the boys and girls are in a twitter to know what is going in; so it will be a "truly story" in the main.

Such a long note for a busy woman to read! but your cheery word was my best "starter;" and I'm, more than ever,

Yours truly,
L. M. A.

MAY ALCOTT NIERIKER.

Born at Concord, July, 1840. Died in Paris, December, 1879.

This younger sister became so dear to Louisa, and through the legacy which she left to her of an infant child, exercised so great an influence over the last ten years of her life, that it will not be uninteresting to trace out the course of her life and the development of her character. May was born before the experiments at Fruitlands, and her childhood passed during the period when the fortunes of the family were at the lowest ebb; but she was too young to feel in all their fulness the cares which weighed upon the older sisters. Her oldest sister — the affectionate, practical Anna — almost adopted May as her own baby, and gave her a great deal of the attention and care which the mother had not time for amid her numerous avocations. The child clung to Anna with trust and affection; but with her quick fancy and lively spirit, she admired the brilliant qualities of Louisa. Hasty in temperament, quick and impulsive in action, she quarrelled with Louisa while she adored her, and was impatient with her rebukes, which yet had great influence over her. She had a more facile nature than the other sisters, and a natural, girlish love of attention, and a romantic fondness for beauty in person and style in living. Graceful in figure and manners, with a fine complexion, blue eyes, and a profusion of light wavy hair, she was attractive in appearance; and a childish frankness, and acceptance of sympathy or criticism.

disarmed those who were disposed to find fault with her.

May is very truly described in "Little Women," and her character is painted with a discerning but loving hand: "A regular snow maiden, with blue eyes, and yellow hair curling on her shoulders, pale and slender, and always carrying herself like a young lady mindful of her manners." Many little touches of description show the consciousness of appearance and love of admiration which she innocently betrayed, and illustrate the relation of the sisters: "'Don't stop to quirk your little finger and prink over your plate, Amy,' cried Jo." Her mother says of this daughter in her diary: "She does all things well; her capabilities are much in her eyes and fingers. When a child, I observed with what ease and grace she did little things."

According to Louisa, "If anybody had asked Amy what the greatest trial of her life was, she would have answered at once, 'My nose.' No one minded it but herself, and it was doing its best to grow; but Amy felt deeply the want of a Grecian nose, and drew whole sheets of handsome ones to console herself." "Little Raphael," as the sisters called her, very early developed a love and talent for drawing which became the delight of her life. She covered her books with sketches, but managed to escape reprimand by being a model of deportment. Always having in her mind an ideal of elegant life, the many little trials of their times of poverty were of course severe mortifications to her; and the necessity of wearing dresses which came to her from others, and which were ugly in them

selves or out of harmony with her own appearance, caused her much affliction. She was always
generous and easily reconciled after a quarrel, and
was a favorite with her companions, and the heroine of those innocent little love episodes which,
as Tennyson says, —

> " Are but embassies of love
> To tamper with the feelings, ere he found
> Empire for life." [1]

While May was too young to take the part in
the support of the family which fell to Anna and
Louisa, she was yet a blessing and comfort by her
kind, bright nature. After the death of Elizabeth
in 1858, her mother speaks of " turning to the little
May for comfort," and her father's letters show how
dear she was to him, although she never entered
into his intellectual life.

May shared in the blessing of Louisa's first success, for she went to the School of Design in 1859
for the lessons in her art, for which she longed so
eagerly. In 1860 an old friend sent her thirty
dollars for lessons in drawing, and she had the
best instruction she could then receive in Boston.

In 1863, Louisa procured for her the great advantage of study with Dr. Rimmer, who was then
giving his precious lessons in art anatomy in Boston. Under his instructions, May gave some attention to modelling, and completed an ideal bust.
Although she did not pursue this branch of art, it
was undoubtedly of great service in giving her
more thorough knowledge of the head, and a

[1] Gardener's Daughter.

bolder and firmer style of drawing than she would have gained in any other way.

As will be seen from Louisa's journal, May was frequently with her in Boston, engaged in studying or teaching. By the kindness of a friend, she went to Europe in 1870, when Louisa accompanied her. Louisa sent her to Europe for a year of study in 1873, and again in 1877. In London and Paris she had good opportunities for study, and improved rapidly in her art. She made some admirable copies from Turner which attracted the attention of Ruskin; and a picture from still life was accepted at the Paris Salon, which event gave great happiness to the family circle and friends at home.

May was very generous in giving to others help in the art she loved. While at home, in the intervals of her studies in Europe, she tried to form an art centre in Concord, and freely gave her time, her instruction, and the use of her studio to young artists. She wrote a little book to aid them in prosecuting their studies abroad, called "Studying Art Abroad, and How to do it Cheaply."

Like the rest of the family, May composed with great ease, and sometimes wrote little stories. Her letters are very sprightly and agreeable.

While residing in London, May had become acquainted with a young Swiss gentleman, whose refined and artistic tastes were closely in unison with her own. During the sad days of bereavement caused by her mother's death he was a kind and sympathetic friend, soothing her grief and cheering her solitude by his music. Thus, frequently together, their friendship became love, and they were betrothed. The course of this true love, which for a time ran swiftly and smoothly, is most exquisitely depicted in May's letters to her family. The charming pictures of herself and her young lover are so like Amy and her Laurie in his happiest moods, that we almost feel as if Miss Alcott had been prophetic in her treatment of these characters in " Little Women."

I wish I could give her own natural, frank account of this event. May had the secret of perpetual youth, at least in spirit; and in reading her letters, one has no consciousness that more than thirty years had passed over her head, for they had taken no drop of freshness from her heart.

The union of this happy pair was not a surprise to the friends at home, who had read May's heart, revealed in her frank, innocent letters, more clearly than she had supposed. When the claims of business called Mr. Nieriker from London, the hearts of the young couple quailed before the idea of separation, and they decided to be married at once, and go together. The simple ceremony was performed in London, March 22, 1878; and May started on her journey, no longer alone, but with a loving friend by her side.

May's letters are full of the most artless joy in her new life. The old days of struggle and penury are gone; the heart-loneliness is no more; the world is beautiful, and everybody loving and kind. Life in the modest French home is an idyllic dream, and she writes to her sisters of every detail of her household. The return of her husband at sunset is a feast, and the evening is delightful with poetry and music. Her blue dress, her crimson furniture, satisfy her artistic sense. She does not neglect her art, but paints with fresh inspiration, and waits for his criticism and praise. She says, " He is very ambitious for my artistic success, and is my most severe critic." In the morning she finds her easel set out for her, a fire burning ready for her comfort, and her husband in the big arm-chair waiting to read to her, or to take his violin and pose for his picture in gray velvet paletot and red slippers.[1]

For the time conjugal love is all sufficient, and May wonders at herself that the happiness of the moment can so drown every remembrance of sorrow. Yet a pathetic note is occasionally heard, as she mourns for the mother who is gone, or yearns for the sister who has been such a strength to her through life. The picturesqueness and ease of French life make America look stupid and forlorn, and she has no wish to go home, but only to have her dear ones share in her happiness. Her work in art was successful; and the money she received for it was not unacceptable, although her husband's income sufficed for their modest wants. She was justified in her grateful feeling that she was singularly blessed. Her husband's family were German-Swiss of high standing, artistic temperament, and warm affections. His mother and sister came to visit them, and took May to their hearts with cordial love.

Among the pictures painted by May at this time the most remarkable is the portrait of a negro girl,

[1] This interesting picture is in the possession of her sister.

which is a very faithful study from life, and gives the color and characteristic traits of a beautiful negro without exaggeration. The expression of the eyes is tender and pathetic, well-suited to the fate of a slave girl. Such earnest study would have borne richer fruit if longer life had been hers.

May's own nature seems to have blossomed out like a flower in this sunny climate. In her youth at home she was impulsive, affectionate, and generous, but quick in temper and sometimes exacting; but the whole impression she made upon her husband and his family was of grace and sweetness, and she herself declares that her sisters at home would not recognize her, she has " become so sweet in this atmosphere of happiness."

We would gladly linger over these records of a paradisiacal home where Adam and Eve renewed their innocent loves and happy labors. When musing over the sorrows of humanity it refreshes us to know that such joy is possible, and needs only love and simple hearts to make it real.

May's note of happiness is touchingly echoed from the heart of her bereaved father, who recalls the days of his own courtship. He cherished every tender word from her; and the respectful and loving words of his new son, to whom he responds affectionately, were like balm to his stricken heart.

May's joy was heightened by the expectation of motherhood. Her health was excellent, and she had the loving care of her new mother and sister. The anxious family at home received the news of the birth of a daughter with heartfelt delight. It was a great disappointment to Louisa that she could not be with her sister at this time; but her health was not equal to the voyage, and she felt that May had most loving and sufficient care. An American friend in Paris kindly wrote to Louisa full details of the little niece and of the mother's condition. " It is difficult," she says, " to say which of that happy household is the proudest over that squirming bit of humanity."

For about two weeks all seemed well ; but alarming symptoms began to appear, and the mother's strength failed rapidly. The brain was the seat of disease; and she was generally unconscious, although she had intervals of apparent improvement, when she recognized her friends. She passed away peacefully December 29, 1879.

An American clergyman in Paris took charge of the funeral service, which according to May's expressed desire was very simple, and she was laid in the tranquil cemetery of Montrouge outside of the fortifications.

Foreseeing the possibility of a fatal termination to her illness, May had made every preparation for the event, and obtained a promise from her sister-in-law that she would carry the baby to Louisa to receive the devoted care that she knew would be given it. The child became a source of great comfort to Miss Alcott as will be seen from the journals. After her death Mr. Nieriker visited his little girl in America, and in June, 1889, her aunt took her to his home in Zurich, Switzerland.

Before the sad letters describing May's illness could reach America, came the cable message of her death. It was sent to Mr. Emerson, the never failing friend of the family, who bore it to Louisa, her father being temporarily absent. His thoughtfulness softened the blow as much as human tenderness could, but still it fell with crushing weight upon them all.

The father and sister could not sleep, and in the watches of the night he wrote that touching ode, the cry of paternal love and grief entitled " Love's Morrow."

To Mrs. Bond.

CONCORD, Jan. 1, 1880.

DEAR AUNTIE, — It is hard to add one more sorrow to your already full heart, particularly one of this sort, but I did not want you to hear it from any one but us. Dear May is dead. Gone to begin the new year with Mother, in a world where I hope there is no grief like this. Gone just when she seemed safest and happiest, after nearly two years of such sweet satisfaction and love that she wrote us, " If I die when baby comes, remember I have been so unspeakably happy for a year that I ought to be content . . ."

And it is all over. The good mother and sister have done everything in the most devoted way. We can never repay them. My May gave me her little Lulu, and in the spring I hope to get my sweet legacy. Meantime the dear grandma takes her to a home full of loving friends and she is safe. I will write more when we know, but the cruel sea divides us and we must wait.

Bless you dear Auntie for all your love for May; she never forgot it, nor do we.

Yours ever,

LOUISA.

JANUARY 4.

DEAR AUNTIE, — I have little further news to tell, but it seems to comfort me to answer the shower of tender sympathetic letters that each mail brings us. . . .

So we must wait to learn how the end came at last, where the dear dust is to lie, and how soon the desolate little home is to be broken up. It only remains for May's baby to be taken away to fill our cup to overflowing. But perhaps it would be best so, for even in Heaven with Mother, I know May will yearn for the darling so ardently desired, so tenderly welcomed, bought at such a price.

In all the troubles of my life I never had one so hard to bear, for the sudden fall from such high happiness to such a depth of sorrow finds me unprepared to accept or bear it as I ought.

Sometime I shall know why such things are; till then must try to trust and wait and hope as you do. . . . Sorrow has its lonely side, and sympathy is so sweet it takes half its bitterness away.

Yours ever, L.

After May's marriage and death Louisa remained awhile in Concord, trying to forget her grief in care for others. She went to the prison in Concord, and told a story to the prisoners which touched their hearts, and was long remembered by some of them.

She wrote some short stories for "St. Nicholas," among them "Jimmy's Cruise in the Pinafore," called out by the acting of the popular opera of that name by a juvenile troupe.

She spent some weeks at Willow Cottage, Magnolia, which she has described in her popular story of " Jack and Jill." The scene of the story is mostly laid in Concord, or " Harmony " as she calls it, and she has introduced many familiar scenes and persons into the book.

This summer, too, the long-dreamed of School of Philosophy was established. The opening of the School was a great event to Mr. Alcott, as it was the realization of the dream of years. Louisa enjoyed his gratification, and took pains to help him to reap full satisfaction from it. She carried flowers to grace the opening meeting, and was friendly to his guests. She occasionally attended lectures given by her friends, — Dr. Bartol, Mrs. Howe, and others, — and she could not fail to enjoy meeting many of the bright people who congregated there; but she did not care for the speculative philosophy. Her keen sense of humor led her to see all that was incongruous or funny or simply novel in the bearing of the philosophers. She felt that her father had too much of the trying details, and perhaps did not appreciate how much joy of recognition it brought him. She had not much faith in the practical success of the experiment. Philosophy was much associated in her mind with early poverty and suffering, and she did not feel its charms. She was usually at the seashore at this season, as she suffered from the heat at Concord. Frequent allusions to the school appear in her journal. The following anecdote is given by a friend.

" It was at Concord on Emerson day. After a morning with Bartol and Alcott and Mrs. Howe, I lunched with the Alcotts', who had for guest the venerable Dr. McCosh. Naturally the conversation turned on the events of the morning. 'I was thinking,' said the Doctor, 'as I looked among your audience, that there were no young men; and that with none but old men your school would soon die with them. By the way, madam,' he continued, addressing Miss Alcott, 'will you tell me what is your definition of a philosopher?'

" The reply came instantly, ' My definition is of a man up in a balloon, with his family and friends holding the ropes which confine him to earth and trying to haul him down.'

" The laugh which followed this reply was heartily joined in by the philosopher himself."

Journal.

March, 1878. — A happy event, — May's marriage to Ernest Nieriker, the " tender friend " who has consoled her for Marmee's loss, as John consoled Nan for Beth's. He is a Swiss, handsome, cultivated, and good; an excellent family living in Baden, and E. has a good business. May is old enough to choose for herself, and seems so happy in the new relation that we have nothing to say against it.

They were privately married on the 22d, and went to Havre for the honeymoon, as E. had business in France; so they hurried the wedding. Send her $1,000 as a gift, and all good wishes for the new life.

April. — Happy letters from May, who is enjoying life as one can but once. E. writes finely to Father, and is a son to welcome I am sure. May sketches and E. attends to his business by day, and both revel in music in the evening, as E. is a fine violin player.

How different our lives are just now ! — I so lonely, sad, and sick ; she so happy, well, and blest. She always had the cream of things, and deserved it. My time is yet to come somewhere else, when I am ready for it.

Anna clears out the old house ; for we shall never go back to it ; it ceased to be " home " when Marmee left it.

I dawdle about, and wait to see if I am to live or die. If I live, it is for some new work. I wonder what?

May. — Begin to drive a little, and enjoy the spring. Nature is always good to me.

May settles in her own house at Meudon, — a pretty apartment, with balcony, garden, etc. . . . I plan and hope to go to them, if I am ever well enough, and find new inspiration in a new life. May and E. urge it, and I long to go, but cannot risk the voyage yet. I doubt if I ever find time to lead my own life, or health to try it.

June and July. — Improving fast, in spite of dark predictions and forebodings. The Lord has more work for me, so I am spared.

Tried to write a memoir of Marmee ; but it is too soon, and I am not well enough.

.   .   .   .

May has had the new mother and brother-in-law with her, and finds them most interesting and lovable. They seem very proud of her, and happy in her happiness. Bright times for our youngest ! May they last !

[They did. — L. M. A.]

.   .   .   .

Got nicely ready to go to May in September ; but at the last moment gave it up, fearing to undo all the good this weary year of ease has done for me, and be a burden on her. A great disappointment ; but I 've learned to wait. I long to see her happy in her own home.

Nan breaks her leg; so it is well I stayed, as there was no one to take her place but me. Always a little chore to be done.

October, November. — Nan improved. Rode, nursed, kept house, and tried to be contented, but was not. Make no plans for myself now; do what I can, and should be glad not to have to sit idle any longer.

On the 8th, Marmee's birthday, Father and I went to Sleepy Hollow with red leaves and flowers for her. A cold, dull day, and I was glad there was no winter for her any more.

November 25th. — A year since our beloved Marmee died. A very eventful year. May marries, I live instead of dying, Father comes to honor in his old age, and Nan makes her home our refuge when we need one.

December. — A busy time. Nan gets about again. I am so well I wonder at myself, and ask no more.

Write a tale for the " Independent," and begin on an art novel, with May's romance for its thread. Went to B. for some weeks, and looked about to see what I could venture to do. . . .

So ends 1878, — a great contrast to last December. Then I thought I was done with life; now I can enjoy a good deal, and wait to see what I am spared to do. Thank God for both the sorrow and the joy.

January, 1879. — At the Bellevue in my little room writing.

Got two books well started, but had too many interruptions to do much, and dared not get into a vortex for fear of a break-down.

Went about and saw people, and tried to be jolly. Did Jarley for a fair, also for Authors' Carnival at Music Hall. A queer time; too old for such pranks. A sad heart and a used-up body make play hard work, I find.

Read "Mary Wollstonecraft," "Dosia," "Danieli,"
"Helène," etc. I like Gréville's books.

Invest $1,000 for Fred's schooling, etc. Johnny has
his $1,000 also safely in the bank for his education and
any emergency.

February. — Home to Concord rather used up. Find
a very quiet life is best; for in B. people beset me to do
things, and I try, and get so tired I cannot work. Dr. C.
says rest is my salvation; so I rest. Hope for Paris in
the spring, as May begs me to come. She is leading
what she calls "an ideal life," — painting, music, love,
and the world shut out. People wonder and gossip; but
M. and E. laugh and are happy. Wise people to enjoy
this lovely time!

Went to a dinner, at the Revere House, of the Papyrus
Club. Mrs. Burnett and Miss A. were guests of honor.
Dr. Holmes took me in, and to my surprise I found myself at the president's right hand, with Mrs. B., Holmes,
Stedman, and the great ones of the land. Had a gay
time. Dr. H. very gallant. "Little Women" often
toasted with more praise than was good for me.

Saw Mrs. B. at a lunch, and took her and Mrs. M. M.
Dodge to Concord for a lunch. Most agreeable women.

A visit at H. W.'s. Mission time at Church of the
Advent. Father Knox-Little preached, and waked up
the sinners. H. hoped to convert me, and took me to
see Father K.-L., a very interesting man, and we had a
pleasant talk; but I found that we meant the same thing,
though called by different names; and his religion had
too much ceremony about it to suit me. So he gave me
his blessing, and promised to send me some books.

[Never did. — L. M. A.]

Pleasant times with my "rainy-day friend," as I call
Dr. W. She is a great comfort to me, with her healthy

common-sense and tender patience, aside from skill as a doctor and beauty as a woman. I love her much, and she does me good.

. . . .

Happy letters from May. Her hopes of a little son or daughter in the autumn give us new plans to talk over. I *must* be well enough to go to her then.

April. — Very poorly and cross; so tired of being a prisoner to pain. Long for the old strength when I could do what I liked, and never knew I had a body. Life not worth living in this way ; but having over-worked the wonderful machine, I must pay for it, and should not growl, I suppose, as it is just.

To B. to see Dr. S. Told me I was better than she ever dreamed I could be, and need not worry. So took heart, and tried to be cheerful, in spite of aches and nerves. Warm weather comforted me, and green grass did me good.

Put a fence round A.'s garden. Bought a phaeton, so I might drive, as I cannot walk much, and Father loves to take his guests about.

May and June. — Go to B. for a week, but don't enjoy seeing people. Do errands, and go home again. Saw " Pinafore ; " a pretty play.

Much company.

E.'s looked at the Orchard House and liked it ; will hire it, probably. Hope so, as it is forlorn standing empty. I never go by without looking up at Marmee's window, where the dear face used to be, and May's, with the picturesque vines round it. No golden-haired, blue-gowned Diana ever appears now ; she sits happily sewing baby-clothes in Paris. Enjoyed fitting out a box of dainty things to send her. Even lonely old spinsters take an interest in babies.

June. — A poor month. Try to forget my own worries, and enjoy the fine weather, my little carriage, and good friends. Souls are such slaves to bodies it is hard to keep up out of the slough of despond when nerves jangle and flesh aches.

Went with Father on Sunday to the prison, and told the men a story. Thought I could not face four hundred at first; but after looking at them during the sermon, I felt that I could at least *amuse* them, and they evidently needed something new. So I told a hospital story with a little moral to it, and was so interested in watching the faces of some young men near me, who drank in every word, that I forgot myself, and talked away "like a mother." One put his head down, and another winked hard, so I felt that I had caught them; for even one tear in that dry, hard place would do them good. Miss McC. and Father said it was well done, and I felt quite proud of my first speech. [Sequel later.]

July. — Wrote a little tale called "Jimmy's Cruise in the Pinafore," for "St. Nicholas;" $100.

14th. — The philosophers begin to swarm, and the buzz starts to-morrow. How much honey will be made is still doubtful, but the hive is ready and drones also.

On the 15th, the School of Philosophy began in the study at Orchard House, — thirty students; Father, the dean. He has his dream realized at last, and is in glory, with plenty of talk to swim in. People laugh, but will enjoy something new in this dull old town; and the fresh Westerners will show them that all the culture of the world is not in Concord. I had a private laugh when Mrs. —— asked one of the new-comers, with her superior air, if she had ever looked into Plato. And the modest lady from Jacksonville answered, with a twinkle at me, "We have been reading Plato in *Greek* for the past six years." Mrs. ——— subsided after that.

[Oh, wicked L. M. A., who hates sham and loves a joke. —L. M. A.]

Was the first woman to register my name as a voter.

August. — To B. with a new "Scrap Bag." "Jimmy" to the fore. Wrote a little tale.

The town swarms with budding philosophers, and they roost on our steps like hens waiting for corn. Father revels in it, so we keep the hotel going, and try to look as if we liked it. If they were philanthropists, I should enjoy it; but speculation seems a waste of time when there is so much real work crying to be done. Why discuss the "unknowable" till our poor are fed and the wicked saved?

A young poet from New York came; nice boy.

Sixteen callers to-day. Trying to stir up the women about suffrage; so timid and slow.

Happy letters from May. Sophie N. is with her now. All well in the Paris nest.

Passed a week in Magnolia with Mrs. H. School ended for this year. Hallelujah !

September. — Home from the seaside refreshed, and go to work on a new serial for "St. Nicholas," — "Jack and Jill." Have no plan yet but a boy, a girl, and a sled, with an upset to start with. Vague idea of working in Concord young folks and their doings. After two years of rest, I am going to try again; it is so easy to make money now, and so pleasant to have it to give. A chapter a day is my task, and not that if I feel tired. No more fourteen hours a day; make haste slowly now.

Drove about and drummed up women to my suffrage meeting. So hard to move people out of the old ruts.

I haven't patience enough; if they won't see and work,
I let 'em alone, and steam along my own way.

May sent some nice little letters of an "Artist's Holiday," and I had them printed; also a book for artists
abroad, — very useful, and well done.

Eight chapters done.   Too much company for work.

October 8th. — Dear Marmee's birthday.   Never forgotten.   Lovely day.   Go to Sleepy Hollow with flowers.
Her grave is green; blackberry vines with red leaves
trail over it.   A little white stone with her initials is at
the head, and among the tall grass over her breast a little
bird had made a nest; empty now, but a pretty symbol
of the refuge that tender bosom always was for all feeble
and sweet things.   Her favorite asters bloomed all about,
and the pines sang overhead.   So she and dear Beth are
quietly asleep in God's acre, and we remember them
more tenderly with each year that brings us nearer them
and home.

Went with Dr. W. to the Woman's Prison, at Sher-
burne.   A lovely drive, and very remarkable day and
night.   Read a story to the four hundred women, and
heard many interesting tales.   A much better place than
Concord Prison, with its armed wardens, and "knock
down and drag out" methods.   Only women here, and
they work wonders by patience, love, common-sense, and
the belief in salvation for all.

First proof from Scribner of "Jack and Jill."   Mrs. D.
likes the story, so I peg away very slowly.   Put in Elly
D. as one of my boys.   The nearer I keep to nature,
the better the work is.   Young people much interested
in the story, and all want to "go in."   I shall have a
hornet's nest about me if all are not *angels*.

Father goes West.

I mourn much because all say I must not go to May;

not safe; and I cannot add to Mamma Nieriker's cares at this time by another invalid, as the voyage would upset me, I am so sea-sick.

Give up my hope and long-cherished plan with grief. May sadly disappointed. I know I shall wish I had gone; it is my luck.

November. — Went to Boston for a month, as some solace for my great disappointment. Take my room at the Bellevue, and go about a little. Write on "J. and J." Anxious about May.

8th. — Little Louisa May Nieriker arrived in Paris at 9 P. M., after a short journey. All doing well. Much rejoicing. Nice little lass, and May very happy. Ah, if I had only been there! Too much happiness for me.

25th. — Two years since Marmee went. How she would have enjoyed the little granddaughter, and all May's romance! Perhaps she does.

Went home on my birthday (forty-seven). Tried to have a little party for Nan and the boys, but it was rather hard work.

Not well enough to write much, so give up my room. Can lie round at home, and it 's cheaper.

December. — May not doing well. The weight on my heart is not all imagination. She was too happy to have it last, and I fear the end is coming. Hope it is my nerves; but this peculiar feeling has never misled me before.

Invited to the breakfast to O. W. H. No heart to go.

8th. — Little Lu one month old. Small, but lively. Oh, if I could only be there to see, — to help! This is a penance for all my sins. Such a tugging at my heart to be by poor May, alone, so far away. The N.'s are devoted, and all is done that can be; but not one of her "very own" is there.

Father came home.

29th. — May died at 8 A. M., after three weeks of fever and stupor. Happy and painless most of the time. At Mr. W.'s funeral on the 30th, I *felt* the truth before the news came.

Wednesday, 31st. — A dark day for us. A telegram from Ernest to Mr. Emerson tells us " May is dead." Anna was gone to B. ; Father to the post-office, anxious for letters, the last being overdue. I was alone when Mr. E. came. E. sent to him, knowing I was feeble, and hoping Mr. E. would soften the blow. I found him looking at May's portrait, pale and tearful, with the paper in his hand. " My child, I wish I could prepare you ; but alas, alas ! " There his voice failed, and he gave me the telegram.

I was not surprised, and read the hard words as if I knew it all before. " I *am* prepared," I said, and thanked him. He was much moved and very tender. I shall remember gratefully the look, the grasp, the tears he gave me ; and I am sure that hard moment was made bearable by the presence of this our best and tenderest friend. He went to find Father but missed him, and I had to tell both him and Anna when they came. A very bitter sorrow for all.

The dear baby may comfort E., but what can comfort us ? It is the distance that is so hard, and the thought of so much happiness ended so soon. " Two years of perfect happiness " May called these married years, and said, " If I die when baby comes, don't mourn, for I have had as much happiness in this short time as many in twenty years." She wished me to have her baby and her pictures. A very precious legacy ! Rich payment for the little I could do for her. I see now why I lived, — to care for May's child and not leave Anna all alone.

January 1st, 1880. — A sad day mourning for May. Of all the trials in my life I never felt any so keenly as this, perhaps because I am so feeble in health that I cannot bear it well. It seems so hard to break up that happy little home and take May just when life was richest, and to leave me who had done my task and could well be spared. Shall I ever know why such things happen?

Letters came telling us all the sad story. May was unconscious during the last weeks, and seemed not to suffer. Spoke now and then of "getting ready for Louy," and asked if she had come. All was done that love and skill could do, but in vain. E. is brokenhearted, and good Madame N. and Sophie find their only solace in the poor baby.

May felt a foreboding, and left all ready in case she died. Some trunks packed for us, some for the N. sisters. Her diary written up, all in order. Even chose the graveyard where she wished to be, out of the city E. obeys all her wishes sacredly.

Tried to write on "J. and J." to distract my mind; but the wave of sorrow kept rolling over me, and I could only weep and wait till the tide ebbed again.

February. — More letters from E. and Madame N. Like us, they find comfort in writing of the dear soul gone, now there is nothing more to do for her. I cannot make it true that our May is dead, lying far away in a strange grave, leaving a husband and child whom we have never seen. It all reads like a pretty romance, now death hath set its seal on these two happy years; and we shall never know all that she alone could tell us.

Many letters from friends in France, England, and America, full of sympathy for us, and love and pride and gratitude for May, who was always glad to help, forgive, and love every one. It is our only consolation now.

Father and I cannot sleep, but he and I make verses as we did when Marmee died. Our grief seems to flow into words. He writes "Love's Morrow" and "Our Madonna."

Lulu has gone to Baden with Grandmamma.

Finish "J. and J." The world goes on in spite of sorrow, and I must do my work. Both these last serials were written with a heavy heart, — "Under the Lilacs" when Marmee was failing, and "Jack and Jill" while May was dying. Hope the grief did not get into them.

Hear R. W. E. lecture for his one hundredth time. Mary Clemmer writes for a sketch of my life for a book of "Famous Women." Don't belong there.

Read "Memoirs of Madame de Rémusat." Not very interesting. Beauties seldom amount to much. Plain Margaret Fuller was worth a dozen of them. "Kings in Exile," a most interesting book, a very vivid and terrible picture of Parisian life and royal weakness and sorrow.

Put papers, etc., in order. I feel as if one should be ready to go at any moment. . . .

March. — A box came from May, with pictures, clothes, vases, her ornaments, a little work-basket, and, in one of her own sepia boxes, her pretty hair tied with blue ribbon, — all that is now left us of this bright soul but the baby, soon to come. Treasures all.

A sad day, and many tears dropped on the dear dress, the blue slippers she last wore, the bit of work she laid down when the call came the evening Lulu was born. The fur-lined sack feels like May's arms round me, and I shall wear it with pleasure. The pictures show us her great progress these last years.

To Boston for a few days on business, and to try to forget. Got gifts for Anna's birthday on the 16th, — forty-nine years old. My only sister now, and the best God ever made. Repaired her house for her.

Lulu is not to come till autumn. Great disappointment; but it is wiser to wait, as summer is bad for a young baby to begin here.

29th. — Town meeting. Twenty women there, and voted first, thanks to Father. Polls closed, — in joke, we thought, as Judge Hoar proposed it; proved to be in earnest, and *we* elected a good school committee. Quiet time; no fuss.

JANUARY 20, 1880.

DEAR MRS. DODGE, — I have been so bowed down with grief at the loss of my dear sister just when our anxiety was over that I have not had a thought or care for anything else.

The story is done; but the last chapters are not copied, and I thought it best to let them lie till I could give my mind to the work.

I never get a good chance to do a story without interruption of some sort. "Under the Lilacs" was finished by my mother's bedside in her last illness, and this one when my heart was full of care and hope and then grief over poor May.

I trust the misery did not get into the story; but I'm afraid it is not as gay as I meant most of it to be.

I forgot to number the pages of the last two chapters, and so cannot number these. I usually keep the run, but this time sent off the parcel in a hurry. Can you send me the right number to go on with in chapter seventeen? I can send you four more as soon as I hear.

I don't believe I shall come to New York this winter.

May left me her little daughter for my own; and if she comes over soon, I shall be too busy singing lullabies to one child to write tales for others, or go anywhere, even to see my kind friends.

A sweeter little romance has just ended in Paris than any I can ever make; and the sad facts of life leave me no heart for cheerful fiction.

Yours truly,　　　L. M. ALCOTT.

CHAPTER XI.

LAST YEARS.

MY PRAYER.

(Written October, 1886.)

COURAGE and patience, these I ask,
  Dear Lord, in this my latest strait;
For hard I find my ten years' task,
  Learning to suffer and to wait.

Life seems so rich and grand a thing,
  So full of work for heart and brain,
It is a cross that I can bring
  No help, no offering, but pain.

The hard-earned harvest of these years
  I long to generously share;
The lessons learned with bitter tears
  To teach again with tender care;

To smooth the rough and thorny way
  Where other feet begin to tread;
To feed some hungry soul each day
  With sympathy's sustaining bread.

So beautiful such pleasures show,
  I long to make them mine;
To love and labor and to know
  The joy such living makes divine.

But if I may not, I will only ask
  Courage and patience for my fate,
And learn, dear Lord, thy latest task, —
  To suffer patiently and wait.

THE early part of the year 1880 was in the deep shadow of sadness, from the death of Louisa's sister. Boxes full of May's pictures, clothes, and books came home to call up anew all the memories of the bright spirit who had blossomed into such beautiful life so quickly to fade away.

Miss Alcott tried to rise above her grief and busy herself with new interests. She took an active part in the voting of the women in Concord, and rejoiced in the election of a good school committee. In April she returned to her old rooms at the Bellevue, where she busied herself with dramatizing " Michael Strogoff," which she never completed. She kept up her interest in young girls, and received with pleasure a visit from thirty pupils of the Boston University, and she helped to give the children of the North End Mission a happy day at Walden Pond. She went to York for rest and refreshment during the summer. Her heart was filled with longing for the child, and everything was done with reference to its coming.

As September brought cooler weather, over the sea came the little babe to the warm hearts that were longing to welcome her. No woman as true and loving as Louisa Alcott but has the mother-nature strong in her heart; and she could not help feeling a new spring of love and life when the child of one so dear was put into her arms to be her very own. Rosy and healthy, full of life and energy, — not a model of sainthood, but a real human nature, with a will to be regulated, not broken, with impulses to be trained, talents and tendencies to be studied, and a true, loving heart to be filled with joy, — Louisa found the child a constant source of interest and pleasure. She brought her up as she herself had been trained, — more by influences than by rules, — and sought to follow the leadings which she found in the young nature rather than to make it over after a plan of her own. This new care and joy helped to fill up the void in her life from the loss of the mother for whom she had worked so faithfully and the pet sister to whom she had ever been a good providence.

The principal interest of the next few years was the care of this child. It was a pleasant occupation to Louisa, occupying her heart, and binding her with new ties to younger generations. The journal tells all the simple story of the "voyage across the seas."

Miss Alcott was very attractive to children, especially to the little ones, who thronged about her and pleaded for stories; but this was the first one who ever really filled the mother-longing in her heart. She was now truly a " marmee; " and remembering the blessing which her own mother had been to her, her standard of motherhood must have been very high. Much care was now also given to her father, and she speaks with pride of her handsome old philosopher in his new suit of clothes.

Miss Alcott was gratified by a visit from one of the men to whom she had spoken at Concord Prison. He told her his story, and she assisted him to find work, and had the satisfaction of hearing of his well-doing.

There is little record of writing done at this period, Louisa's time and thoughts being absorbed by the child. In the autumn of 1881 she wrote a preface to a new edition of the " Prayers of Theodore Parker," and also one to the new edition of " Moods."

Louisa kept the birthdays of November, though with saddened heart. She wrote a tale for the Soldiers' Home, — " My Red Cap," in " Proverb Stories," — and another for the New England Hospital fair, — " A Baby's Birthday; " and also one for her old publisher. Such was the feeling toward her as a universal benefactor, that a poor woman wrote her begging her to send some Christmas gifts to her children, as they had asked her to write to Santa Claus for some. With Lulu's help she got up a box for the poor family, and then made a story out of the incident, for which she received a hundred dollars.

A new project was that of a temperance society, which was felt to be needed in Concord.

Louisa occupied herself much in looking over her mother's papers, and unfortunately destroyed them, instead of preparing a memoir of her as she had intended to do. It is a matter of great regret that she did not feel able to do this work, for Mrs. Alcott's letters would have been a most valuable record of the life of her time, as well as a treasury of bright thought and earnest feeling. Louisa was not willing to commit the task to any other hand, and the opportunity is gone.

To Mrs. Dodge.

CONCORD, May 29.

DEAR MRS. DODGE, — I was away from home, so your letter did not reach me till I got back yesterday.

Thanks for your kind thought of me, and recollections of the pleasant week when the L. L.'s had a lark. I should like another; but in this work-a-day world busy folk don't get many, as we know.

If I write a serial, you shall have it; but I have my doubts as to the leisure and quiet needed for such tasks being possible with a year-old baby. Of course little Lu is a *very* remarkable child, but I fancy I shall feel as full of responsibility as a hen with one chick, and cluck and scratch industriously for the sole benefit of my daughter.

She may, however, have a literary turn, and be my assistant, by offering hints and giving studies of character for my work. She comes in September, if well.

If I do begin a new story, how would " An Old-Fashioned Boy " and his life do? I meant that for the title of a book, but another woman took it. You proposed a revolutionary tale once, but I was not up to it; for this I have quaint material in my father's journals, letters, and recollections. He was born with the century, and had an uncle in the war of 1812 ; and his life was very pretty and pastoral in the early days. I think a new sort of story would n't be amiss, with fun in it, and the queer old names and habits. I began it long ago, and if I have a chance will finish off a few chapters and send them to you, if you like.

Yours cordially,

L. M. ALCOTT.

*To Mr. Niles, about the new illustrated edition of
" Little Women."*

YORK, July 20, 1880.

The drawings are all capital, and we had great fun
over them down here this rainy day. . . . Mr. Merrill
certainly deserves a good penny for his work. Such a
fertile fancy and quick hand as his should be well paid,
and I shall not begrudge him his well-earned compensation, nor the praise I am sure these illustrations will earn.
It is very pleasant to think that the lucky little story has
been of use to a fellow-worker, and I am much obliged
to him for so improving on my hasty pen-and-ink
sketches. What a dear rowdy boy Teddy is with the
felt basin on !

The papers are great gossips, and never get anything
quite straight, and I do mean to set up my own establishment in Boston (D. V.). Now I have an excuse for
a home of my own, and as the other artistic and literary
spinsters have a house, I am going to try the plan, for a
winter at least.

Come and see how cosey we are next October at 81
Pinckney Street. Miss N. will receive.

Yours truly, L. M. A.

To Mrs. Dodge.

81 PINCKNEY STREET, 1880.

DEAR MRS. DODGE, — The editor of " Harper's Young
People " asked for a serial, and I declined ; then they
wanted a short story for Christmas, and I sent one. But
it was not long enough, though longer than most of my
short $100 tales.

So I said, "If you don't want it, send it to 'Saint Nicholas.'"

Therefore if "How It Happened" comes straying along, you will know what it means. If you don't want it, please send it to me in Boston, 81 Pinckney Street; for Christmas tales are always in demand, and I have no time to write more.

You will like to know that my baby is safely here, — a healthy, happy little soul, who comes like sunshine to our sad hearts, and takes us all captive by her winning ways and lovely traits.

I shall soon be settled for the winter, and I hope have good times after the hard ones.

Affectionately yours,

L. M. A.

Journal.

April, 1880. — So sad and poorly; went to B. for a change. Old room at the Bellevue.

Amused myself dramatizing "Michael Strogoff;" read, walked, and rested. Reporters called for story of my life; did not get much. Made my will, dividing all I have between Nan and the boys, with Father as a legacy to Nan, and to Lulu her mother's pictures and small fortune of $500.

May. — Thirty girls from Boston University called; told stories, showed pictures, wrote autographs. Pleasant to see so much innocent enthusiasm, even about so poor a thing as a used-up old woman. Bright girls! simple in dress, sensible ideas of life, and love of education. I wish them all good luck.

Ordered a stone for May's grave like Marmee's and Beth's, for some day I hope to bring her dust home.

Twenty-third is the anniversary of Mother's wedding. If she had lived, it would have been the golden wedding.

Went to see St. Botolph's Club rooms. Very prim and neat, with easy chairs everywhere; stained glass, and a pious little *bar*, with nothing visible but a moral ice-pitcher and a butler like a bishop. The reverend gentlemen will be comfortable and merry, I fancy, as there is a smoking-room and card-tables, as well as a library and picture-gallery. Divines nowadays are not as godly as in old times, it seems.

Mrs. Dodge wants a new serial, but I doubt if I can do it; boys, babies, illness, and business of all sorts leave no time for story-telling.

June. — We all enjoy the new rooms very much, and Father finds his study delightful. Prepare the Orchard House for W. T. Harris, who is to rent it.

North End Mission children at Walden Pond. Help give them a happy day, — eleven hundred of them. Get Anna and John off to Walpole. Cleaned house.

Madame N. sends a picture of Lulu, — a funny, fat little thing in her carriage. Don't realize that it is May's child, and that she is far away in a French cemetery, never to come home to us again.

It is decided that Baby is to come to us in September.

24th. — Lizzie's birthday and Johnny's. He is fifteen, — a lovely, good boy, whom every one loves. Got the Dean a new suit of clothes, as he must be nice for his duties at the School. Plato's toga was not so costly, but even he did not look better than my handsome old philosopher.

July and August. — To York with boys. Rest and enjoy the fine air. Home in August, and let Anna go down. Four hundred callers since the School began. Philosophy is a bore to outsiders.

Got things ready for my baby, — warm wrapper, and all the dear can need on her long journey. On the 21st saw Mrs. Giles (who went for baby) off; the last time I went, it was to see May go. She was sober and sad, not gay as before; seemed to feel it might be a longer voyage than we knew. The last view I had of her, was standing alone in the long blue cloak waving her hand to us, smiling with wet eyes till out of sight. How little we dreamed what an experience of love, joy, pain, and death she was going to !

A lonely time with all away. My grief meets me when I come home, and the house is full of ghosts.

September. — Put papers in order, and arrange things generally, to be in order when our Lulu comes. Make a cosey nursery for the darling, and say my prayers over the little white crib that waits for her, if she ever comes. God watch over her !

Paid my first *poll*-tax. As my *head* is my most valuable piece of property, I thought $2 a cheap tax on it. Saw my townswomen about voting, etc. Hard work to stir them up ; cake and servants are more interesting.

18*th.* — In Boston, waiting for the steamer that brings my treasure. The ocean seems very wide and terrible when I think of the motherless little creature coming so far to us.

19*th.* — Lulu and Sophie N. arrived with poor G., worn out by anxiety. A stormy passage, and much care, being turned out of the stateroom I had engaged for them and paid for, by a rude New York dressmaker. No help for it, so poor G. went to a rat-hole below, and did her best.

As I waited on the wharf while the people came off the ship, I saw several babies, and wondered each time if that was mine. At last the captain appeared, and in his arms a little yellow-haired thing in white, with its hat half off as it looked about with lively blue eyes and babbled prettily. Mrs. G. came along by it, and I knew it was Lulu. Behind, walked a lovely brown-eyed girl with an anxious face, all being new and strange to Sophie.

I held out my arms to Lulu, only being able to say her name. She looked at me for a moment, then came to me, saying " Marmar " in a wistful way, and resting close as if she had found her own people and home at last, — as she had, thank Heaven ! I could only listen while I held her, and the others told their tale. Then we got home as soon as we could, and dear baby behaved very well, though hungry and tired.

The little princess was received with tears and smiles. and being washed and fed went quietly to sleep in her new bed, while we brooded over her and were never tired of looking at the little face of " May's baby."

She is a very active, bright child, not pretty yet, being browned by sea air, and having a yellow down on her head, and a pug nose. Her little body is beautifully formed, broad shoulders, fine chest, and lovely arms. A happy thing, laughing and waving her hands, confiding and bold, with a keen look in the eyes so like May, who hated shams and saw through them at once. She always comes to me, and seems to have decided that I am really " Marmar." My heart is full of pride and joy, and the touch of the dear little hands seems to take away the bitterness of grief. I often go at night to see if she is really *here,* and the sight of the little head is like sunshine to me. Father adores her, and she loves to sit in his strong arms. They make a pretty picture as he walks in the garden with her to "see birdies." Anna tends her as she did May, who was her baby once, being ten years younger, and we all find life easier to live now the baby has come. Sophie is a sweet girl, with much character and beauty. A charming sister in love as in law.

October. — Happy days with Lulu and Sophie; getting acquainted with them. Lulu is rosy and fair now, and grows pretty in her native air, — a merry little lass, who seems to feel at home and blooms in an atmosphere of adoration. People come to see " Miss Alcott's baby," and strangers waylay her little carriage in the street to look at her; but she does not allow herself to be kissed.

As Father wants to go West I decide to hire Cousin L. W.'s house furnished for the winter, so that Sophie and the boys can have a pleasant time. S. misses the gayety of her home-life in stupid Concord, where the gossip and want of manners strike her very disagreeably. Impertinent questions are asked her, and she is amazed at the queer, rude things people say.

November 8th. — Lulu's birthday. One year old. Her gifts were set out on a table for her to see when she came down in the afternoon, — a little cake with *one* candle, a rose crown for the queen, a silver mug, dolly, picture-books, gay ball, toys, flowers, and many kisses. She sat smiling at her treasures just under her mother's picture. Suddenly, attracted by the sunshine on the face of the portrait which she knows is " Marmar," she held up a white rose to it calling " Mum ! Mum !" and smiling at it in a way that made us all cry. A happy day for her, a sad one to us.

Thanksgiving. — Family dinner.

Father at Syracuse, having conversations at Bishop Huntington's and a fine time everywhere.

December. — Too busy to keep much of a journal. My life is absorbed in my baby. On the twenty-third she got up and walked alone; had never crept at all, but when ready ran across the room and plumped down, laughing triumphantly at her feat.

Christmas. — Tried to make it gay for the young folks, but a heavy day for Nan and me. Sixty gifts were set out on different tables, and all were much pleased. Sophie had many pretty things, and gave to all generously.

A hard year for all, but when I hold my Lulu I feel as if even death had its compensations. A new world for me.

Called down one day to see a young man. Found it one of those to whom I spoke at the prison in Concord last June. Came to thank me for the good my little story did him, since it kept him straight and reminded him that it is never too late to mend. Told me about himself, and how he was going to begin anew and wipe out the past. He had been a miner, and coming East met some fellows who made him drink; while tipsy he stole something in a doctor's office, and having no friends here was sentenced to three years in prison. Did well, and was now out. Had a prospect of going on an expedition to South America with a geological surveying party. An interesting young man. Fond of books, anxious to do well, intelligent, and seemed eager to atone for his one fault. Gave him a letter to S. G. at Chicago. Wrote to the warden, who confirmed D.'s story and spoke well of him. Miss Willard wrote me later of him, and he seemed doing well. Asked if he might write to me, and did so several times, then went to S. A. and I hear no more. Glad to have said a word to help the poor boy.

March, 1881. — Voted for school committee.

October. — Wrote a preface for Parker's Prayers, just got out by F. B. Sanborn.

November. — Forty-nine on 29th. Wrote a preface to the new edition of " Moods."

8th. — Gave my baby *two* kisses when she woke, and escorted her down to find a new chair decked with ribbons, and a doll's carriage tied with pink ; toys, pictures, flowers, and a cake, with a red and a blue candle burning gayly.

Wrote a tale for the Soldiers' Home, — " My Red Cap," — and one for the Woman's Hospital fair, — " A Baby's Birthday." Also a tale for F.

December. — A poor woman in Illinois writes me to send her children some Christmas gifts, being too poor and ill to get any. They asked her to write to Santa Claus and she wrote to *me.* Sent a box, and made a story about it, — $100. Lulu much interested, and kept bringing all her best toys and clothes " for poor little boys." A generous baby.

To Mr. Niles.

FEBRUARY 12, 1881.

DEAR MR. NILES, — Wendell Phillips wrote me a letter begging me to write a preface for Mrs. Robinson's " History of the Suffrage Movement ; " but I refused him, as I did Mrs. R., because I don't write prefaces well, and if I begin to do it there will be no end. . . .

Cannot you do a small edition for her? All the believers will buy the book, and I think the sketches of L. M. Child, Abby May, Alcott, and others will add much to the interest of the book.

Has she seen you about it? Will you look at the manuscripts by and by, or do you scorn the whole thing? Better not ; for we are going to win in time, and the friend of literary ladies ought to be also the friend of women generally.

We are going to meet the Governor, council, and legislature at Mrs. Tudor's next Wednesday eve and have a grand set-to. I hope he will come out of the struggle alive.

Do give Mrs. R. a lift if you can, and your petitioners will ever pray.

Yours truly,   **L. M. A.**

FEBRUARY 19, 1881.

DEAR MR. NILES,—Thank you very much for so kindly offering to look at Mrs. R.'s book. It is always pleasant to find a person who can conquer his prejudices to oblige a friend, if no more.

I think we shall be glad by and by of every little help we may have been able to give to this reform in its hard times, for those who take the tug now will deserve the praise when the work is done.

I can remember when Antislavery was in just the same state that Suffrage is now, and take more pride in the very small help we Alcotts could give than in all the books I ever wrote or ever shall write.

"Earth's fanatics often make heaven's saints," you know, and it is as well to try for that sort of promotion in time.

If Mrs. R. does send her manuscripts I will help all I can in reading or in any other way. If it only records the just and wise changes Suffrage has made in the laws for women, it will be worth printing; and it is time to keep account of these first steps, since they count most.

I, for one, don't want to be ranked among idiots, felons, and minors any longer, for I am none of the three, but very gratefully yours,

L. M. A.

To Mrs. Stearns.

DEAR MRS. STEARNS, — Many thanks for the tender thoughtfulness which sends us the precious little notes from the dear dead hands.

They are so characteristic that they bring both Mother and May clearly up before me, alive and full of patient courage and happy hopes. I am resigned to my blessed mother's departure, since life was a burden, and the heroic past made a helpless future very hard to think of. But May's loss, just when life was fullest and sweetest, seems very bitter to me still, in spite of the sweet baby who is an unspeakable comfort. I wish you could see the pretty creature who already shows many of her mother's traits and tastes. Her love of pictures is a passion, but she will not look at the common gay ones most babies enjoy. She chooses the delicate, well-drawn, and painted figures of Caldecott and Miss Greenaway; over these she broods with rapture, pointing her little fingers at the cows or cats, and kissing the children with funny prattlings to these dumb playmates. She is a fine, tall girl, full of energy, intelligence, and health; blonde and blue-eyed like her mother, but with her father's features, for which I am glad, for he is a handsome man. Louisa May bids fair to be a noble woman; and I hope I may live to see May's child as brave and bright and talented as she was and, much happier in her fate.

Father is at the West, busy and well. Anna joins me in thanks and affectionate regards.

Ever yours,   L. M. ALCOTT.

Journal.

March, 1882. — Helped start a temperance society; much needed in C. A great deal of drinking, not among the Irish, but young American gentlemen, as well as farmers and mill hands. Women anxious to do something, but find no interest beyond a few. Have meetings, and try to learn how to work. I was secretary, and wrote records, letters, and sent pledges, etc.; also articles in "Concord Freeman" and "Woman's Journal" about the union and town meetings.

April. — Read over and destroyed Mother's diaries, as she wished me to do so. A wonderfully interesting record of her life, from her delicate, cherished girlhood through her long, hard, romantic married years, old age, and death. Some time I will write a story or a memoir of it.

Lulu's teeth trouble her; but in my arms she seems to find comfort, for I tell stories by the dozen; and lambs, piggies, and "tats" soothe her little woes. Wish I were stronger, so that I might take all the care of her. We seem to understand each other, but my nerves make me impatient, and noise wears upon me.

Mr. Emerson ill. Father goes to see him. E. held his hand, looking up at the tall, sorry old man, and saying, with that smile of love that has been Father's sunshine for so many years, "*You* are very well, — keep so, keep so." After Father left, he called him back and grasped his hand again, as if he knew it was for the last time, and the kind eyes said, "Good-by, my friend!"

April 27, 1882, Louisa speaks most tenderly of the death of Mr. Emerson. He had been to her and to her family the truest and best of friends; and her own profound reverence for him had been a strong influence, from the time when she played games with his children in the barn until she followed him to his honored grave. Let critics and philosophers judge him by his intellect; in the hearts of this family, and in many an humble home besides, he will always be remembered as the tenderest, most sympathetic, most loyal of all friends, whose bounty fell on them silently as the dew from heaven, and whose presence could brighten the highest joy and soothe the keenest sorrow they could ever know.

Journal.

Thursday, 27th. — Mr. Emerson died at 9 P. M. suddenly. Our best and greatest American gone. The nearest and dearest friend Father has ever had, and the man who has helped me most by his life, his books, his society. I can never tell all he has been to me, — from the time I sang Mignon's song under his window (a little girl) and wrote letters *à la* Bettine to him, my Goethe, at fifteen, up through my hard years, when his essays on Self-Reliance, Character, Compensation, Love, and Friendship helped me to understand myself and life, and God and Nature. Illustrious and beloved friend, good-by !

Sunday, 30th. — Emerson's funeral. I made a yellow lyre of jonquils for the church, and helped trim it up. Private services at the house, and a great crowd at the church. Father read his sonnet, and Judge Hoar and others spoke. Now he lies in Sleepy Hollow among his brothers, under the pines he loved.

I sat up till midnight to write an article on R. W. E. for the "Youth's Companion," that the children may know something of him. A labor of love.

May. — Twenty-seven boys signed pledge. Temperance work. Meetings. I give books to schools. Wrote an article for Mrs. Croly on R. W. E.

June. — I visited A. B. in Mattapoisset for a week. A queer time, driving about or talking over our year in Europe. School children called upon me with flowers, etc.

24th. — John's seventeenth birthday. A dear boy, good and gay, full of love, manliness, and all honest and lovely traits, like his father and mother. Long life to my boy!

July. — School of Philosophy opens on the 17th in full force. I arrange flowers, oak branches, etc., and then fly before the reporters come. Father very happy. Westerners arrive, and the town is full with ideal speculators. Penny has a new barge; we call it the "Blue Plato" (not the "Black Maria"), and watch it rumble by with Margaret Fullers in white muslin and Hegels in straw hats, while stout Penny grins at the joke as he puts money in his purse. The first year Concord people stood aloof, and the strangers found it hard to get rooms. Now every one is eager to take them, and the School is pronounced a success because it brings money to the town. Even philosphers can't do without food, beds, and washing; so all rejoice, and the new craze flourishes. If all our guests paid we should be well off; several hundred a month is rather wearing. Father asked why we never went, and Anna showed him a long list of four hundred names of callers, and he said no more.

October. — To Hotel Bellevue with John.

Missed my dear baby, but need quiet. Brain began to work, and plans for tales to simmer. Began "Jo's Boys," as Mrs. Dodge wants a serial.

In the autumn of 1882 Mr. Alcott was attacked by a severe stroke of paralysis, from which he never fully recovered; and for the rest of his life his daughters shared in the duty of tending and caring for him in his enfeebled state. It had been the great reward of Louisa's years of hard work that she could surround her mother with every comfort that could make her happy in her last declining years. Not less had she delighted to gratify every wish of her father. His library was fitted up with exquisite taste, his books and manuscripts bound, and he was "throned in philosophic ease" for the rest of his days. What a relief it was now that she could have the faithful nurse ready at his call; that she could give him the pleasant drives which he enjoyed so much; and lighten her sister's labors with every assistance that money could procure!

The Orchard House, which had been the family home for twenty-five years, was sold to Mr. Harris, and Mrs. Pratt's house was the home of all. Louisa spent part of the summer at the seashore, and finally bought a small house at Nonquit, where the children could all spend the summer, while she and her sister alternated in the care of her father.

In the autumn of 1885, Miss Alcott decided to take a furnished house in Louisburg Square. Her nephews were established in Boston, and their mother wished to be with them. Mr. Alcott bore the moving well, and they found many comforts in the arrangement. Louisa's health was very feeble. She had great trouble in the throat, and her old dyspeptic symptoms returned to annoy her. Still she cannot give up work, and busies herself in preparing "Lulu's Library" for publication, and hopes to be able to work on "Jo's Boys."

"Lulu's Library" was a collection of stories which had been the delight of the child. The first series was published in 1885, the second in 1887, and the third in 1889. They are full of Louisa's charming qualities, and have a special interest from the tender feeling with which she gathereᴅ them up for her niece. The touching preface to " Jo's Boys " tells of the seven years of occasional work on this book, and reveals the depth of feeling which would not allow her to write as formerly of Marmee and Amy, who were no longer here to accept their own likenesses. During the latter part of her work on this book, she could only write from half an hour to one or two hours a day. This was published in September, 1886. It contains an engraving of her from a bas-relief by Mr. Ricketson.

This book was written under hard circumstances, and cost its author more effort perhaps than any other. It is evidently not the overflow of her delight and fun in life like " Little Women," but it is full of biographical interest. Her account of her own career, and of the annoyances to which her celebrity exposed her, is full of her old spirit and humor. She has expressed many valuable thoughts on education, and her spirit is as hopeful for her boys as in her days of youth and health. She has too many characters to manage; but we feel a keen interest in the fortunes of Dan and Emil, and in the courtship by the warm-hearted Tom of his medical sweetheart.

Preface to " *Jo's Boys.*"

Having been written at long intervals during the past seven years, this story is more faulty than any of its very imperfect predecessors; but the desire to atone for an unavoidable disappointment, and to please my patient little friends, has urged me to let it go without further delay.

To account for the seeming neglect of Amy, let me add, that, since the original of that character died, it has been impossible for me to write of her as when she was here to suggest, criticise, and laugh over her namesake. The same excuse applies to Marmee. But the folded leaves are not blank to those who knew and loved them and can find memorials of them in whatever is cheerful, true, or helpful in these pages.

L. M. ALCOTT.

CONCORD, July 4, 1886.

To Mr. Horace Chandler.

DEAR MR. CHANDLER, — The corrections are certainly rather peculiar, and I fear my struggles to set them right have only produced greater confusion.

Fortunately punctuation is a free institution, and all can pepper to suit the taste. I don't care much, and always leave proof-readers to quibble if they like.

Thanks for the tickets. I fear I cannot come till Thursday, but will try, and won't forget the office, since I am not that much-tried soul the editor.

Yours truly,

L. M. A.

To Mrs. Williams (Betsey Prig).

NONQUIT, August 25.

DEAR BETSEY, — I am so sorry the darling Doll is ill! Brood over him, and will him well; for mother-love works wonders.

My poppet is a picture of health, vigor, and delightful naughtiness. She runs wild in this fine place with some twenty other children to play with, — nice babies, well-bred, and with pleasant mammas for me to gossip with.

It would be a good place for your little people, as the air is delicious, bathing safe and warm, and cottages to be quiet in if one cares to keep house. Do try it next year. Let me know early. I can get a nice little cot for you (near mine) for $100, or perhaps less, from June to October, — if you care to stay; I do. . . .

We have been here since July, and are all hearty, brown, and gay as larks.

" John Inglesant " was too political for me. I am too lazy here to read much; mean to find a den in Boston and work for a month or two; then fly off to New York, and perhaps run over and see my Betsey. I shall be at home in October, and perhaps we may see you then, if the precious little shadow gets nice and well again, and I pray he may.

Lulu has some trifling ail now and then, — just enough to show me how dear she is to us all, and what a great void the loss of our little girl would make in hearts and home. She is very intelligent and droll. When I told her the other day that the crickets were hopping and singing in the grass with their mammas, she said at once, " No; their Aunt Weedys." Aunty is nearer than mother to the poor baby; and it is very sweet to have it so, since it must be.

Now, my blessed Betsey, keep a brave heart, and I am sure all will be well in the nest. Love and kisses to the little birds, and all good wishes to the turtle-dove and her mate.

Yours ever,   L. M. A.

The older birthdays are 29th of November, Lulu's the 8th; so we celebrate for Grandpa, Auntie, and Lulu all at once, in great style, — eighty-three, fifty, and three years old.

When I get on my pins I 'm going (D. V.) to devote myself to settling poor souls who need a gentle boost in hard times.

To Mr. Niles.

JUNE 23, 1883.

DEAR MR. NILES, — Thanks for the Goethe book. I want everything that comes out about him. " Princess Amelia " is charming, and the surprise at the end well done. Did the author of " My Wife's Sister " write it?

I told L. C. M. she might put "A Modern Mephistopheles " in my list of books. Several people had found it out, and there was no use in trying to keep it secret after that.

Mrs. Dodge begged me to consider myself mortgaged to her for tales, etc., and as I see no prospect of any time for writing books, I may be able to send her some short stories from time to time, and so be getting material for a new set of books like " Scrap-bag," but with a new name. You excel in names, and can be evolving one meantime. . . .

Yours truly,   L. M. A.

JULY 15, 1884.

I wish I might be inspired to do those dreadful boys ["Jo's Boys"]; but rest is more needed than money.

Perhaps during August, my month at home, I may take
a grind at the old mill.

Journal.

October 24, 1882. — Telegram that Father had had a
paralytic stroke. Home at once, and found him stricken
down. Anxious days; little hope.

November. — Gave up our rooms, and I went home to
help with the new care. My Lulu ran to meet me, rosy
and gay, and I felt as if I could bear anything with this
little sunbeam to light up the world for me.

Poor Father dumb and helpless; feeble mind slowly
coming back. He knows us; but he's asleep most of
the time. Get a nurse, and wait to see if he will rally.
It is sad to see the change one moment makes, turning
the hale, handsome old man into this pathetic wreck.
The forty sonnets last winter and the fifty lectures at the
School last summer were too much for a man of eighty-
three. He was warned by Dr. W., but thought it folly
to stop ; and now poor Father pays the penalty of breaking the laws of health. I have done the same : may I
be spared this end !

January, 1883. — Too busy to keep a diary. Can
only jot down a fact now and then.

Father improving. Much trouble with nurses; have
no idea of health ; won't walk ; sit over the fire, and drink
tea three times a day ; ought to be an intelligent, hearty
set of women. Could do better myself; have to fill up
all the deficiencies and do double duty.

People come to see Father; but it excites him, and we
have to deny him.

February. — To B. for a week of rest, having got Mrs.
H. settled with Father, and all comfortable for November.

Began a book called " Genius." Shall never finish it,

I dare say, but must keep a vent for my fancies to escape at. This double life is trying, and my head will work as well as my hands.

March. — To give A. rest I took Lulu and maid to the Bellevue for a month. Lulu very happy with her new world. Enjoys her walks, the canary I got her, and the petting *she* gets from all. Showed her to friends; want them to know May's child. Had her picture taken by Notman; very good.

April 2d. — Town meeting. Seven women vote. I am one of them, and A. another. A poor show for a town that prides itself on its culture and independence.

6th. — Go home to stay; Father needs me. New nurse; many callers; Lulu fretful, Anna tired, Father feeble, — hard times for all.

Wrote a story for "St. Nicholas" at odd moments. Nurses and doctors take a deal of money.

May. — Take care of Lulu, as we can find no good woman to walk and dress and play with her. The ladies are incapable or proud; the girls vulgar or rough; so my poor baby has a bad time with her little temper and active mind and body. Could do it myself if I had the nerves and strength, but am needed elsewhere, and must leave the child to some one. Long to go away with her and do as I like. Shall never lead my own life.

July. — Go to Nonquit with Miss H. and Lulu for the summer. A quiet, healthy place, with pleasant people and fine air. Turn Lulu loose, with H. to run after her, and try to rest.

Lulu takes her first bath in the sea. Very bold; walks off toward Europe up to her neck, and is much afflicted that I won't let her go to the bottom and see the " little trabs;" makes a cupid of herself, and is very pretty and gay.

The boys revel in the simple pleasures of Nonquit, — a fine place for them to be in.

Wrote a tale for "St. Nicholas," — "Sophie's Secret," — $100.

August. — Home to C., and let A. come for her holiday. Much company.

P. C. Mozoomdar preached, and had a conversation at Mrs. Emerson's; a most interesting man. Curious to hear a Hindu tell how the life of Christ impressed him.

November 27th. — Decide to lessen care and worry at home; so take rooms in Boylston Street, and with Lulu set forth to make a home of our own. The whole parlor floor gives my lady room to run in doors, and the Public Garden opposite is the out-door play-ground. Miss C. comes as governess, and we settle down. Fred boards with us. Heard Mathew Arnold.

29th. — Birthday, — fifty-one. Home with gifts to poor Father, — eighty-four. Found a table full for myself.

December 25th. — Home with gifts for all; sad day. See H. Martineau's statue; very fine.

January, 1884. — New Year's Day is made memorable by my solemnly spanking my child. Miss C. and others assure me it is the only way to cure her wilfulness. I doubt it; but knowing that mothers are usually too tender and blind, I correct my dear in the old-fashioned way. She proudly says, "Do it, do it!" and when it is done is heartbroken at the idea of Aunt Weewee's giving her pain. Her bewilderment was pathetic, and the effect, as I expected, a failure. Love is better; but also endless patience.

February 2d. — Wendell Phillips died. I shall mourn for him next to R. W. E. and Parker.

6th. — Funeral at Hollis Street Church. Sat between

Fred Douglas and his wife. A goodly gathering of all left of the old workers. Glad and proud to be among them.

. . . .

June. — Sell the Orchard House to W. T. Harris. Glad to be done with it, though after living in it twenty-five years, it is full of memories; but places have not much hold on me when the dear persons who made them dear are gone. . . .

Bought a cottage at Nonquit, with house and furniture. All like it, and it is a good investment I am told.

24th. — To Nonquit with Lulu and K. and John. Fixed my house, and enjoyed the rest and quiet immensely. Lulu wild with joy at the freedom. . . .

July and August. — Restful days in my little house, which is cool and quiet, and without the curse of a kitchen to spoil it.

Lulu happy and well, and every one full of summer fun.

On the 7th of August I went home, and let A. go for her holiday.

Took care of Father and house, and idled away the hot days with books and letters. Drove with Father, as he enjoyed it very much. . . .

October. — To Boston with John, and take rooms at the Bellevue. Very tired of home-worry, and fly for rest to my old refuge, with J. and L. to look after and make a home for.

Saw Irving. Always enjoy him, though he is very queer. Ellen Terry always the same, though charming in her way.

November. — Find Bellevue uncomfortable and expensive, so take rooms in Chestnut Street for self and boys.

8th. — My Lulu's birthday. Go home with flowers, gifts, and a grateful heart that the dear little girl is so well and happy and good. A merry day with the little queen of the house.

29th. — Our birthday, — Father eighty-five; **L. M. A.** fifty-two. Quiet day; always sad for thinking of Mother and John and May, who all left us at this season.

December. — Began again on "Jo's Boys," as T. N. wants a new book very much, and I am tired of being idle. Wrote two hours for three days, then had a violent attack of vertigo, and was ill for a week. Head won't bear work yet. Put away papers, and tried to dawdle and go about as other people do.

Pleasant Christmas with Lulu and Nan and poor Father, who loves to see us about him. A narrow world now, but a happy one for him.

Last day of the year. All well at home except myself; body feeble, but soul improving.

Jaunary 1, 1885. — Pleasant greeting from brother Ernest by telegram, — never forgets us. Opera in the evening, — Emma Nevada. Sent box home. Very cold.

John had his first dress-suit. Happy boy! Several pleasant Sunday evenings at E. P. W.'s. See Mrs. Burnett, and like her.

Visit Blind Asylum and North End Mission. Lulu passed a week with me for a change.

19th. — An old-fashioned party in an old-time house. All in antique costume; Lulu very pretty in hers. Country kitchen and country fare; spinning and weaving; old songs and dances; tally-ho coach with P. as an ancient Weller, — very funny.

. . . .

June. — Read Life of Saint Elizabeth by D'Alembert, — quaint and sweet; also French novels. Write out the little tales I tell Lulu for a new Christmas book, having nothing else. Send one, "The Candy Country," to "St. Nicholas."

. . . .

August 8th. — Go home, and A. goes to N. Take care of Father, arrange the little tales, and look at houses in B. Have a plan to take a furnished house for the winter, and all be together. A. is lonely in C.; boys must be near business. I want Lulu, and Father will enjoy a change.

Sorted old letters, and burned many. Not wise to keep for curious eyes to read and gossip-lovers to print by and by.

Lived in the past for days, and felt very old, recalling all I have been through. Experiences go deep with me, and I begin to think it might be well to keep some record of my life, if it will help others to read it when I'm gone. People seem to think our lives interesting and peculiar.

September. — After a lively time with house-brokers, I take a house in Louisburg Square for two years. It is a large house, furnished, and well suited to our needs, — sunny, trees in front, good air, and friends near by. All are pleased, and we prepare to move October 1st. . . .

Father drove down very nicely. Pleased with his new room; Lulu charmed with her big, sunny nursery and the play-house left for her; boys in clover; and Nan ready for the new sort of housekeeping.

I shall miss my quiet, care-free life in B.; but it is best for all, so I shall try to bear the friction and the worry many persons always bring me.

It will be an expensive winter; but T. N. tells me the books never sold better, so a good run in January will make all safe.

"Lulu's Library" as a "pot-boiler" will appease the children, and I may be able to work on "Jo's Boys."

March, 1886. — To Mrs. H.'s to hear Mr. Snyder read the "Iliad;" enjoyed it.

Sixteen little girls call, and the autograph fiend is abroad.

27th. — Another attack of vertigo, — ill for a week; sleepless nights. Head worked like a steam-engine; would not stop. Planned "Jo's Boys" to the end, and longed to get up and write it. Told Dr. W. that he had better let me get the ideas *out*, then I could rest. He very wisely agreed, and said, " As soon as you can, write half an hour a day, and see if it does you good. Rebellious brains want to be attended to, or trouble comes." So I began as soon as able, and was satisfied that we were right; for my head felt better very soon, and with much care about not overdoing, I had some pleasant hours when I forgot my body and lived in my mind.

April. — Went on writing one or two hours a day, and felt no ill effects.

May. — Began to think of Concord, and prepare to go back for the summer. Father wants his books; Lulu, her garden; Anna, her small house; and the boys, their friends. I want to go away and rest.

Anna goes up the last of the month and gets the house ready. We send Lulu and Father later, and the boys and I shut up No. 10. . . .

June. — Home in C., — sunny, clean, and pleasant. Put Lulu in order, and get ready for a month in Princeton with Mrs. H. Very tired.

A quiet three weeks on the hillside, — a valley pink with laurel in front, Mount Wachusett behind us, and green hills all round. A few pleasant people. I read, sleep, walk, and write, — get fifteen chapters done. Instinct was right; after seven years of rest, the old brain was ready for work and tired of feeding on itself, since work it must at something. Enjoyed Hedge's " Hours with German Classics," and " Baldwin," by Vernon Lee.

Home in time to get Anna and Lulu off to N. for the summer. A. needs the rest very much, and Lulu the freedom. I shall revel in the quiet, and finish my book.

July. — The seashore party get off, and peace reigns. I rest a day, and then to work. Finish "Jo's Boys," and take it to T. N. Much rejoicing over a new book. Fifty thousand to be the first edition; orders coming in fast. Not good, — too great intervals between the parts, as it was begun long ago; but the children will be happy, and my promise kept. Two new chapters were needed, so I wrote them, and gladly corked my inkstand.

What next? Mrs. Dodge wants a serial, and T. N. a novel. I have a dozen plots in my head, but think the serial better come first. Want a great deal of money for many things; every poor soul I ever knew comes for help, and expenses increase. I am the only money-maker, and must turn the mill for others, though my own grist is ground and in the barn.

The School begins. Father feeble, but goes, — for the last time, I think.

A series of letters to her father's friend, Mrs. Stearns, show how tenderly and carefully Louisa watched over the slow decline of the stricken man, but they are too full of details of the sick-room for publication. A few extracts will give her feeling.

MAY 23 [1885].

DEAR MRS. STEARNS, — Many thanks for the sweet nosegay you sent me. It came in good time, for to-day is the anniversary of Father's wedding-day and my sister's silver wedding. Rather sad for both mateless ones; but we have done our best to cheer them up, and the soft rain is very emblematic of the memories their own quiet tears keep green.

Father remembered you, and smelled his flowers with pleasure. He is very tired of living, and wants to "go up," as he expresses it. A little more or little less light would make him happier; but the still active mind beats against the prison bars, and rebels against the weakness of body that prevents the old independent life. I am afraid the end is not to be peaceful unless it is sudden, as I hope it may be for all our sakes; it is so wearing to see this slow decline, and be able to do little but preach and practise patience.

. . . .

Affectionately yours,   L. M. A.

SUNDAY.

. . . .

It is only a temporary change, perhaps; but I still hope that it will last, and his mind grow still clearer. These painless, peaceful days have a certain sweetness, sad as it is to see the dear, hale old man so feeble. If he can know us, and enjoy something of the old life, it is worth having, though the end may come at any moment. . . .

Now and then a word comes without effort. "Up!" was the first one, and seems very characteristic of this beautiful, aspiring soul, almost on the wing for heaven.

To Mr. Niles.

NONQUIT, July 13, 1885.

DEAR MR. NILES, — I want to know if it is too late to do it and if it is worth doing; namely, to collect some of the little tales I tell Lulu and put them with the two I shall have printed the last year and the "Mermaid Tale" to match the pictures we bought, and call it "Lulu's Library"? I have several tiny books written down for L.; and as I can do no great work, it occurred to me that I might venture to copy these if it would do for a Christmas book for the younger set.

I ache to fall on some of the ideas that are simmering in my head, but dare not, as my one attempt since the last "Jo's Boys" break-down cost me a week or two of woe and $30 for the doctor. I have lovely long days here, and can copy these and see 'em along if you want them. One has gone to "Harper's Young People," and one is for "St. Nicholas" when it is done, — about the Kindergarten for the blind. These with Lulu's would make a little book, and might begin a series for small folks. Old ladies come to this twaddle when they can do nothing else. What say you? . . .

Yours truly,

L. M. A.

September 18, 1885.

DEAR MR. NILES, — I send you some funny sketches by Mrs. L. She seems to be getting on. How would it do to ask her to illustrate the fairy book? She has a pretty taste in elves, and her little girl was good. I hope to touch up the other stories this winter, and she can illustrate, and next Christmas (or whenever it is ready) we can have a little book out. This sort of work being all I dare do now, I may as well be clearing the decks for action when the order comes to "Up, and at 'em!" again, if it ever does.

I'd like to help Mrs. L. if I could, as we know something of her, and I fancy she needs a lift. Perhaps we could use these pictures in some way if she liked to have

———•———

Jan, 2 ond 1886

Dear Mr Niles.

Thanks for the good wishes & news. Now that I cannot work it is very agreeable to hear that the books go so well. & that the lazy woman need not worry about things.

I appreciate my blessings
I assure you, & heartily
wish I could "swamp the
book room with Jo's
Boys" as I did say, & hope
to do it by & by when head
& hand can safely obey,
the desire of the heart
which will never be too
tired or too old to
remember & be grateful.

Your friend
L. M. Alcott.

us. Maybe I could work them into a story of our "cullud bredren."

Thanks for the books. Dear Miss —— is rather prim in her story, but it is pretty and quite *correct.* So different from Miss Alcott's slap-dash style.

The " H. H." book [" Ramona "] is a noble record of the great wrongs of her chosen people, and ought to wake up the sinners to repentance and justice before it is too late. It recalls the old slavery days, only these victims are red instead of black. It will be a disgrace if " H. H." gave her work and pity all in vain.

Yours truly,   L. M. A.

[1885.]

DEAR MR. NILES, — Thanks for the book which I shall like to read.

Please tell Miss N. that she will find in Sanborn's article in " St. Nicholas " or Mrs. Moulton's in the " Eminent Women " book all that I wish to have said about myself. You can add such facts about editions, etc., as you think best. I don't like these everlasting notices ; one is enough, else we poor people feel like squeezed oranges, and nothing is left sacred.

George Eliot's new life and letters is well done, and we are not sorry we have read them. Mr. Cross has been a wise man, and leaves us all our love and respect instead of spoiling them as Froude did for Carlyle,

Yours truly,   L. M. A.

JANUARY 2, 1886.

DEAR MR. NILES, — Thanks for the good wishes and news. Now that I cannot work, it is very agreeable to hear that the books go so well, and that the lazy woman need not worry about things.

I appreciate my blessings, I assure you. I heartily wish I could "swamp the book-room with 'Jo's Boys,'" as Fred says, and hope to do it by and by when head and hand can safely obey the desire of the heart, which will never be too tired or too old to remember and be grateful.

Your friend,   L. M. ALCOTT.

MONDAY, A. M. [1886].

DEAR MR. NILES, — My doctor forbids me to begin a long book or anything that will need much thought this summer. So I must give up "Tragedy of To-day," as it will need a good deal of thinking to be what it ought.

I can give you a girls' book however, and I think that will be better than a novel. I have several stories done, and can easily do more and make a companion volume for "Spinning-Wheel Stories" at Christmas if you want it.

This, with the Lulu stories, will be better than the set of novels I am sure. . . . Wait till I can do a novel, and then get out the set in style, if Alcott is not forgotten by that time.

I was going to send Mrs. Dodge one of the tales for girls, and if there is time she might have more. But nearly all new ones would make a book go well in the holiday season. You can have those already done now if you want them. "Sophie's Secret" is one, "An Ivy Spray: or Cinderella's Slippers" another, and "Mountain Laurel" is partly done. "A Garland for Girls" might do for a title perhaps, as they are all for girls.

Yours truly,   L. M. A.

In the spring of 1886, Dr. Rhoda Lawrence took charge of Miss Alcott's health, and gave her treat-

ment by massage and other appropriate means, from
which she received benefit. The summer was spent
at Concord with her father, and was varied by a
pleasant trip to the mountains. Miss Alcott finished "Jo's Boys," which was published in September. She occupied herself also in looking
over old journals and letters, and destroyed many
things which she did not wish to have come under
the public eye. She had enjoyed her life at Princeton, and said that she felt better than for fifteen
years; but in August she was severely attacked
with rheumatism and troubled with vertigo. She
suffered very much, and was in a very nervous
condition.

Miss Alcott always looked bravely and calmly
upon all the possibilities of life, and she now made
full preparations for the event of her own death.
Her youngest nephew had always been especially
beloved, and she decided to take out papers of
adoption, to make him legally her son and heir.
She wished him to assume the name of Alcott, and
to be her representative.

Louisa's journal closes July, 1886, with the old
feeling, — that she must grind away at the mill and
make money to supply the many claims that press
upon her from all sides. She feels the burden
of every suffering human life upon her own soul.
She knew that she could write what was eagerly
desired by others and would bring her the means
of helping those in need, and her heart and head
united in urging her to work. Whether it would
have been possible for her to have rested more
fully, and whether she might then have worked

longer and better, is one of those questions which
no one is wise enough to answer. Yet the warning
of her life should not be neglected, and the eager
brain should learn to obey the laws of life and
health while it is yet time.

In September, 1886, Miss Alcott returned to
Louisburg Square, and spent the winter in the care
of her father, and in the society of her sister and
nephews and the darling child. She suffered much
from hoarseness, from nervousness and debility, and
from indigestion and sleeplessness, but still exerted
herself for the comfort of all around her. She had
a happy Christmas, and sympathized with the joy
of her oldest nephew in his betrothal. In December she was so weary and worn that she went out
to Dr. Lawrence's home in Roxbury for rest and
care. She found such relief to her overtasked
brain and nerves from the seclusion and quiet of
Dunreath Place, that she found her home and rest
there for the remainder of her life.

It was a great trial to Louisa to be apart from
her family, to whom she had devoted her life. She
clung to her dying father, and to the dear sister still
left to her, with increasing fondness, and she longed
for her boys and her child; but her tired nerves
could not bear even the companionship of her
family, and sometimes for days she wanted to be
all alone. "I feel so safe out here!" she said
once.

Mr. Alcott spent the summer at Melrose, and
Louisa went there to visit him in June. In June
and July, 1887, she went to Concord and looked
over papers and completed the plan for adopting

her nephew. She afterward went to Princeton, accompanied by Dr. Lawrence. She spent eight weeks there, and enjoyed the mountain air and scenery with something of her old delight. She was able to walk a mile or more, and took a solitary walk in the morning, which she greatly enjoyed. Her evening walk was less agreeable, because she was then exposed to the eager curiosity of sight-seers, who constantly pursued her.

Miss Alcott had a great intellectual pleasure here in the society of Mr. James Murdock and his family. The distinguished elocutionist took great pains to gratify her taste for dramatic reading by selecting her favorite scenes for representation, and she even attended one of his public readings given in the hall of the hotel. The old pain in her limbs from which she suffered during her European journey again troubled her, and she returned to Dr. Lawrence's home in the autumn, where she was tenderly cared for.

Miss Alcott was still continually planning stories. Dr. Lawrence read to her a great deal, and the reading often suggested subjects to her. She thought of a series to be called "Stories of All Nations," and had already written "Trudel's Siege," which was published in "St. Nicholas," April, 1888, the scene of which was laid at the siege of Leyden. The English story was to be called "Madge Wildfire," and she had thought of plots for others. She could write very little, and kept herself occupied and amused with fancy work, making flowers and pen-wipers of various colors, in the form of pinks, to send to her friends.

On her last birthday Louisa received a great many flowers and pleasant remembrances, which touched her deeply, and she said, " I did not mean to cry to-day, but I can't help it, everybody is so good." She went in to see her father every few days, and was conscious that he was drawing toward the end.

While riding with her friend, Louisa would tell her of the stories she had planned, one of which was to be called " The Philosopher's Wooing," referring to Thoreau. She also had a musical novel in her mind. She could not be idle, and having a respect for sewing, she busied herself with it, making garments for poor children, or helping the Doctor in her work. She insisted upon setting up a work-basket for the Doctor, amply supplied with necessary materials, and was pleased when she saw them used. A flannel garment for a poor child was the last work of her hands. Her health improved in February, especially in the comfort of her nights, as the baths she took brought her the long-desired sleep. " Nothing so good as sleep," she said. But a little too much excitement brought on violent headaches.

During these months Miss Alcott wrote part of the " Garland for Girls," one of the most fanciful and pleasing of her books. These stories were suggested by the flowers sent to her by different friends, which she fully enjoyed. She rode a great deal, but did not see any one.

Her friends were much encouraged; and although they dared not expect full recovery, they hoped that she might be " a comfortable invalid, able to enjoy life, and give help and pleasure to

24

others." She did not suffer great pain, but she was very weak; her nervous system seemed to be utterly prostrated by the years of work and struggle through which she had passed. She said, " I don't want to live if I can't be of use." She had always met the thought of death bravely; and even the separation from her dearest friends was serenely borne. She believed in their continued presence and influence, and felt that the parting was for a little time. She had no fear of God, and no doubt of the future. Her only sadness was in leaving the friends whom she loved and who might yet need her.

A young man wrote asking Miss Alcott if she would advise him to devote himself to authorship; she answered, " Not if you can do anything else. Even dig ditches." He followed her advice, and took a situation where he could support himself, but he still continued to write stories. A little boy sent twenty-five cents to buy her books. She returned the money, telling him it was not enough to buy books, but sent him " Little Men." Scores of letters remained unanswered for want of strength to write or even to read.

Early in March Mr. Alcott failed very rapidly. Louisa drove in to see him, and was conscious that it was for the last time. Tempted by the warm spring-like day, she had made some change in her dress, and absorbed in the thought of the parting, when she got into the carriage she forgot to put on the warm fur cloak she had worn.

The next morning she complained of violent pain in her head, amounting to agony. The physician who had attended her for the last weeks was called. He felt that the situation was very serious. She herself asked, "Is it not meningitis?" The trouble on the brain increased rapidly. She recognized her dear young nephew for a moment and her friendly hostess, but was unconscious of everything else. So, at 3.30 P. M., March 6, 1888, she passed quietly on to the rest which she so much needed. She did not know that her father had already preceded her.

The friends of the family who gathered to pay their last tribute of respect and love to the aged father were met at the threshold by the startling intelligence, "Louisa Alcott is dead," and a deeper sadness fell upon every heart. The old patriarch had gone to his rest in the fulness of time, "corn ripe for the sickle," but few realized how entirely his daughter had worn out her earthly frame. Her friends had hoped for renewed health and strength, and for even greater and nobler work from her with her ripened powers and greater ease and leisure.

Miss Alcott had made every arrangement for her death; and by her own wish the funeral service was very simple, in her father's rooms at Louisburg Square, and attended only by a few of her family and nearest friends. They read her exquisite poem to her mother, her father's noble tribute to her, and spoke of the earnestness and truth of her life. She was remembered as she would have wished to be. Her body was carried to Concord and placed in the beautiful cemetery of Sleepy Hollow where her dearest ones were already laid to rest. "Her boys" went beside her as "a guard of honor," and stood around as she was placed across the feet of father, mother, and sister, that she might "take care of them as she had done all her life."

Of the silent grief of the bereaved family I will not speak, but the sound of mourning filled all the land, and was re-echoed from foreign shores. The children everywhere had lost their friend. Miss Alcott had entered into their hearts and revealed them to themselves. In her childish journal her oldest sister said, " I have not a secret from Louisa; I tell her everything, and am not afraid she will think me silly." It was this respect for the thought and life of children that gave Louisa Alcott her great power of winning their respect and affection. Nothing which was real and earnest to them seemed unimportant to her.

LAST LETTERS.

To Mr. Niles.

SUNDAY, 1886.

DEAR MR. NILES, — The goodly supply of books was most welcome; for when my two hours pen-work are over I need something to comfort me, and I long to go on and finish "Jo's Boys" by July 1st.

My doctor frowns on that hope, and is so sure it will do mischief to get up the steam that I am afraid to try, and keep Prudence sitting on the valve lest the old engine run away and have another smash-up.

I send you by Fred several chapters, I wish they were neater, as some were written long ago and have knocked about for years; but I can't spare time to copy, so hope the printers won't be in despair.

I planned twenty chapters and am on the fifteenth. Some are long, some short, and as we are pressed for time we had better not try to do too much.

. . . I have little doubt it will be done early in July, but things are so contrary with me I can never be sure of carrying out a plan, and I don't want to fail again; so far I feel as if I could, without harm, finish off these dreadful boys.

Why have any illustrations? The book is not a child's book, as the lads are nearly all over twenty, and pretty pictures are not needed. Have the bas-relief if you like, or one good thing for frontispiece.

I can have twenty-one chapters and make it the size of "Little Men." Sixteen chapters make two hundred and sixteen pages, and I may add a page here and there later, — or if need be, a chapter somewhere to fill up.

I shall be at home in a week or two, much better for the rest and fine air; and during my quiet days in C. I can touch up proofs and confer about the book. Sha'n't we be glad when it is done?

Yours truly,

L. M. A.

To Mrs. Dodge.

JUNE 29.

DEAR MRS. DODGE, — I will evolve something for December (D. V.) and let you have it as soon as it is done.

Lu and I go to Nonquit next week; and after a few days of rest, I will fire up the old engine and see if it will run a short distance without a break-down.

There are usually about forty young people at N., and I think I can get a hint from some of them.

Had a call from Mr. Burroughs and Mr. Gilder last eve. Mr. G. asked if you were in B., but I did n't know.

Father remains comfortable and happy among his books. Our lads are making their first visit to New York, and may call on " St. Nick," whom they have made their patron saint.

I should like to own the last two bound volumes of " St. Nicholas," for Lulu. She adores the others, and they are nearly worn out with her loving but careless luggings up and down for " more towries, Aunt Wee-wee." Charge to

Yours affectionately,

L. M. A.

P. S. — Was n't I glad to see you in my howling wilderness of wearisome domestic worrits ! Come again.

CONCORD, August 15.

DEAR MRS. DODGE, — I like the idea of " Spinning-Wheel Stories," and can do several for a series which can come out in a book later. Old-time tales, with a thread running through all from the wheel that enters in the first one.

A Christmas party of children might be at an old farm-house and hunt up the wheel, and grandma spins and tells the first story ; and being snow-bound, others amuse the young folks each evening with more tales. Would that do ? The mother and child picture would come in nicely for the first tale, — " Grandma and her Mother."

Being at home and quiet for a week or so (as Father is nicely and has a capable nurse), I have begun the serial, and done two chapters ; but the spinning-tales come tumbling into my mind so fast I 'd better pin a few while " genius burns." Perhaps you would like to start the set Christmas. The picture being ready and the first story can be done in a week, "Sophie's Secret" can come later. Let me know if you would like that, and about how many pages of the paper "S. S." was written on you think would make the required length of tale (or tail?). If you don't want No. 1 yet, I will take my time and do several.

The serial was to be "Mrs. Gay's Summer School," and have some city girls and boys go to an old farm-house, and for fun dress and live as in old times, and learn the good, thrifty old ways, with adventures and fun thrown in. That might come in the spring, as it takes me longer to grind out yarns now than of old.

Glad you are better. Thanks for kind wishes for the little house; come and see it, and gladden the eyes of forty young admirers by a sight of M. M. D. next year.

Yours affectionately,

L. M. A.

31 CHESTNUT ST., DECEMBER 31.

DEAR MRS. DODGE, — A little cousin, thirteen years old, has written a story and longs to see it in print. It is a well written bit and pretty good for a beginner, so I send it to you hoping it may find a place in the children's corner. She is a grandchild of S. J. May, and a bright lass who paints nicely and is a domestic little person in spite of her budding accomplishments. Good luck to her!

I hoped to have had a Christmas story for some one, but am forbidden to write for six months, after a bad turn of vertigo. So I give it up and take warning. All good wishes for the New Year.

From yours affectionately,

L. M. ALCOTT.

To Mr. Niles.

1886.

DEAR MR. NILES, — Sorry you don't like the bas-relief [of herself] ; I do. A portrait, if bright and comely, would n't be me, and if like me would disappoint the children ; so we had better let them imagine "Aunt Jo young and beautiful, with her hair in two tails down her back," as the little girl said.

In haste, L. M. A.

To Mrs. Bond.

CONCORD, Tuesday, 1886.

DEAR AUNTIE, — I want to find Auntie Gwinn, and don't know whom to ask but you, as your big motherly heart yearns over all the poor babies, and can tell them where to go when the nest is bare. A poor little woman has just died, leaving four children to a drunken father. Two hard-working aunts do all they can, and one will take the oldest girl. We want to put the two small girls and boy into a home till we can see what comes next. Lulu clothes one, and we may be able to put one with a cousin. But since the mother died last Wednesday they are very forlorn, and must be helped. If we were not so full I'd take one ; but Lu is all we can manage now.

There is a home at Auburndale, but it is full ; and I know of no other but good Auntie Gwinn's. What is her address, please? I shall be in town on Saturday, and can go and see her if I know where.

Don't let it be a bother ; but one turns at once in such cases to the saints for direction, and the poor aunts don't known what to do ; so this aunt comes to the auntie of all.

I had a pleasant chat with the Papa in the cars, and was very glad to hear that W. is better. My love to both and S.

Thanks for the news of portraits. I 'll bear them in mind if G. H. calls. Lulu and Anna send love, and I am as always,

Your   LOUISA ALCOTT.

To Mrs. Dodge.

APRIL 13, 1886.

DEAR MRS. DODGE, — I am glad you are going to have such a fine outing. May it be a very happy one.

I cannot promise anything, but hope to be allowed to write a little, as my doctor has decided that it is as well to let me put on paper the tales "knocking at the saucepan lid and demanding to be taken out" (like Mrs. Cratchit's potatoes), as to have them go on worrying me inside. So I 'm scribbling at "Jo's Boys," long promised to Mr. Niles and clamored for by the children. I may write but one hour a day, so cannot get on very fast; but if it is ever done, I can think of a serial for "St. Nicholas." I began one, and can easily start it for '88, if head and hand allow. I will simmer on it this summer, and see if it can be done. Hope so, for I don't want to give up work so soon.

I have read "Mrs. Null," but don't like it very well, — too slow and colorless after Tolstoi's "Anna Karanina."

I met Mr. and Mrs. S. at Mrs. A.'s this winter. Mr. Stockton's child-stories I like very much. The older ones are odd but artificial.

Now, good-by, and God be with you, dear woman, and bring you safely home to us all.

Affectionately yours,   L. M. ALCOTT.

To Mrs. Bond.

DEAR AUNTIE, — I have been hoping to get out and see you all winter, but have been so ill I could only live on hope as a relish to my gruel, — that being my only food, and not of a nature to give me strength. Now I am beginning to live a little, and feel less like a sick oyster at low tide. The spring days will set me up I trust, and my first pilgrimage shall be to you ; for I want you to see how prettily my May-flower is blossoming into a fine off-shoot of the old plant.

Lizzy Wells has probably told you our news of Fred and his little bride, and Anna written you about it as only a proud mamma can.

Father is very comfortable, but says sadly as he looks up from his paper, " Beecher has gone now ; all go but me." Please thank Mr. Bond for the poems, which are interesting, even to a poor, ignorant worm who does not know Latin. Mother would have enjoyed them very much. I should have acknowledged his kindness sooner ; but as I am here in Roxbury my letters are forwarded, and often delayed.

I was sorry to hear that you were poorly again. Is n't it hard to sit serenely in one's soul when one's body is in a dilapidated state ? I find it a great bore, but try to do it patiently, and hope to see the why by and by, when this mysterious life is made clear to me. I had a lovely dream about that, and want to tell it you some day.

Love to all.

Ever yours,			L. M. A.

Her publisher wished to issue a new edition of " A Modern Mephistopheles," and to add to it her story " A Whisper in the Dark," to which she consented.

MAY 6, 1887.

DEAR MR. NILES. — This is about what I want to say. You may be able to amend or suggest something. I only want it understood that the highfalutin style was for a disguise, though the story had another purpose ; for I'm not ashamed of it, and like it better than " Work " or " Moods."

Yours in haste,   L. M. A.

P. S. — Do you want more fairy tales?

Preface.

" A Modern Mephistopheles " was written among the earlier volumes of the No Name Series, when the chief idea of the authors was to puzzle their readers by disguising their style as much as possible, that they might enjoy the guessing and criticism as each novel appeared. This book was very successful in preserving its incognito ; and many persons still insist that it could not have been written by the author of " Little Women." As I much enjoyed trying to embody a shadow of my favorite poem in a story, as well as the amusement it has afforded those in the secret for some years, it is considered well to add this volume to the few romances which are offered, not as finished work by any means, but merely attempts at something graver than magazine stories or juvenile literature.

L. M. ALCOTT.

SATURDAY A. M., May 7, 1887.

DEAR MR. NILES, — Yours just come. " A Whisper " is rather a lurid tale, but might do if I add a few lines to

Fac-simile of Preface to "A Modern
Mephistopheles."

Preface.

—

A Modern Mephistopheles
was written among the earlier
volumes of the No Name Series
when the chief idea of the
authors was to puzzle their
readers by disguising their
style as much as possible, that
they might enjoy the guessing
& criticism as each novel offer
ed. This book was very successful in preserving its incognito
& many persons still insist that
it could not have been written
by the author of Little Women.
As I much enjoyed trying to
embody a shadow of my
favorite poem in a story, as
well as the amusement it has
afforded those in the secret, I

some years; it is considered
well to add this volume to the
small essays of few romances which
are offered not as finished work
by any means but merely attempts
at something graver than
magazine stories or juvenile
tales literature,

L. M. Alcott.

the preface of "Modern Mephistopheles," saying that this is put in to fill the volume, or to give a sample of Jo March's necessity stories, which many girls have asked for. Would that do?

It seems to me that it would be better to wait till I can add a new novel, and then get out the set. Meantime let "Modern Mephistopheles" go alone, with my name, as a summer book before Irving comes [Irving as Faust].

I hope to do "A Tragedy of To-day" this summer, and it can come out in the fall or next spring, with "Modern Mephistopheles," "Work," and "Moods."

A spunky new one would make the old ones go. "Hospital Sketches" is not cared for now, and is filled up with other tales you know. . . .

Can that plan be carried out? I have begun my tragedy, and think it will be good; also a shorter thing called "Anna: An Episode," in which I do up Boston in a jolly way, with a nice little surprise at the end. It would do to fill up "Modern Mephistopheles," as it is not long, unless I want it to be.

I will come in next week and see what can be done. Yours truly,

L. M. A.

To Mrs. Bond.

SUNDAY, Oct. 16, [1887].

DEAR AUNTIE, — As you and I belong to the "Shut-in Society," we may now and then cheer each other by a line. Your note and verse are very good to me to-day, as I sit trying to feel all right in spite of the stiffness that won't walk, the rebel stomach that won't work, and the tired head that won't rest.

My verse lately has been from the little poem found under a good soldier's pillow in the hospital.

I am no longer eager, bold, and strong, —
  All that is past ;
I am ready not to do
  At last — at last.
My half-day's work is done,
  And this is all my part.
I give a patient God
  My patient heart.

The learning not to do is so hard after being the hub to the family wheel so long. But it is good for the energetic ones to find that the world can get on without them, and to learn to be still, to give up, and wait cheerfully.

As we have " fell into poetry," as Silas Wegg says, I add a bit of my own; for since you are Marmee now, I feel that you won't laugh at my poor attempts any more than she did, even when I burst forth at the ripe age of eight.

Love to all the dear people, and light to the kind eyes that have made sunshine for others so many years.

Always your   Lu.

*To Mrs. Bond, with first copy of "Lulu's Library,"
second volume.*

OCTOBER, 1887.

DEAR AUNTIE, — I always gave Mother the first author's copy of a new book. As her representative on earth, may I send you, with my love, the little book to come out in November?

The tales were told at sixteen to May and her playmates ; then are related to May's daughter at five ; and for the sake of these two you may care to have them for the little people.

I am still held by the leg, but seem to gain a little, and hope to be up by and by. Slow work, but part of

the discipline I need, doubtless; so I take it as well as
I can.

You and I won't be able to go to the golden wedding
of S. J. May. I have been alone so long I feel as if I 'd
like to see any one, and be in the good times again.
L. W. reports you as " nicely, and sweet as an angel; "
so I rejoice, and wish I could say the same of

Your loving   Lu.

To Mrs. Dodge.

DECEMBER 22, 1887.

DEAR MRS. DODGE, — I send you the story your assistant editor asked for. As it is needed at once I do not
delay to copy it, for I can only write an hour a day and
do very little. You are used to my wild manuscript, and
will be able to read it. I meant to have sent the Chinese
tale, but this was nearly done, and so it goes, as it does
not matter where we begin. . . . I hope you are well,
and full of the peace which work well done gives the
happy doer.

I mend slowly, but surely, and my good Doctor says
my best work is yet to ~ome; so I will be content with
health if I can get it. W.th all good wishes,

Yours aff ctionately,   L. M. A.

To Mrs. Bond.

FEBRUARY 7 [1888].

DEAR AUNTIE, — My blessed Anna is so busy, and I
can do so little to help her, I feel as if I might take upon
me the pleasant duty of writing to you.

Father is better, and we are all so grateful, for just
now we want all to be bright for our boy.

The end is not far off, but Father rallies wonderfully from each feeble spell, and keeps serene and happy through everything.

I don't ask to keep him now that life is a burden, and am glad to have him go before it becomes a pain. We shall miss the dear old white head and the feeble saint so long our care; but as Anna says, "He will be with Mother." So we shall be happy in the hope of that meeting.

Sunday he seemed very low, and I was allowed to drive in and say "good-by." He knew me and smiled, and kissed "Weedy," as he calls me, and I thought the drowsiness and difficulty of breathing could not last long. But he revived, got up, and seemed so much as usual, I may be able to see him again. It is a great grief that I am not there as I was with Lizzie and Mother, but though much better, the shattered nerves won't bear much yet, and quiet is my only cure.

I sit alone and bless the little pair like a fond old grandmother. You show me how to do it. With love to all,

Yours ever,   LU·

Her last note. To Mrs. Bond.

FEBRUARY 8, 1888.
Air, — "Haste to the Wedding."

DEAR AUNTIE, — I little knew what a sweet surprise was in store for me when I wrote to you yesterday.

As I awoke this morning my good Doctor L. came in with the lovely azalea, her round face beaming through the leaves like a full moon.

It was very dear of you to remember me, and cheer up my lonely day with such a beautiful guest.

It stands beside me on Marmee's work-table, and reminds me tenderly of her favorite flowers; and among those used at her funeral was a spray of this, which lasted for two weeks afterward, opening bud after bud in the glass on her table, where lay the dear old "Jos. May" hymn book, and her diary with the pen shut in as she left it when she last wrote there, three days before the end, "The twilight is closing about me, and I am going to rest in the arms of my children."

So you see I love the delicate flower, and enjoy it very much.

I can write now, and soon hope to come out and see you for a few minutes, as I drive out every fine day, and go to kiss my people once a week for fifteen minutes.

Slow climbing, but I don't slip back; so think up my mercies, and sing cheerfully, as dear Marmee used to do, "Thus far the Lord has led me on!"

Your loving　　　　Lu.

CHAPTER XII.

CONCLUSION.

TO MY FATHER,

ON HIS EIGHTY-SIXTH BIRTHDAY.

DEAR Pilgrim, waiting patiently,
 The long, long journey nearly done,
Beside the sacred stream that flows
 Clear shining in the western sun;
Look backward on the varied road
 Your steadfast feet have trod,
From youth to age, through weal and woe,
 Climbing forever nearer God.

Mountain and valley lie behind;
 The slough is crossed, the wicket passed;
Doubt and despair, sorrow and sin,
 Giant and fiend, conquered at last.
Neglect is changed to honor now;
 The heavy cross may be laid down;
The white head wins and wears at length
 The prophet's, not the martyr's, crown.

Greatheart and Faithful gone before,
 Brave Christiana, Mercy sweet,
Are Shining Ones who stand and wait
 The weary wanderer to greet.
Patience and Love his handmaids are,
 And till time brings release,
Christian may rest in that bright room
 Whose windows open to the east.

The staff set by, the sandals off,
 Still pondering the precious scroll,
Serene and strong, he waits the call
 That frees and wings a happy soul.
Then, beautiful as when it lured
 The boy's aspiring eyes,
Before the pilgrim's longing sight
 Shall the Celestial City rise.

November 29, 1885.   L. M. A.

MISS ALCOTT'S appearance was striking and impressive rather than beautiful. Her figure was tall and well-proportioned, indicating strength and activity, and she walked with freedom and majesty. Her head was large, and her rich brown hair was long and luxuriant, giving a sense of fulness and richness of life to her massive features. While thoroughly unconventional, and even free and easy in her manner, she had a dignity of deportment which prevented undue liberties, and made intruders stand in awe of her. Generous in the extreme in serving others, she knew her own rights, and did not allow them to be trampled on. She repelled "the spurns that patient merit of the unworthy takes," and had much of the Burns spirit that sings "A man's a man for a' that" in the presence of insolent grandeur.

Miss Alcott always took her stand not for herself, but for her family, her class, her sex. The humblest writer should not be imposed upon in her person; every woman should be braver and stronger from her attitude. She was careless of outward distinctions; but she enjoyed the attentions which her fame brought her with simple pleasure, and was delighted to meet bright, intelligent, distinguished people, who added to her stores of observation and thought. She had the rare good fortune, which an heir of millions might envy, of living all her life in the society of the noblest men and women. The Emersons, the Thoreaus, the Hawthornes, and Miss Elizabeth Peabody were the constant companions of her childhood and youth. It was from them that her standard of character was formed, and she could never enter any circle higher than that in which she had breathed freely from a child. She was quite capable of hero-worship, but her heroes were few.

With all her imagination and romance, Miss Alcott was a tremendous destroyer of illusions; she remorselessly tore them away from herself, persisting in holding a lens before every fault and folly of her own, and she did the same for those she loved best. Only what was intrinsically noble and true could stand the searching test of her intellectual scrutiny and keen perception of the incongruous and ridiculous.

This disposition was apparent in Louisa's relation to her father, whom she did not always fully understand. Perhaps he had a perception of this when he wrote —

" I press thee to my heart, as Duty's faithful child."

She had little sympathy with his speculative fancy, and saw plainly the impracticability of his schemes, and did not hesitate to touch with light and kindly satire his little peculiarities; yet in her deepest heart she gave him not only affection, but deep reverence. She felt the nobility and grandeur of his mind and heart. In "Little Women" the portrait of the father is less vivid and less literal than that of any other member of the family, and is scarcely recognizable; but it was impossible to make the student and idealist a part of the family life as she painted it, — full of fun, frolic, and adventure. In the second part she has taken pains to make up for this seeming neglect, and pays homage to the quiet man at the end of the house, whose influence was so potent and so sweet over all within it.

Mrs. Alcott was a rich and noble nature, full of zeal and impulse, daily struggling with a temper threatening to burst out into fire, ready to fight like a lioness for her young, or to toil for them till Nature broke down under the burden. She had a rich appreciation of heroism and beauty in all noble living, a true love of literature, and an overflowing sympathy with all suffering humanity, but was also capable of righteous indignation and withering contempt. To this mother, royal in her motherhood, Louisa was bound by the closest ties of filial love and mutual understanding. She early believed herself to be her mother's favorite child, knew she was close to her heart, her every struggle watched, her every fault rebuked, every aspiration encouraged, every effort after good recognized. I think Louisa felt no pride in this preference. She knew that she was dear to her mother, because her stormy, wayward heart was best understood by her; and hence the mother, wiser for her child than for herself, watched her unfolding life with anxious care. Throughout the childish journal this relation is evident: the child's heart lies open to the mother, and the mother can help her because she understands her, and holds sacred every cry of her heart.

Such a loving relation to a mother — so rich, so full, so enduring — was the greatest possible blessing to her life. And richly did Louisa repay the care. From her earliest years she was her mother's confidante, friend, and comforter. Her dream of success was not of fame and glory, but of the time when she could bring this weary pilgrim into "that chamber whose name is Peace," and there bid her sit with folded hands, listening to the loving voices of her children, and drinking in the fulness of life without care or anxiety.

And it all came true, like the conclusion of a fairy story; for good fairies had been busy at work for many years preparing the way. Who that saw that mother resting from her labors, proud in her children's success, happy in her husband's contentment, and in the love that had never faltered in the darkest days, can ever forget the peace of her countenance, the loving joy of her heart ?

The relation of Miss Alcott to her older sister was of entire trust and confidence. Anna inherited the serene, unexacting temper of her father, with much of the loving warmth of her mother. She loved to hide behind her gifted sister, and to keep the ingle-side warm for her to retreat to when she was cold and weary. Anna's fine intellectual powers were shown more in the appreciation of others than in the expression of herself; her dramatic skill and her lively fancy, combined with her affection for Louisa, made her always ready to second all the plans for entertainment or benevolence. She appears in her true light in the sweet, lovable Meg of "Little Women;" and if she never had the fame and pecuniary success of her sister, she had the less rare, but equally satisfying, happiness of wifehood and motherhood. And thus she repaid to Louisa what she had so generously done for the family, by giving her new objects of affection, and connecting her with a younger generation.

Louisa was always very fond of boys, and the difference of nature gave her an insight into their trials and difficulties without giving her a painful sense of her own hard struggles. In her nephews she found objects for all her wise and tender care, which they repaid with devoted affection. When boys became men, " they were less interesting to her; she could not understand them."

Elizabeth was unlike the other sisters. Retiring in disposition, she would gladly have ever lived in the privacy of home, her only desire being for the music that she loved. The father's ideality was in her a tender religious feeling; the mother's passionate impulse, a self-abnegating affection. She was in the family circle what she is in the book, — a strain of sweet, sad music we long and love to hear, and yet which almost breaks the heart with its forecasting of separation. She was very dear to both the father and mother, and the picture of the father watching all night by the marble remains of his child is very touching. He might well say, —

> " Ah, me ! life is not life deprived of thee."

Of the youngest of all, — bright, sparkling, capricious May, — quick in temper, quick in repentance, affectionate and generous, but full of her own plans, and quite inclined to have the world go on according to her fancies, — I have spoken elsewhere. Less profound in her intellectual and religious nature than either of her sisters, she was like a nymph of Nature, full of friendly sportiveness, and disposed to live out her own life, since it might be only a brief summer day. She was Anna's special child, and Louisa was not always so patient with her as the older sister; yet how well Louisa understood her generous nature is shown by the beautiful sketch she has made of her in "Little Women." She was called the lucky one of the family, and she reaped the benefit of her generous sister's labors in her opportunities of education.

Miss Alcott's literary work is so closely interwoven with her personal life that it needs little separate mention. Literature was undoubtedly her true pursuit, and she loved and honored it. That she had her ambitious longings for higher forms of art than the pleasant stories for children is evident from her journals, and she twice attempted to paint the life of mature men and women struggling with great difficulties. In "Moods" and "A Modern Mephistopheles" we have proof of her interest in difficult subjects. I have spoken of them in connection with her life ; but while they evince great power, and if standing alone would have stamped her as an author of original observation and keen thought, they can hardly be considered as thoroughly successful, and certainly have not won the sanction of the public like "Hospital Sketches" and "Little Women." Could she ever have commanded quiet leisure, with a tolerable degree of health, she might have wrought her fancies into a finer fabric, and achieved the success she aimed at.

Much as Miss Alcott loved literature, it was not an end in itself to her, but a means. Her heart was so bound up in her family, — she felt it so fully to be her sacred mission to provide for their wants, — that she sacrificed to it all ambitious dreams, health, leisure, — everything but her integrity of soul. But as " he that loseth his life shall find it," she has undoubtedly achieved a really greater work than if she had not had this constant stimulus to exertion. In her own line of work she is unsurpassed. While she paints in broad, free strokes the life of her own day, represented mostly by children and young people, she has always a high moral purpose, which gives strength and sweetness to the delineation; yet one never hears children complain of her moralizing, — it is events that reveal the lesson she would enforce. Her own deep nature shines through all the experiences of her characters, and impresses upon the children's hearts a sense of reality and truth. She charms them, wisely, to love the common virtues of truth, unselfishness, kindness, industry, and honesty. Dr. Johnson said children did not want to hear about themselves, but about giants and fairies ; but while Miss Alcott could weave fairy fancies for them, they are quite as pleased with her real boys and girls in the plainest of costumes.

An especial merit of these books for young boys and girls is their purity of feeling. The family affection which was so predominant in the author's own life, always appears as the holiest and sweetest phase of human nature. She does not refuse to paint the innocent love and the happy marriage which it is natural for every young heart to be interested in, but it is in tender, modest colors. She does not make it the master and tyrant of the soul, nor does she ever connect it with sensual imagery; but it appears as one of " God's holy ordinances," — natural and beautiful, — and is not separated from the thought of work and duty and self-sacrifice for others. No mother fears that her books will brush the bloom of modesty from the faces of her young men or maidens.

Even in the stories of her early period of work for money, which she wisely renounced as trash, while there is much that is thoroughly worthless as art, and little that has any value, Miss Alcott never falls into grossness of thought or baseness of feeling. She is sentimental, melodramatic, exaggerated, and unreal in her descriptions, but the stories leave no taint of evil behind them. Two of these stories, "The Baron's Gloves" and "A Whisper in the Dark," have been included in her published works, with her permission. Her friends are disposed to regret this, as they do not add to her reputation; but at least they serve to show the quality of work which she condemned so severely, and to satisfy the curiosity of readers in regard to it. It would be easy to point out defects in her style, and in some of her books there is evidence of the enforced drudgery of production, instead of the spontaneous flow of thought. The most serious defect is in her style of expression, which certainly passes the fine line between colloquial ease and slang; it is her own natural, peculiar style, which appears in her journals and letters. That it is attractive to children is certain, but it offends the taste of those who love purity and elegance of speech. It does not appear in Louisa's more ambitious novels; here she sometimes falls into the opposite extreme of labored and stilted expression. But much of these books is written in a pure and beautiful style, showing that she could have united ease with elegance if she had not so constantly worked at high speed and with little revision. She was a great admirer of Dickens's writings; and although she has never imitated him, she was perhaps strengthened in her habit of using dashing, expressive language by so fascinating a model.

I have placed at the head of each chapter one of Miss Alcott's own poems, usually written at the period of which the chapter treats, and characteristic of her life at that time. Her first literary essay was the "Little Robin." But although her fond mother saw the future of a great poet in these simple verses, Louisa never claimed the title for herself. Her thoughts ran often into rhyme, and she sent many birthday and Christmas verses to her friends and especially to her father. They are usually playful. She always wrote to express some feeling of the hour, and I find no objective or descriptive poetry. But a few of her sacred poems, for we may certainly call them so, are very tender and beautiful, and deserve a permanent place among the poems of feeling, — those few poems which a true heart writes for itself. "Thoreau's Flute" was originally published in the "Atlantic Monthly." It is the least personal of her poems. The lines to her father on his eighty-sixth birthday, the verses dedicated to her mother, and "My Prayer," the last poem that she wrote, breathe her deepest religious feeling in sweet and fitting strains. They will speak to the hearts of many in the hours of trial which are common to humanity. The long playful poem called "The Lay of the Golden Goose" was sent home from Europe as an answer to many questions from her admirers and demands for new stories. It has never been published, and is an interesting specimen of her playful rhyming.

While to Miss Alcott cannot be accorded a high rank as a poet, — which, indeed, she never claimed for herself, — it would be hard to deny a place in our most select anthology to "Thoreau's Flute" or "Transfiguration," the "Lines to my Father on his Eighty-sixth Birthday" and "My Prayer." I have therefore thought it well to preserve her best poems in connection with her life, where they properly belong; for they are all truly autobiographical, revealing the inner meaning of her life.

The pecuniary success of Miss Alcott's books enabled her to carry out her great purpose of providing for the comfort and happiness of her family. After the publication of "Little Women," she not only received a handsome sum for every new story, but there was a steady income from the old ones. Her American publishers estimate that they " have sold of her various works a million volumes, and that she realized from them more than two hundred thousand dollars." While her own tastes were very simple, her expenses were large, for she longed to gratify every wish of those she loved, and she gave generously to every one in need. She had a true sense of the value of money. Her early poverty did not make her close in expending it, nor her later success lavish. She never was enslaved by debt or corrupted by wealth. She always held herself superior to her fortune, and made her means serve her highest purposes.

Of Miss Alcott's own reading she says: —

"Never a student, but a great reader. R. W. E. gave me Goethe's works at fifteen, and they have been my delight ever since. My library consists of Goethe, Emerson, Shakespeare, Carlyle, Margaret Fuller, and George Sand. George Eliot I don't care for, nor any of the modern poets but Whittier; the old ones — Herbert, Crashaw, Keats, Coleridge, Dante, and a few others — I like."

She gives this account of the beginning of her literary career: —

"This gem ['The Robin'] my proud mother preserved with care, assuring me that if I kept on in this way I might be a second Shakespeare in time. Fired with this modest ambition, I continued to write poems upon dead butterflies, lost kittens, the baby's eyes, and other simple subjects till the story-telling mania set in; and after frightening my sisters out of their wits by awful tales whispered in bed, I began to write down these histories of giants, ogres, dauntless girls, and magic transformations till we had a library of small paper-covered volumes illustrated by the author. Later the poems grew gloomy and sentimental, and the tales more fanciful and less tragic, lovely elves and spirits taking the places of the former monsters."

Of her method of work she says : —

" I never had a study. Any pen and paper do, and an old atlas on my knee is all I want. Carry a dozen plots in my head, and think them over when in the mood. Sometimes keep one for years, and suddenly find it all ready to write. Often lie awake and plan whole chapters word for word, then merely scribble them down as if copying.

" Used to sit fourteen hours a day at one time, eating little, and unable to stir till a certain amount was done.

" Very few stories written in Concord ; no inspiration in that dull place. Go to Boston, hire a quiet room and shut myself up in it."

The following letter gives her advice to young writers : —

To Mr. J. P. True.

CONCORD, October 24.

DEAR SIR, — I never copy or " polish," so I have no old manuscripts to send you ; and if I had it would be of little use, for one person's method is no rule for another. Each must work in his own way ; and the only drill needed is to keep writing and profit by criticism. Mind grammar, spelling, and punctuation, use short words, and express as briefly as you can your meaning. Young people use too many adjectives and try to " write fine." The strongest, simplest words are best, and no *foreign* ones if it can be helped.

Write, and print if you can; if not, still write, and improve as you go on. Read the best books, and they will improve your style. See and hear good speakers and wise people, and learn of them. Work for twenty years, and then you may some day find that you have a style and place of your own, and can command good pay for the same things no one would take when you were unknown.

I know little of poetry, as I never read modern attempts, but advise any young person to keep to prose, as only once in a century is there a true poet; and verses are so easy to do that it is not much help to write them. I have so many letters like your own that I can say no more, but wish you success, and give you for a motto Michael Angelo's wise words: "Genius is infinite patience."

Your friend,   L. M. ALCOTT.

P. S. — The lines you send are better than many I see; but boys of nineteen cannot know much about hearts, and had better write of things they understand. Sentiment is apt to become sentimentality; and sense is always safer, as well as better drill, for young fancies and feelings.

Read Ralph Waldo Emerson, and see what good prose is, and some of the best poetry we have. I much prefer him to Longfellow.

"Years' afterward," says Mr. True, "when I had achieved some slight success, I once more wrote, thanking her for her advice; and the following letter shows the kindliness of heart with which she extended ready recognition and encouragement to lesser workers in her chosen field:"—

CONCORD, Sept. 7, 1883.

MY DEAR MR. TRUE, — Thanks for the pretty book, which I read at once and with pleasure; for I still enjoy boys' pranks as much as ever.

I don't remember the advice I gave you, and should judge from this your first story that you did not need much. Your boys are real boys; and the girls can run, — which is a rare accomplishment nowadays I find. They are not sentimental either; and that is a good example to set both your brother writers and the lasses who read the book.

I heartily wish you success in your chosen work, and shall always be glad to know how fast and how far you climb on the steep road that leads to fame and fortune.

Yours truly,

L. M. ALCOTT.

Roberts Brothers, Miss Alcott's publishers for nearly twenty years, have collected all her stories in a uniform edition of twenty-five volumes. They are grouped into different series according to size and character, from her novels to "Lulu's Library" for very small children, and may be enumerated as follows: —

Novels (four volumes). — Work, Moods, A Modern Mephistopheles, Hospital Sketches.

Little Women Series (eight volumes). — Little Women, An Old-Fashioned Girl, Little Men, Eight Cousins, Rose in Bloom, Under the Lilacs, Jack and Jill, Jo's Boys.

Spinning-Wheel Stories Series (four volumes). — Silver Pitchers, Proverb Stories, Spinning-Wheel Stories, A Garland for Girls.

Aunt Jo's Scrap-Bag (six volumes). — My Boys, Shawl-

Straps, Cupid and Chow-Chow, My Girls, Jimmy's Cruise in the Pinafore, An Old-Fashioned Thanksgiving.

Lulu's Library (three volumes).

Many of these stories were originally published in various magazines, — the popular " St. Nicholas," for which Miss Alcott wrote some of her best things in her later years, the " Youth's Companion," and others. Her works have been republished in England ; and through her English publishers, Messrs. Sampson Low and Company, of London, she has reaped the benefit of copyright there, and they have been translated into many languages. Her name is familiar and dear to the children of Europe, and they still read her books with the same eagerness as the children of her own land.

This extract from a letter written by the translator of Miss Alcott's books into Dutch will show how she is esteemed in Holland : —

" Miss Alcott was and is so much beloved here by her books, that you could scarce find a girl that had not read one or more of them. Last autumn I gave a translation of ' Lulu's Library ' that appeared in November, 1887 ; the year before, a collection of tales and Christmas stories that appeared under the name of ' Gandsbloempje ' (' Dandelion '). Yesterday a young niece of mine was here, and said, ' Oh, Aunt, how I enjoyed those stories ! but the former of " Meh Meh " I still preferred.' A friend wrote : ' My children are confined to the sick-room, but find comfort in Alcott's " Under the Lilacs." ' Her fame here was chiefly caused by her ' Little Women ' and ' Little Women Wedded,' which in Dutch were called ' Under Moedervleugels ' (' Under Mother's Wings ') and ' Op Eigen Wieken ' (' With Their Own Wings '). Her ' Work ' was translated as ' De Hand van den Ploey ' (' The Hand on the Plough ')."

How enduring the fame of Louisa M. Alcott will be, time only can show; but if to endear oneself to two generations of children, and to mould their minds by wise counsel in attractive form entitle an author to the lasting gratitude of her country, that praise and reward belong to LOUISA MAY ALCOTT.

TERMINUS.

It is time to be old,
To take in sail :
The god of bounds,
Who sets to seas a shore,
Came to me in his fatal rounds,
And said, " No more !
No farther shoot
Thy broad ambitious branches, and thy root;
Fancy departs : no more invent,
Contract thy firmament
To compass of a tent.
There 's not enough for this and that,
Make thy option which of two ;
Economize the failing river,
Not the less revere the Giver ;
Leave the many, and hold the few.
Timely wise, accept the terms ;
Soften the fall with wary foot :
A little while
Still plan and smile.

And, fault of novel germs,
Mature the unfallen fruit."

.　.　.　.　.　.　.

As the bird trims her to the gale,
I trim myself to the storm of time;
I man the rudder, reef the sail,
Obey the voice at eve obeyed at prime:
Lowly faithful, banish fear,
Right onward drive unharmed;
The port, well worth the cruise, is near,
And every wave is charmed.

EMERSON.

A close friend of the entire Alcott family, EDNAH D. CHENEY had a privileged view of Louisa May. The two women moved in the same influential Boston-Concord literary circle. Organizing reforms that ranged from women's suffrage to the rights of blacks, Cheney accumulated an admirable record of public service while pursuing a career as a writer. Primarily a biographer, Cheney won both fame and respect with her intimate portrait of Alcott.

ANN DOUGLAS is Associate Professor of English at Columbia University and the author of *The Feminization of American Culture.*